Implementing Deeper Learning and 21st Century Education Reforms

Fernando M. Reimers
Editor

Implementing Deeper Learning and 21st Century Education Reforms

Building an Education Renaissance After a Global Pandemic

 Springer

Editor
Fernando M. Reimers
Harvard Graduate School of Education
Harvard University
Cambridge, MA, USA

ISBN 978-3-030-57041-5   ISBN 978-3-030-57039-2   (eBook)
https://doi.org/10.1007/978-3-030-57039-2

This Springer imprint is published by the registered company Springer Nature Switzerland AG
The registered company address is: Gewerbestrasse 11, 6330 Cham, Switzerland

Contents

Contributors

Somaia Abdulrazzak International Education Policy, Harvard Graduate School of Education, Cambridge, MA, USA

Cristina Aparicio Harvard Graduate School of Education, Cambridge, MA, USA

Jayanti Bhatia International Education Policy, Harvard Graduate School of Education, Cambridge, MA, USA

Taylor Boyd Harvard Graduate School of Education, Cambridge, MA, USA

Anne K. Calef Massachusetts Institute of Technology, Cambridge, MA, USA

Emma Cameron International Education Policy, Harvard Graduate School of Education, Cambridge, MA, USA

Rastee Chaudhry Harvard University Graduate School of Education, Cambridge, MA, USA

Jeļena Fomiškina International Education Policy, Harvard Graduate School of Education, Cambridge, MA, USA

Djénéba Gory Harvard Kennedy School, Cambridge, MA, USA

Paul Moch Islas Harvard Graduate School of Education, Cambridge, MA, USA

Ama Peiris International Education Policy, Harvard Graduate School of Education, Cambridge, MA, USA

Durgesh Rajandiran Harvard Graduate School of Education, Cambridge, MA, USA

Venkatesh Reddy Mallapu Reddy International Education Policy, Harvard Graduate School of Education, Cambridge, MA, USA

Fernando M. Reimers Harvard Graduate School of Education, Cambridge, MA, USA

Abdullah Waqar Tajwar Harvard University Graduate School of Education, Cambridge, MA, USA

Eve Woogen International Education Policy, Harvard Graduate School of Education, Cambridge, MA, USA

The original version of this book was revised: This book was inadvertently published with incorrect book title which has been corrected now in the cover and throughout the book. The correction to this book is available at https://doi.org/10.1007/978-3-030-57039-2_9

Chapter 1
In Search of a Twenty-First Century Education Renaissance after a Global Pandemic

Fernando M. Reimers

1.1 The Coronavirus Disease Pandemic and a New Consciousness About the Power of Education to Improve the World

On March 11, 2020 the World Health Organization declared the Coronavirus outbreak a pandemic, likely to spread to every country in the globe. At that time, 114 countries had reported that 118,000 people had contracted COVID-19, the illness caused by the SARS-CoV2 virus and that 4300 people had died (Branswell & Joseph, 2020). Over the subsequent months, the Pandemic would ravage the world, infecting people, causing deaths, stressing the capacity of hospitals to care for the sick, and significantly disrupting many domains of human activity, as a result of the social distancing measures imposed by public health authorities in an attempt to slow down the velocity of the transmission of the virus. These measures were deeply disruptive to education systems as, in country after country, schools closed down.

The closure of schools led many to express concerns about the potential learning loss and about the lack of sustained engagement with learning that would result, and about the fact that there would be significant differences among groups of children within countries and across countries in the amount of learning loss and in the level of school disengagement and potential dropout. This concern is noteworthy because it indicates that, around the world, schooling had become widely ingrained as an expectation of the normal experience of growing up. That amidst a global Pandemic in which lives were at stake, serious attention focused on what this would do to the opportunities of children and youth to study is significant. A similar concern with education as a priority would have been unlikely during the Influenza Pandemic of 1918–1919, a time when only 39% of the world population over the age of 15 had accessed some formal

F. M. Reimers (✉)
Harvard Graduate School of Education, Cambridge, MA, USA
e-mail: Fernando_Reimers@harvard.edu

© The Author(s) 2021
F. M. Reimers (ed.), *Implementing Deeper Learning and 21st Century Education Reforms*, https://doi.org/10.1007/978-3-030-57039-2_1

education, compared to 86% in 2020 (Roser & Ortiz-Ospina, 2013). The concern over education during COVID-19 demonstrates that the notion that all children should be schooled had become normalized, a significant global achievement.

To mitigate learning loss and learning disengagement, schools and education systems created alternative means to sustain opportunities for students to continue learning remotely. These involved using a variety of resources and technologies, from instructional packages, to radio and television, to online learning. In two survey studies I conducted, in partnership with Andreas Schleicher at the OECD, I found that between the end of March of 2020 and the end of April of 2020, many countries around the world had gone from not having a strategy of educational continuity, to having put in place strategies of educational continuity using alternative means of delivery (Reimers & Schleicher, 2020a, b). Notwithstanding the fact that these alternative delivery systems reached different children with various levels of success, and that many questions remain about their efficacy in supporting learning, these strategies demonstrated remarkable capacity of educators for rapid innovation. As educators developed these alternative means of delivery, the question of what should be taught, whether new priorities should be established in the curriculum to account for the diminished capacities of the alternative systems deployed, became critical. Should the strategies of continuity focus on 'the basics', perhaps the basic literacies of reading, math and science, or should they instead focus on emotional and social development, or some other combination of 'breadth of skills'? The timeless question of 'what is education for' received renewed and considerable attention as schools and governments sought to sustain educational opportunity even as children could not attend school.

In addition, as many children were confined to their homes with their parents or guardians, the interruption of school attendance created a widely shared experience, for a vast number of people around the world, of observing up-close the process of engaging with school curriculum, as delivered by these quickly put together alternative means. In many cases, parents or guardians supported their children with their studies at home. This everyday experience with schooling for many, furthered interest on the question of what knowledge and skills students were gaining and, by extension, also interest on what skills they should be gaining, particularly as the alternative forms of continuity made evident that some children were better prepared than others to learn independently and remotely.

These questions about education purposes and the means to best achieve them are likely to stay with us not just during the Pandemic, but in the immediate post-Pandemic aftermath and beyond. Anticipating that the Pandemic will leave a number of lingering challenges, it is likely that even after the Pandemic is under control, a return to schooling will involve not just resuming formal education as it was left before the Pandemic, but to schools that will have to be reimagined to better address needs created by the Pandemic or made more evident by it, such as helping students develop the skills to learn independently, or addressing visible societal challenges such as poverty, social inequality, racism and bigotry, political polarization, national and international conflicts, or climate change.

Furthermore, the question of how to make schools more relevant will be intertwined with the question of how to develop institutional capacity and of resources, as it becomes apparent that the Pandemic will be followed by a period of financial austerity, in which societies will have to meet many needs with resources that are now further constrained by the slowdown in economic activity and by the costs of attending to the public health crisis. Schools will have to meet the new scrutiny and heightened expectations of how to better prepare students for a volatile and rapidly changing world in a context of clear resource and institutional constraints. The purpose of this book is to contribute to address these questions with some lessons drawn from the comparative analysis of several recent large scale education reforms that attempted to make schools more relevant to the needs of a changing world.

1.2   How Should We Educate All Children?

The concern over educational continuity during the Pandemic made evident that there is today widespread global agreement that all children should be educated. That we have reached such consensus should not be underestimated, for such consensus was elusive not just during the Pandemic of 1918–1919, but even at the time the goal of educating all children was included as one of the thirty rights contained in the Universal Declaration of Human Rights, adopted at the United Nations in 1948. In the seven decades since its adoption few of the ideas reflected in the remaining twenty-nine articles have seen greater universal adoption.

The seismic shift represented by the universalization of the idea that all children should be educated, however, has not translated into the same agreement with respect to how to do this. To be sure, as the institution of schooling has emerged as the preferred mean to advance the right to education, schools have become ubiquitous and policies and programs have managed to include most children in school for a significant period of their lives. The universal consensus ends here, for the schooling experiences of children differ vastly for different children born into different circumstances in the same societies, and for children across the world. In part those differences result from lack of capacity of some schools to achieve their goals. For public schools, these differences reflect limited institutional capacity of governments to support all schools as necessary. But the differences are also by design, reflecting contention regarding what goals schools should advance, and what particular learning outcomes they should pursue for different students.

One such contention, arguably at the root of many others, concerns whether schools should provide students a fundamental instruction in the basic literacies of reading and writing, and numeracy, or whether they should endeavor to equip students with a broader set of capacities. The contention is aggravated by limitations in education funding and in the capacities of the public system. It is one thing to argue that all children should be broadly educated, but quite another to reach consensus on how to fund the necessary level of resources to be able to do this or to know how to organize schools and support teachers so that this aspiration translates into real learning experiences for students.

The question then of determining how to educate all children sits at the intersection of questions about goals, institutional capacity and resources. Facing the obvious challenge of resource constraints priorities are essential, anticipating greater complexity and costs in implementing reforms with ambitious goals, it may be tempting to argue that the basics should come first. From that line of thought one would argue that the first order of business for school systems should be to teach the foundational literacies and that more expansive goals should only be considered after succeeding at teaching the basics. An expression of that argument is found in the recent World Bank Development report documenting a 'global learning crisis' focusing on basic literacy and numeracy (World Bank, 2018). Aligned with this concept, the World Bank has introduced the concept of learning poverty, understood as the capacity to read a simple text by the age of 10. Given that 53% of all children in low and middle income countries are unable to read a simple text (World Bank, 2019), the urgency of addressing this target is self-evident. In practice, many governments and international development institutions prioritize the basic literacies. A recent report from the Global Partnership for Education, the largest partnership to support and fund education in the developing world, states that 'the learning outcomes that are the focus of GPE 2020 [their current strategic plan] are de facto in relation to the foundational areas of literacy and numeracy' (Global Partnership for Education, 2020, 1). Similar priorities are observed in countries such as the United States in which governments have pursued reform strategies that heighten accountability for schools to deliver on the basic literacies, an approach which has been shown to limit the breath of the curriculum, teach to the test, and lower assessment standards to show spurious improvement (Ravitch, 2010).

What the argument of prioritizing basic literacy or numeracy means in practice, in spite of its face value appeal, is that students attending the most endowed or better functioning schools, or school systems, have opportunities to develop a breath of skills which are denied children attending more precarious systems. This makes clear how the self-evident need to prioritize the basics because it is what is most 'feasible' quickly becomes an issue of 'equity'. This is arguably the situation we are at present: some children have opportunities to develop a breath of skills that others lack. These inequities are found within countries as well as across countries. As the expanded range of skills that only some students develop translates into economic advantages, those educational inequalities in turn translate into socio-economic inequalities (Deming, 2017; Taylor et al., 2017).

Confirming such limitations of an approach to focus on the basics, a recent study of education reform in Massachusetts, widely considered a national leader in the standards based education reform movement in the United States, demonstrated that over the last 20 years, even as overall educational attainment had increased, the gaps between White and Latino students and between White and Black students and between Low and High income students in access to college and college completion had increased, with considerable impact in subsequent labor market earnings post college graduation, even for students who had comparable levels of performance in the Massachusetts Comprehensive Assessment System (MCAS).

Among students with the same performance in the MCAS, students from low-income families are significantly less likely to complete a 4-year college degree than their peers from high-income families (Papay et al., 2020 p. 22). The authors of the study offer several complementary explanations for these gaps, beginning with the different experiences of students in high school:

> Low-income students are increasingly concentrated in schools in which most of their class-mates also are living in poverty. Such schools tend to have fewer resources for college guidance and fewer students who plan to attend a 4-year college. These schools are also more likely to be at risk of sanctions because of low MCAS scores, which may lead educators to focus on increasing scores using strategies that do not promote mastery of critical academic and social skills important in college. (Papay et al., 2020, p. 23).

There are similar gaps associated with race. While Black students are 2% more likely to enroll in a 4 year college than their white peers, they are 11% less likely to graduate, and Hispanic students are 15% less likely to enroll in a 4 year college and 20% less likely to graduate than their white peers. (Papay et al., 2020, p. 24).

Given that focusing on 'basic skills' limits opportunities for students, it follows that in a world demanding breath of skills for full economic and civic participation, there is no choice but to provide all children the opportunity to develop an expanded range of skills, as anything else would amount to giving the most marginalized children access to the opportunity to gain skills that are increasingly irrelevant, of little value to advance oneself and one's community while their more advantaged peers receive opportunities to gain skills that truly matter. Such view in favor of expanding the goals of education for all is reflected in the United Nations Development Goal for Education, goal 4, and in particular in target 4.7

> 4.7 by 2030 ensure all learners acquire knowledge and skills needed to promote sustainable development, including among others through education for sustainable development and sustainable lifestyles, human rights, gender equality, promotion of a culture of peace and non-violence, global citizenship, and appreciation of cultural diversity and of culture's contribution to sustainable development (UN, 2020)

1.3 The Need for a Science of Implementing Twenty-First Century Education and Deeper Learning Reforms

While the moral argument to provide all children the opportunity to develop a breath of skills is compelling, there is no easy way to resolve the conundrum of whether to align education systems to teach the basics or to teach more advanced skills, when the needs are many, the resources few and institutional capacity is limited. This conundrum is aggravated by limitations in our knowledge of how to translate this aspiration of teaching a broad range of skills in practice, for all students, at scale. This is the kind of dilemma the creation of alternative education systems to sustain educational opportunity during the Pandemic made painfully clear, some systems narrowed down curricular goals because lack of knowledge of how to achieve them with the precarious systems which had been rapidly developed during the emergency.

But for many children, the education systems they experience are always precarious. This is most often because of lack of resources of one sort or another, but also because of lack of knowledge of how to do better withing those constrains. This dilemma will continue in the coming years of austerity as we wrestle with the question of what should we teach all children and how. Examining how different countries approached the challenge of elevating the goals of education for all children at scale in recent years is one way to inform the policy debate on this topic. The purpose of this book is to explain what strategies where followed by six system level reforms to broaden curricular goals, and to examine their implementation.

The reforms studied in this book preceded the Covid-19 Pandemic, and there may be inherent limitations in that sense in extrapolating from even that recent past to a world that may be considerably changed as a result of the Pandemic. In some respect however these reforms wrestled with the dilemma of what does it mean to expand the goals of education in ways that anticipated the thorny challenges now confronted by most nations because of the new consciousness about the importance of intentionally leading educational change with clear goals for what students should learn and why caused by the Pandemic.

More than knowledge about what goals for education are pursued by various nations is needed to develop sound strategies of educational change to help all students gain the breadth of skills necessary in a rapidly changing world. What is direly needed is knowledge about how the strategies to advance more ambitious goals are implemented in practice. Even if the knowledge of what goals countries pursue is accompanied by knowledge about the levels of student achievement in assessments of those domains, there are limits to such type of comparative analysis because countries face different education needs and their education systems have differing resources and institutional capacity. For example, some countries still grapple with completing the provision of access to all students of school going age, some facing growing populations of children which create demands to recruit more teachers, while others benefit from demographic transitions, which allow them to concentrate resources on fewer children.

Because education systems are at different stages of institutional development, knowing what goals are pursued by high performing systems can be of limited value to inform efforts of improvement. An education leader cannot just wish that their education system looked like Singapore's, one of the nations where students perform at high levels in international assessments of knowledge and skills in the areas of language, math and science. In order to develop clear action steps to make progress in educating all children in a particular system it is necessary to understand how the institutions of education develop over time, how developmental trajectories through which school staff, teachers and education leaders, and schools as organizations, lead to greater capacity to take on more ambitious goals. Ideas about those institutional developmental trajectories must define the details of implementation, including sequence and speed of change. Are there some elements in the development of the capacity of an education system which must be in place before others can be? How quickly can education systems progress towards greater capacity? While, arguably, a system needs a basic capacity to deliver the fundamentals of literacy and math education before it takes on more challenging education goals, is it the case that once they build that capacity that they will be better able to help students gain twenty-first century skills? We lack a sound theory of the development of education systems which can help answer those questions. We also need more knowledge about the details of implementing reforms to help students gain twenty-first century skills.

Since countries are at various stages of educational development, in terms of their education priorities and institutional capacity, understanding how systems at various stages of educational development implement strategies to serve the learning needs of students can contribute to theorize what kind of strategies are appropriate at various stages. This can help understand how systems can build the capacity of teachers and administrators to pursue ambitious goals, and how such efforts at capacity building are supported by other institutional reforms.

In spite of such absence of sound theories that can inform the development of strategies of system level transformation, governments around the world are embracing broader goals for the curriculum in many different nations. Predictably, the absence of an adequate theory to inform the development of strategies to achieve the adoption of more ambitious education goals, results in a gap between policy intent, implementation and practice. A recent study of national education mission statements in 113 countries, found that 86% of them included evidence of a commitment to the development of a broader range of skills with significantly less evidence of implementation of efforts to translate those goals into changed educational cultures in schools.

> This suggests that countries are recognizing the importance of breadth of skills, at least in terms of aspirational statements reflected in policy documents. However, only a few countries are consistently identifying skills at both policy and practice levels. (Care, Kim, Anderson, & Gustafsson-Wright, 2017, p. 5).

> The scan establishes conclusively the ubiquity of the breadth of skills movement through education systems. However, it is very much a work in progress. Many countries do not yet delineate how skills are expected to align with curriculum, nor do they include expectations for how these skills are to develop and mature, in the way they do for traditional subjects. (Ibid, p. 6).

Similar conclusions regarding the growing interest in twenty-first century skills and the challenges in implementation are presented in a landscape review conducted by the Global Partnership for Education, which works to support educational reform in countries with low levels of income per capita. The review notes that in a sample of education sector plans in 15 countries in Africa and Asia supported by the Partnership, all of them mention twenty-first century skills as education priorities, however the same review also notes that only three of those fifteen countries had implementation plans that included activities that could support the implementation of twenty-first century skills (Global Partnership for Education, 2020, vi).

> In addition, while existing implementation may focus on some components (for example, teacher training), it appears that there is a lack of knowledge and experience of how to approach implementation at a whole sector or system level, including practical frameworks and guidance for doing so. (Ibid).

> What appears to be absent in this ecosystem is work on integrating 21 century skills from a systemwide implementation lens. Despite the proliferation of initiatives across the partnership, there is little in the way of research, knowledge sharing, capacity development and advocacy around what it means to integrate and promote 21 century skills throughout an education system, particularly in developing countries. (Ibid).

Also reflecting this growing interest in broadening the curriculum, the International Association for the Evaluation of Educational Achievement, responsible for the oldest comparative cross-national surveys of student knowledge and skills, is planning a comparative, curriculum mapping study to examine opportunities to develop twenty-first century skills in the curriculum of participating countries.

Given this growing interest in broadening the goals of the curriculum, and the observed gap in implementation strategies to advance such goals, it is helpful to take stock of how governments implement reforms that broaden curriculum goals. What are the particular competencies they emphasize? What strategies do they adopt to support teachers and schools so they can help their students develop those competencies? Do countries that prioritize the basic literacies eventually transition to teaching twenty-first century skills, once they have succeeded in teaching the basics? How do they sequence those reforms? How do they pace them? What are the results in countries with low levels of institutional capacity and resources, when they prioritize twenty-first century skills?

Examining these questions is the purpose of this book, as we study reforms aimed at broadening curriculum goals in a group of diverse countries. We look at system level reforms in jurisdictions where students already achieve at high levels in international assessments of the basic literacies, such as Singapore and Ontario, Canada, as well as in nations where students achieve a much lower levels, such as Kenya, Mexico, Punjab-Pakistan and Zimbabwe. We examine system level reforms which focus on strengthening the capacity to teach the basics, as in Ontario and Punjab, as well as reforms that aim at building the capacity to teach a much broader set of competencies and skills, such as Kenya, Mexico, Singapore and Zimbabwe. We look at systems at very different levels of spending per student, and at reforms at various points in the cycle of policy implementation, some just starting as in Kenya and Zimbabwe, others such as Mexico's struggling to survive a governmental transition, and others such as Ontario, Punjab and Singapore that have been in place for an extended period of time. From the comparative study of these reforms we draw lessons on the implementation of reforms to teach twenty-first century skills at scale in diverse settings.

The choice of these countries is to some extent arbitrary. The studies of the reforms presented in this book originated in a graduate course I teach on comparative education policy analysis at Harvard University. The course draws a very diverse group of students, many of them in the International Education Policy Program I direct at the Harvard Graduate School of Education. Students are naturally drawn to carry out studies in countries in which they have experience or contacts to access the kind of information that this study required. Through this somewhat serendipitous approach, we ended with a collection of countries that are diverse in various useful ways, in this way expanding the knowledge drawn from existing studies of large system change which focus on countries all at similar levels of economic and institutional development, of which a preponderance are based on a narrow set of high income countries.

In examining these various reforms, we draw on a theoretical framework that sees the process of educational change as encompassing five perspectives, five ways of thinking about reform: cultural, psychological, professional, institutional and political (Reimers, 2020c). This comparative study of six large scale reforms examines which of these perspectives are reflected in the strategies pursued by governments as they seek to strengthen the capacity of the public education system to teach ambitious goals.

1.4 The Global Education Movement and the Right to Education in a Changing World

The current consensus on the universal right to education is squarely a result of the international architecture to promote development created at the end of World War II. The same international institutions have played a pivotal role in shaping ideas about how students should be educated and to what ends. The inclusion of education as a right in the Universal Declaration adopted at the third session of the United Nations General Assembly on December 10, 1948 spearheaded a global movement to educate all children (Reimers, 2017). The United Nations Education, Culture and Science Organization (UNESCO), the specialized agency established to support the advancement of that right, has played a pivotal role leading this global education movement through the strategic exercise of five functions:

(a) **Generating and disseminating ideas** – anticipating and responding to emerging trends and needs in education, and developing education policies based on research and country priorities,
(b) **Developing and promoting the adoption of education standards** – developing policies and practices,
(c) **Serving as a clearinghouse** – promoting the development, implementation and dissemination of successful educational policies and practices setting norms and standards and providing support in their implementation,
(d) **Building capacity** – providing technical co-operation to develop the capacity of member states to achieve their national education goals,
(e) **Catalyzing international co-operation** – initiating and promoting dialogue and exchange among education leaders and stakeholders.

Those actions by UNESCO, as representative and steward of the global commitment to the right of education, and of national and local governments, organizations of civil society and other international organizations, steered a global education movement which transformed the experience of humanity, creating an institution, the school, designed to provide children and youth opportunities to learn and norming that all children would spend a significant period early in their lives in that institutional creation. The concern over the education of children during the COVID-19 Pandemic demonstrated the success of that global education movement in normalizing the idea that education was a human right.

As a result of this global education movement, global access to education increased dramatically, especially in the developing world. In the 1950s and 1960s

UNESCO convened meetings of Ministers of Education, and of Finance, to advocate for the universalization of basic education. This advocacy, and the adoption of global norms and resolutions incorporating that right, resulted in legal and regulatory reforms in many countries enshrining the right of education. UNESCO then promoted the adoption of specific standards, stipulating for example the duration of compulsory education or creating the International Standard Classification of Education, a framework to organize information on access at different levels and modalities of education. UNESCO also monitors country's enrollment rates and disseminates such information, as a way to further reinforce country's commitments to implement programs to achieve the agreed upon resolutions. In its role as a clearinghouse of ideas and good practices, UNESCO documents practices which have contributed to the achievement of the goal of universalizing access or closing equity gaps, for example the creation of double shift schools, or cluster schools to rapidly expand access through better utilization of existing infrastructure. Through a variety of courses and training programs it developed the capacity of government staff who could help design and implement policies and programs that contributed to the achievement of the universalization of the right to education. Finally, UNESCO mobilized other international agencies to support countries in the achievement of those goals.

The impact of this global education movement is nothing short of remarkable. I have elsewhere defined it as the most significant silent revolution experienced by humanity (Reimers, 2017). Whereas prior to the creation of UNESCO less than half of all children had the opportunity to attend school, seven decades later, most of them had the same opportunity as shown in Fig. 1.1.

Figure 1.1 shows the percentage of world the population over 15 years of age which had accessed at least some formal education, increasing from under 20% in 1820 to 85% in 2015. The figure shows that most of the expansion in access to school took place during the 1950s and 1960s. Note that those increases in relative access took place even as population grew considerably. The most dramatic increases, in population as well as in access, were in the developing world, where levels of access to school were lower. The result was a significant increase in the average level of educational attainment of the population. As the global education movement brought to school children whose families had not traditionally been schooled, and as the demands for meaningful participation in society increased, new questions emerged about what should be the purpose of educating all children.

With respect to this question of purpose, UNESCO played also an important guiding role. The foundational answer to the question of why should all children be educated is provided in the text of the Universal Declaration of Human Rights itself, in article 26 which spells out the right to education and which directs the expansion of education to the full development of the human personality and to promoting understanding, tolerance and friendship among nations, racial or religious groups, as well as to furthering the activities of the United Nations to maintain peace:

Article 26.

(1) Everyone has the right to education. Education shall be free, at least in the elementary and fundamental stages. Elementary education shall be compulsory. Technical and professional

Share of the world population older than 15 years with at least basic education

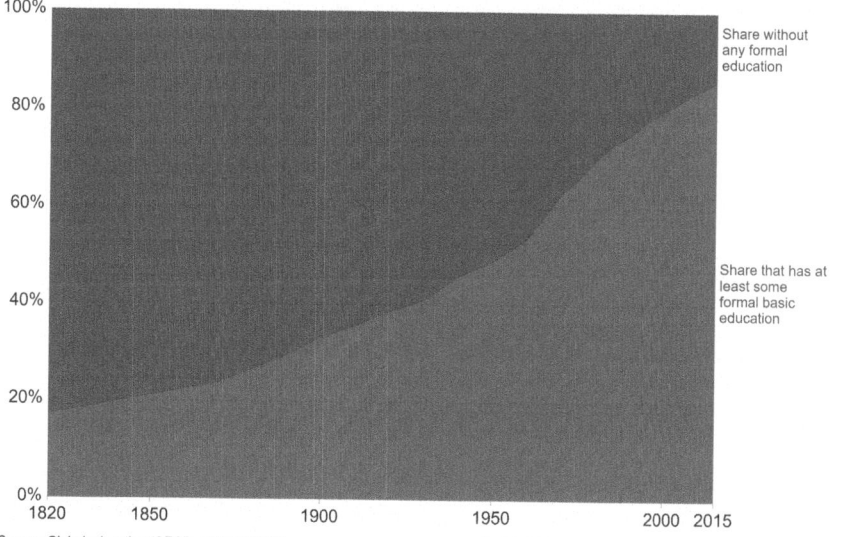

Source: Global education (OECD + IIASA (2016))   OurWorldInData.org/primary-and-secondary-education • CC BY

Fig. 1.1 Share of the world population older than 15 years with at least basic education. (Source: Roser, M. and E. Ortiz-Ospina (2013). "Primary and Secondary Education" Published online at OurWorldInData.org   Retrieved   from   https://ourworldindata.org/primary-and-secondary-education)

education shall be made generally available and higher education shall be equally accessible to all on the basis of merit.

(2) Education shall be directed to the full development of the human personality and to the strengthening of respect for human rights and fundamental freedoms. It shall promote understanding, tolerance and friendship among all nations, racial or religious groups, and shall further the activities of the United Nations for the maintenance of peace.

(3) Parents have a prior right to choose the kind of education that shall be given to their children. (United Nations, 1948)

This emphasis on educating all in order to advance human rights, tolerance and peace has been an ongoing concern of UNESCO, reaffirmed at the 1974 General Conference in the "Recommendation concerning Education for International Understanding, Co-operation and Peace and Education relating to Human Rights and Fundamental Freedoms". The recommendation proposed the following guidelines for education policy:

(a) An international dimension and a global perspective in education at all levels and in all its forms;

(b) Understanding and respect for all peoples, their cultures, civilizations, values and ways of life, including domestic ethnic cultures and cultures of other nations;

(c) Awareness of the increasing global interdependence between peoples and nations;

(d) Abilities to communicate with others;

(e) Awareness not only of the rights but also of the duties incumbent upon individuals, social groups and nations towards each other;

(f) Understanding – of the necessity for international solidarity and cooperation;

(g) Readiness on the part of the individual to participate in solving the problems of his commu-
     nity, his country and the world at large.
       5. Combining learning, training, information and action, international education should
     further the appropriate intellectual and emotional development of the individual. It should
     develop a sense of social responsibility and of solidarity with less privileged groups and
     should lead to observance of the principles of equality in everyday conduct. It should also
     help to develop qualities, aptitudes and abilities which enable the individual to acquire a
     critical understanding of problems at the national and the international level; to understand
     and explain facts, opinions and ideas; to work in a group; to accept and participate in free
     discussions; to observe the elementary rules of procedure applicable to any discussion; and
     to base value judgments and decisions on a rational analysis of relevant facts and factors.
       6. Education should stress the inadmissibility of recourse to war for purposes of expan-
     sion, aggression and domination, or to the use of force and violence for purposes of repres-
     sion, and should bring every person to understand and assume his or her responsibilities for
     the maintenance of peace. It should contribute to international understanding and strength-
     ening of world peace and to the activities in the struggle against colonialism and neo-
     colonialism in all their forms and manifestations, and against all forms and varieties of
     racialism, fascism, and apartheid as well as other ideologies which breed national and racial
     hatred and which are contrary to the purposes of this recommendation. (UNESCO, 1974).

To advance ideas about the purpose of education for all, throughout its history,
UNESCO has thrice established commissions tasked with producing guiding frameworks. The first commission established at UNESCO's General Conference in 1970
and chaired by former minister of education of France Edgar Faure, produced a
report titled 'Learning to Be' which made the case for lifelong learning as a way to
contribute to the full development of people as capable of agency to direct their own
lives, promoters of democracy and world citizens (Faure et al., 1972, 158). The
second commission, established at the 1991 General Conference, was chaired by
Jacques Delors, a former President of the European Commission, proposed that
education should be organized around four goals: learning to know; learning to do;
learning to live together; and learning to be, of which the report assigned the greatest importance to learning to live together (Delors, 1996). In 2019, UNESCO established another commission to produce a report on the goals of education, The
Education on the Futures of Education Commission, chaired by the President of the
Federal Democratic Republic of Ethiopia Sahle-Work Zewde. The Faure and Delors
reports reflect a humanist vision of education, very much in line with the values of
the Enlightenment that emphasize the equal rights of all people, the capacity of
people to become architects of their lives, and their ability to rule themselves and
improve the world.

   The ideas contained in the Delors report, that the purposes for school learning
should be broadened to prepare students for a changing and uncertain world, found
resonance throughout the world. While the Delors report was not discussed by the
Executive Board of UNESCO, it was translated into about 30 languages, and generated initiatives in 50 countries, stimulating the development of indicators of lifelong
learning, and position papers on education, as well as pilot projects, and the four
pillars of learning became a catchphrase in policy documents (Elfert, 2015, 94).

   Alongside this work of UNESCO, since the early 1990 a number of international
organizations, governments and other institutions developed frameworks and advocated to broaden the range of skills that schools should cultivate. These reflected

several strands of ideas: a growing interest in the socio-emotional development of learners and in the development of life skills, an interest in more active forms of civic engagement, and an interest in the development of skills that allowed economic participation as workplaces were transformed by technology.

In 1994, a group of educators in the United States, formed a consortium to establish high quality evidence on ways to support socio emotional learning in schools, the Collaborative for Academic, Social, and Emotional Learning (CASEL). In 1997, CASEL partnered with the Association for Supervision and Curriculum Development, a large professional association of educators in the United States, producing guidelines for educators on how to promote socio-emotional learning in schools (CASEL, 2020). CASEL defines five core socio-emotional competencies: Self-awareness, Self-management, Social-awareness, Relationship skills and Responsible decision making.

Self-awareness consists of "the ability to recognize one's own emotions, thoughts, and values and how they influence behavior. The ability to accurately assess one's strengths and limitations, with a well-grounded sense of confidence, optimism, and a 'growth mindset'" (CASEL, 2020)

Self-management is "The ability to successfully regulate one's emotions, thoughts, and behaviors in different situations – effectively managing stress, controlling impulses, and motivating oneself. The ability to set and work toward personal and academic goals." (Ibid.)

Social-awareness is "The ability to take the perspective of and empathize with others, including those from diverse backgrounds and cultures. The ability to understand social and ethical norms for behavior and to recognize family, school, and community resources and supports." (Ibid.)

Relationship skills comprise "The ability to establish and maintain healthy and rewarding relationships with diverse individuals and groups. The ability to communicate clearly, listen well, cooperate with others, resist inappropriate social pressure, negotiate conflict constructively, and seek and offer help when needed." (Ibid).

Responsible decision making involves "The ability to make constructive choices about personal behavior and social interactions based on ethical standards, safety concerns, and social norms. The realistic evaluation of consequences of various actions, and a consideration of the well-being of oneself and others." (Ibid).

Similar socio-emotional goals for schools were advocated in 1999 by the World Health Organization in an inter-agency report underscoring the importance of promoting psycho-social or life skills to help students deal with the demands and challenges of life, in particular to empower children and youth at risk to protect their rights. The report identified five basic areas of life skills: decision making and problem solving, creative and critical thinking, communication and interpersonal skills, self-awareness and empathy and copying with emotions and stress (WHO, 1999, 1).

Also in 1999, UNICEF developed a framework for 'child friendly' schools and educational systems, based on the Convention on the Rights of the Child. The framework reflects a student centered, whole-child vision of education, aligned with a broad set of educational competencies (UNICEF, 2020). Building on UNESCO's Delors Report, UNICEF has also developed a framework of life skills and citizenship to support the development of children in the Middle East that reflects an ambitious set of twelve core life skills aligned to the four pillars in UNESCO's report. Learning to know, for instance, is reflected in Skills for Learning (creativity, critical thinking, problem-solving), learning to do in Skills for Employability (cooperation, negotiation, decision-making), learning to be in Skills for Personal Empowerment (self-management, resilience, communication) and learning to live together in Skills for Active Citizenship (respect for diversity, empathy, participation) (UNICEF, 2017, 4).

The Organization for Economic Cooperation and Development also contributed to the global dialogue on broader goals for education through the project of Definition and Selection of Competencies in the 1990s and the associated Programme of International Student Assessment launched in 1997, and more recently through the OECD 2030 Learning Framework, outlining an expanded set of competencies that could contribute to individual and collective wellbeing (OECD, 2020). This framework consists of a Learning Compass which includes "Core knowledge, skills, attitudes and values for 2030 will cover not only literacy and numeracy, but also data and digital literacy, physical and mental health, and social and emotional skills." (OECD, 2020), building on those foundations are Competencies, which include knowledge, skills, attitudes and values that allow a person to act in coherent and responsible ways that change the future for the better (Ibid). Finally, transformative competencies allow students to develop and reflect on their own perspective and support learning and the capacity to take responsibility to create a better world.

The National Research Council of the United States, commissioned an expert panel to produce a scientific consensus report on skills variously termed 'deeper learning', '21st century skills', 'college and career readiness', 'next generation learning', 'new basic skills' and 'higher order thinking' (National Research Council, 2012). The report, published in 2012, classified these skills as:

1. **Cognitive Skills**

   1.1. Processing and cognitive strategies

   - Critical Thinking
   - Problem Solving
   - Analysis
   - Logical Reasoning
   - Interpretation
   - Decision Making
   - Executive Functioning

   1.2. Knowledge

   - Literacy and communication skills
   - Active listening skills
   - Knowledge of the disciplines
   - Ability to use evidence and assess biases in information
   - Digital Literacy

1.3. Creativity

- Creativity
- Innovation

2. **Interpersonal skills**

2.1. Collaborative group skills

- Communication
- Collaboration
- Team Work
- Cooperation
- Coordination
- Empathy, Perspective Taking
- Trust
- Service Orientation
- Conflict Resolution
- Negotiation

2.2. Leadership

- Leadership
- Responsibility
- Assertive Communication
- Self-Presentation
- Social Influence

3. **Intra-personal skills**

3.1. Intellectual Openness

- Flexibility
- Adaptability
- Artistic and Cultural Appreciation
- Personal and Social Responsibility
- Intercultural competency
- Appreciation for diversity
- Adaptability
- Capacity for lifelong learning
- Intellectual interest and curiosity

3.2. Work Ethic/Responsibility

- Initiative
- Self-direction
- Responsibility
- Perseverance
- Productivity
- Persistence
- Self-Regulation
- Meta-cognitive skills, anticipate future, reflexive skills

- Professionalism
- Ethics
- Integrity
- Citizenship
- Work Orientation

3.3. Self-efficacy

- Self-regulation (self-monitoring and self-assessment)
- Physical and mental health

Additional impetus for the expansion of education goals was provided by the compact of development adopted at the annual general conference of the United Nations, in September of 2015, at which participating governments embraced the goal of sustainable development, identifying seventeen goals and a series of specific targets, and highlighting the pivotal role education should play in the achievement of all other goals. The fourth Sustainable Development Goal 'Ensure inclusive and equitable quality education and promote lifelong learning opportunities for all', includes a target that explicitly focuses on education about sustainable lifestyles, mentioned earlier in this chapter.

More recently, in 2020, the World Economic Forum produced a brief outlining eight essential skills for the fourth industrial revolution:

1. Global citizenship skills: Include content that focuses on building awareness about the wider world, sustainability and playing an active role in the global community.
2. Innovation and creativity skills: Include content that fosters skills required for innovation, including complex problem-solving, analytical thinking, creativity and systems analysis.
3. Technology skills: Include content that is based on developing digital skills, including programming, digital responsibility and the use of technology.
4. Interpersonal skills: Include content that focuses on interpersonal emotional intelligence, including empathy, cooperation, negotiation, leadership and social awareness.
5. Personalized and self-paced learning: Move from a system where learning is standardized, to one based on the diverse individual needs of each learner, and flexible enough to enable each learner to progress at their own pace.
6. Accessible and inclusive learning: Move from a system where learning is confined to those with access to school buildings to one in which everyone has access to learning and is therefore inclusive.
7. Problem-based and collaborative learning: Move from process-based to project- and problem-based content delivery, requiring peer collaboration and more closely mirroring the future of work.
8. Lifelong and student-driven learning: Move from a system where learning and skilling decrease over one's lifespan to one where everyone continuously improves on existing skills and acquires new ones based on their individual needs. (World Economic Forum, 2020, 4).

The advocacy of the various organizations involved in producing these diverse frameworks gradually caused governments around the world to revise and expand national standards and curriculum. A study of how curriculum goals had changed in the twenty first century in Chile, China, India, Mexico, Singapore and the United States found that in all these countries the curriculum had expanded to include a broader focus on cognitive, social and emotional competencies (Reimers & Chung,

2016). The same was found in a study of education reforms in Brazil, Finland, Japan, Mexico, Peru, Poland, Portugal and Russia (Reimers, 2020b).

UNESCO carries out periodic consultations to member states to assess the extent to which the goals of the 1974 recommendation are reflected in education policies and in the curriculum. The most recent consultation, to which 83 out of 195 member states responded, reports improvements in implementing the guiding principles of the 1974 recommendation. Among the respondents, 68% indicate that these principles are fully integrated in education policies, and an additional 51% indicate that they are somewhat reflected. All countries report that the curriculum includes goals reflecting peace and non-violence, 99% include human rights and fundamental freedoms, 96% include cultural diversity and 99% include environmental sustainability goals (UNESCO, 2018, figure 6). The same survey shows that there is a disconnect between the inclusion of these goals in the curriculum and the extent to which they are also incorporated in teacher education programs. Only 19% of the countries report that these goals are fully integrated in teacher preparation programs, and an additional 93% indicate that they are only somewhat integrated (UNESCO, 2018, figure 13).

An in-depth analysis of policy documents in ten countries with an expressed commitment to Education for Sustainable Development and Global Citizenship Education undertaken by UNESCO, revealed that in all these countries there are abundant references to both of these concepts, and that they are expressed in terms of cognitive, socio-emotional and behavioral dimensions (UNESCO, 2019). In the documents examined in these countries –Costa Rica, Japan, Kenya, Lebanon, Mexico, Morocco, Portugal, Republic of Korea, Rwanda and Sweden – there were almost twice as many references to Global Citizenship Education (representing about 60% of the references) than to Education for Sustainable Development (representing about 30%) across national laws, strategic plans and policies, national curriculum frameworks, programmatic documents and subject specific curriculum. These references were present across various subjects in the curriculum, and the emphasis on cognitive dimensions, relative to socio-emotional and behavioral domains, increased in secondary education (Ibid).

1.5 Broader Curriculum Goals Don't Teach Themselves. The Need for Effective Implementation Strategies That Augment Teacher Capacities

As the goals of the curriculum expand to encompass a broader range of skills and capacities, teacher capacity is increasingly recognized as the lynchpin to the success of these efforts to better prepare students for a world in which they will face greater cognitive and skills demands. This is the reason teacher professional preparation has become a crucial policy priority for many nations (Reimers, 2020a; Reimers & Chung, 2016). While there is evidence that teacher professional development can help teachers develop the pedagogical skills to educate the whole child (Reimers & Chung, 2018) and while many teachers receive professional development, it is clear that many teachers lack the capacities to enact the type of pedagogies which are known to cultivate some of the expanded skills considered essential to participate, civically and economically, in the twenty first century. As a result, many students lack opportunities for 'deeper learning' and the opportunities to develop the breadth of skills intended in the curriculum.

Cross national studies show that many students are poorly supported to develop cognitive or socio-emotional skills. In the last PISA study, less than 10% of the students can distinguish facts from opinions (OECD, 2019b, 3). In terms of their literacy skills, the assessment defines a threshold at which 'students can identify the main idea in a piece of text of moderate length. They can understand relationships or construe meaning within a limited part of the text when the information is not prominent by producing basic inferences, and/or when the information is in the presence of some distracting information. They can select and access a page in a set based on explicit though sometimes complex prompts, and locate one or more pieces of information based on multiple, partly implicit, criteria. Readers at level 2 can, when explicitly cued, reflect on the overall purpose, or on the purpose of specific details, in texts of moderate length. They can reflect on simple visual or typographical features. They can compare claims and evaluate the reasons supporting them based on short, explicit statements." (OECD, 2019b, 91). On average, 77% of the students in the OECD can read at this level or above, although there is much variation across countries in the percentage of students reading at various levels. In the Chinese provinces who participated in the study (Beijing, Shanghai, Jiangsu and Zhejiang), close to 95% of the students exceed this literacy threshold, that figure is above 80% in Australia, Denmark, Japan, Korea, New Zealand, Norway, Slovenia, Sweden, Taipei, the United Kingdom and the United States, and above 85% in Canada, Finland, Hong Kong and Poland. In contrast, more than 25% of the students were unable to read at this level in Chile, Colombia, Greece, Hungary, Iceland, Israel, Luxembourg, Mexico, the Slovak Republic and Turkey (OECD, 2019a, 92).

In Mathematics, the PISA study defines proficiency at level two or above as 'students begin to demonstrate the ability and initiative to use mathematics in simple real-life situations… the 'minimum level of proficiency' that all children should acquire by the end of secondary education' (OECD, 2019a, 105). While over 90% of students in Beijing, Shanghai, Jiangsu and Zhejiang, Hong Kong, Macao and Singapore and close to 90% in Estonia achieved at this level, in 21 countries only between 20% and 50% of the students did so (Ibid).

In Science, students below level 2 are unable to 'draw on everyday content knowledge and basic procedural knowledge to identify an appropriate scientific explanation, interpret data, and identify the question being addressed in a simple experimental design'. On average in the OECD 78% of the students demonstrated this basic level of scientific knowledge or higher (OECD, 2019a, 115).

The pedagogical shortcomings of teachers to support their students disproportionally affect poor students. Socioeconomically disadvantaged students are more likely to perform at low levels than their more advantaged peers. For example, whereas on average among OECD countries, one in five students achieved below the threshold level for literacy, this figure was 36% for the poorest 25% of the students but only 11% for the wealthier 25% of the students. Socioeconomic background is significantly associated with student learning outcomes in all countries participating in PISA, with the sole exception of the province of Macao in China (OECD, 2019c, 54).

In spite of the relationship between socioeconomic background and learning outcomes, some disadvantaged students achieve at high levels in PISA, one in ten disadvantaged students achieves in the top 25% of the reading assessment. Those students have supportive parents, enthusiastic teachers, greater sense of self-efficacy and are in schools with a positive disciplinary climate (OECD, 2019c, 66). In half of the countries participating in the study, those students from low socioeconomic backgrounds who achieved at high levels were more likely to feel that they belonged in school (Ibid). These findings underscore the interdependence of various aspects of the educational experience, no one learns very much in a school where they don't feel they belong, and students are more likely to apply themselves to their studies if they have more efficacy, or when they have a growth mindset, and the results of such effort will in turn reinforce their sense of efficacy and growth mindset. Effective teachers are able to educate the whole child, to support the development of their students in the cognitive, emotional and cognitive domains, and to do this for all their students.

These student learning outcomes are reflective of the opportunities they have to learn. Most teachers are better prepared to transmit content than to design and support the learning challenges which develop both higher order cognitive skills as well as socio-emotional skills. A recent study on teacher practices around the world conducted by the OECD, identifies that whereas most teachers report effectively deploying teacher centered strategies such as presenting a summary of recently learned content at the beginning of a lesson, setting goals at the beginning of instruction, explaining what they expected students to learn, or explaining how old and new topics are related, considerable fewer report using student centered pedagogies which engage students with tasks of high cognitive complexity, such as presenting tasks for which there is no obvious solution, giving tasks which require students to think critically, having students work in small groups to solve a problem or task, asking students to design their own procedures to solve problems, or giving students problems which require at least a week to complete. (OECD, 2019a).

These shortcomings in teacher's pedagogical skills are confirmed by a recent survey to students, administered as part of the Programme for International Student Assessment. As a result of the varying levels of teacher skills to educate the whole child, the experience of school can be vastly different for different students. For instance, on average in the OECD 38% of students are in schools where at least 25% of the students are bullied at least a few times a month (OECD, 2019c, Table III. B1.2.3). The climate students experience in their classrooms varies also as a result of different teacher competencies, for instance on average across countries 29% of the students report that they can't listen to the teacher in most or all lessons, 30% report noise and disorder in most or all lessons, 26% say the teachers have to wait a long time for students to quiet down in most or all lessons (Ibid, Table III.B1.3.3).

Only 22% of the students strongly agree with the statement that the teachers enjoyed teaching the lesson, and an additional 50% agreed with the same statement. Only 15% of the students strongly agree with the statement that the enthusiasm of the teachers inspired them, and an additional 40% agree with the same statement. Only 24% of the students strongly agree with the statement that their teachers enjoy teaching the topics they were teaching, and an additional 55% agree with that statement. Only 25% of the students strongly agreed with the statement that teachers demonstrated enjoyment teaching, and an additional 49% agreed with the statement (Ibid, Table III.B1.5.3). These reports suggest that at least 25% of the students are in classrooms they find unsupportive, as confirmed by the fact that 75% of the students report that their teachers provide extra help when students need it (Ibid, Table III.B1.6.4).

These various experiences with teachers lead to various experiences of inclusion in school. Twenty percent of the students in the OECD agree or strongly agree with the statement that they feel like an outsider or left out of things at school; 29% disagree or strongly disagree with the statement that they feel like they belong in school; 20% agree or strongly agree with the statement that they feel awkward and out of place at school (Ibid, Table III.B.1.9.3).

While the student's skills and experiences are indicative of shortcomings of many of their teachers, teachers themselves report a need for more effective professional development to effectively address a number of their professional challenges. For example, as a result of growing mobility and access, classrooms today are increasingly diverse, as shown in the following table displaying the percentage of teachers who teach in classes where more than 10% of the students come from homes where a different language to the language of instruction is spoken. In spite of such diversity, however, only a fraction of the teachers were prepared to teach in multicultural settings in their initial education, or feel well prepared to do so, or received professional development focused on teaching in multicultural settings. On average, for the OECD, 18% of the teachers are in classes with more than 10% of students who are learning in a second language; 35% of the teachers received preparation to teach multicultural classes in their initial preparation; 26% feel well or very well prepared to teach in a multicultural classroom; 22% received professional development addressing this are; 15% feel a high need for professional development in this area; and only 67% feel they can cope with the challenges of teaching a multicultural classroom (Table 1.1).

Similar needs for professional development are observed in teacher responses with respect to using information and communication technologies. On average, for the OECD, only 56% of the teachers indicate that the use of ICT was included in their initial preparation; only 43% feel well prepared or very well prepared to use ICT; only 60% indicate that the use of ICT was included in their recent professional development; 18% express a high need for professional development in using ICT for teaching; only 53% allow students to regularly use ICT for projects, and 25% of principals report shortage of digital technology for instruction. (OECD, 2019a, Figure I.1.1.)

Table 1.1 Teacher preparation to teach in multicultural settings

Countries/economies where the indicator is **above** the OECD average
Countries/economies where the indicator is **not statistically different** from the OECD average
Countries/economies where the indicator is **below** the OECD average

	Percentage of teachers teaching in classes with more than 10% of students whose first language is different from the language of instruction	Percentage of teachers for whom "teaching in a multicultural or multilingual setting" was included in their formal education or training	Percentage of teachers who felt "well prepared" or "very well prepared" for teaching in a multicultural or multilingual setting	Percentage of teachers for whom "teaching in a multicultural setting" was included in their recent professional development activities	Percentage of teachers reporting a high level of need for professional development in teaching in a multicultural or multilingual setting	Percentage of teachers who feel they can cope with the challenges of a multicultural classroom "quite a bit" or "a lot" in teaching a culturally diverse class[1]
	Chapter 3	Chapter 4	Chapter 4	Chapter 5	Chapter 5	Chapter 3
Alberta (Canada)	45	63	38	41	10	67
Australia	27	59	27	23	7	70
Austria	42	31	15	18	14	74
Belgium	35	31	16	13	9	81
Flemish Comm. (Belgium)	39	34	17	18	8	77
Brazil	4	42	44	27	44	81
Bulgaria	40	27	26	31	21	82
CABA (Argentina)	9	35	34	19	25	70
Chile	5	42	37	21	34	57
Colombia	5	47	30	29	45	90
Croatia	8	25	20	19	14	81
Czech Republic	3	16	10	14	6	65
Denmark	21	37	26	14	11	85
England (UK)	27	68	43	19	5	72
Estonia	13	28	16	25	11	70
Finland	15	29	14	20	7	69
France	16	12	8	6	17	66
Georgia	9	30	33	35	12	71
Hungary	2	19	28	15	13	84
Iceland	24	27	13	23	19	62
Israel	17	34	33	21	17	63
Italy	17	26	19	28	14	80
Japan	2	27	11	13	15	17
Kazakhstan	33	48	43	37	13	68
Korea	4	29	24	31	14	31
Latvia	23	33	32	28	11	89
Lithuania	6	23	35	18	10	67
Malta	29	38	23	27	20	65
Mexico	4	27	26	16	46	59
Netherlands	15	30	17	10	4	68
New Zealand	27	78	45	46	7	74
Norway	23	29	15	15	13	59
Portugal	8	21	19	14	22	94
Romania	8	37	43	22	27	72
Russian Federation	12	31	32	24	13	83
Saudi Arabia	11	36	43	40	26	77
Shanghai (China)	3	63	52	43	22	45
Singapore	58	72	61	25	5	65
Slovak Republic	11	26	21	14	9	64
Slovenia	16	12	27	18	14	58
South Africa	62	75	67	54	20	81
Spain	22	29	26	32	18	52
Sweden	41	41	32	24	15	68
Turkey	18	33	39	27	22	55
United Arab Emirates	50	76	80	65	10	90
United States	25	70	48	42	6	66
Viet Nam	20	44	31	41	19	46
OECD average-31	18	35	26	22	15	67

1. The sample is restricted to teachers reporting that they have already taught a classroom with students from different cultures.
Source: OECD, 2019a Figure I.1.2.

Similar needs are evident with respect to teaching students with special needs. On average, for the OECD, 27% of the teachers teach in classrooms where more than 10% of the students have special needs; 67% have received preparation to teach in integrated classrooms as part of their professional development; only 44% feel well prepared or very well prepared to teach in inclusive classrooms; only 43% have received preparation to teach in inclusive classrooms in their recent professional development; 22% report a high level of need for professional development to teach in integrated classrooms and 32% of school principals report a shortage of teachers with competency to teach in integrated environments. Table 1.2 presents these results for all countries participating in the survey.

Even with respect to simple instructional tasks, such as classroom management, many teachers feel inadequately prepared. On average for the OECD, only 72% of the teachers report learning about classroom management in their initial teacher preparation, and only 53% feel well or very well prepared to manage their classrooms; only 50% report that classroom management was addressed in their recent professional development; only 14% of teachers report a high need of professional development in their classrooms; 85% feel they can control disruptive behavior in their classrooms, but 29% report that they lose a lot of time because of student disruptions. Table 1.3 has detailed percentages of teachers who report adequate preparation to manage their classrooms in the countries participating in the study.

1.6 The Limitations of What We Know to Develop More Effective Teacher Capacities to Educate the Whole Child

The fact that teacher education and development are recognized as important but many efforts to support teachers in learning new skills are insufficient to prepare them to meet the broader demands of more ambitious curricula is paradoxical, particularly given that much research has been conducted on teacher professional development and on the process of school improvement. Why is that research insufficient to guide more effective programs of teacher preparation?

An obvious limitation of the existing knowledge base is that it focuses on particular places and programs, and attempts to extrapolate findings from those studies to different places and programs assumes a generalizability beyond the strict empirical boundaries within which such knowledge was gained. In particular, transfering knowledge about teacher professional development across national education systems should be done carefully (Villegas-Reimers, 2003). The varying results observed across different countries in their efforts to improve educational outcomes underscores the limitations of existing knowledge about how to build system capacity. The latest PISA study shows that, among the countries that have participated in the study over the last two decades, there are many different patterns of improvement, as well as many different patterns of decline. In some countries, student performance is today very comparable to what it was two decades ago. In other countries, such performance has declined. In others in has increased. Figure 1.2 shows these various patterns.

These results are helpful to place what is known about strategies to improve systems to teach a broader range of competencies in context. Much of the education

Table 1.2   Teacher preparation to teach in inclusive classrooms

	Percentage of teachers teaching in classes with more than 10% of special needs students	Percentage of teachers for whom the "teaching in a mixed-ability setting" has been included in their formal education or training	Percentage of teachers who felt "well prepared" or "very well prepared" for teaching in a mixed-ability setting	Percentage of teachers for whom "teaching students with special needs" was included in their recent professional development activities	Percentage of teachers reporting a high level of need for professional development in teaching students with special needs	Percentage of principals reporting a shortage of teachers with competence in teaching students with special needs
Alberta (Canada)	32	77	44	47	11	14
Australia*	29	74	38	58	12	18
Austria	23	52	27	23	16	14
Belgium	52	66	37	35	18	56
- Flemish Comm. (Belgium)	53	70	41	38	13	39
Brazil	11	73	71	40	58	60
Bulgaria	8	42	37	39	27	18
CABA (Argentina)	3	57	51	23	36	18
Chile	55	76	68	55	38	27
Colombia	9	70	54	42	55	68
Croatia	10	47	28	67	36	25
Czech Republic	24	34	18	53	15	30
Denmark	33	67	45	29	19	33
England (UK)	41	90	69	57	6	23
Estonia	14	51	24	57	26	47
Finland	26	73	35	30	12	15
France	40	49	25	30	34	70
Georgia	4	35	39	51	22	14
Hungary	21	71	76	45	22	35
Iceland	40	55	26	30	17	13
Israel*	27	73	59	33	25	41
Italy	37	57	37	74	15	48
Japan	21	64	26	56	46	44
Kazakhstan	5	76	67	32	14	17
Korea	6	64	50	25	13	20
Latvia	9	50	42	50	20	26
Lithuania	11	45	52	53	21	20
Malta	23	64	36	31	20	29
Mexico	8	71	72	28	53	34
Netherlands	46	44	27	42	12	21
New Zealand	17	83	49	32	15	24
Norway	35	60	25	31	18	18
Portugal	19	45	39	30	27	48
Romania	12	80	77	33	35	45
Russian Federation	5	73	72	55	15	11
Saudi Arabia	9	77	70	26	29	52
Shanghai (China)	8	80	69	46	25	20
Singapore	19	79	54	35	20	17
Slovak Republic	22	57	36	37	26	30
Slovenia	31	46	57	54	23	28
South Africa	29	76	67	34	39	53
Spain	19	35	28	37	28	25
Sweden	40	73	61	46	18	30
Turkey	11	66	65	52	16	37
United Arab Emirates	16	87	88	69	18	42
United States	51	81	56	56	9	28
Viet Nam	7	88	72	50	26	58
OECD average-31	27	62	44	43	22	32

Source: OECD, 2019a, Figure I.1.3

Table 1.3 Teachers preparation to manage classroom discipline

	Percentage of teachers for whom "student behaviour and classroom management" was included in their formal education or training	Percentage of teachers who felt "well prepared" or "very well prepared" for student behaviour and classroom management	Percentage of teachers for whom "student behaviour and classroom management" was included in their recent professional development activities	Percentage of teachers reporting a high level of need for professional development in student behaviour and classroom management	Percentage of teachers who feel that they can control disruptive behaviour in the classroom	Percentage of teachers who "agree" or "strongly agree" that they lose quite a lot of time because of students interrupting the lesson
Alberta (Canada)	87	56	45	4	87	26
Australia	84	45	44	5	82	29
Austria	54	21	36	17	88	27
Belgium	73	37	40	10	85	42
- Flemish Comm. (Belgium)	77	43	46	8	93	41
Brazil	75	83	64	19	91	50
Bulgaria	50	46	57	22	85	32
CABA (Argentina)	66	65	40	9	90	35
Chile	76	66	52	17	86	40
Colombia	84	77	70	21	98	22
Croatia	54	38	54	23	82	17
Czech Republic	54	30	45	17	83	18
Denmark	63	53	33	6	97	22
England (UK)	94	68	47	3	86	27
Estonia	79	44	59	17	81	17
Finland	71	29	30	9	83	32
France	55	22	24	13	73	40
Georgia	80	80	84	21	86	7
Hungary	76	81	59	13	93	23
Iceland	58	28	37	19	88	41
Israel*	74	59	56	22	84	29
Italy	58	48	65	16	93	24
Japan	81	39	48	43	60	8
Kazakhstan	88	84	83	21	75	10
Korea	66	56	76	28	82	39
Latvia	81	67	66	20	86	21
Lithuania	71	72	69	21	89	16
Malta	83	49	46	11	83	35
Mexico	84	90	62	12	88	20
Netherlands	85	57	58	9	94	33
New Zealand	90	57	47	5	85	31
Norway	74	50	52	11	79	25
Portugal	62	47	42	18	98	43
Romania	85	82	61	17	90	18
Russian Federation	82	82	77	14	m	10
Saudi Arabia	87	81	74	16	91	26
Shanghai (China)	89	76	80	31	92	10
Singapore	91	65	54	9	80	33
Slovak Republic	62	46	33	19	79	31
Slovenia	37	62	46	16	85	30
South Africa	93	82	79	16	88	41
Spain	40	35	48	14	79	45
Sweden	70	55	41	8	81	27
Turkey	92	88	61	6	90	33
United Arab Emirates	92	92	80	8	92	23
United States	85	61	56	5	84	26
Viet Nam	99	95	94	68	94	12
OECD average-31	72	53	50	14	85	29

Source: OECD, 2019a, Figure I.1.4

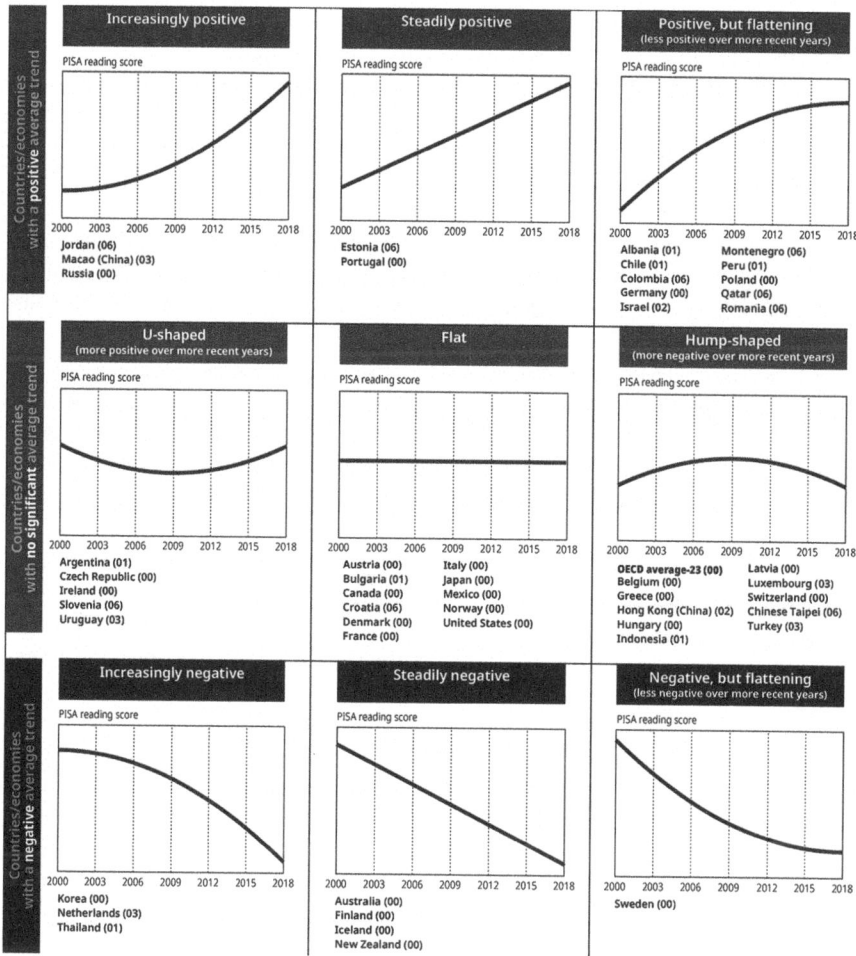

Fig. 1.2 PISA results. (Source: OECD, 2019a Figure I.9.1)

Notes: Figures are for illustrative purposes only. Countries and economies are grouped according to the overall direction of their trend (the sign and significance of the average three-year trend) and to the rate of change in the direction of their trend (the sign and significance of the curvature in the estimate of quadratic trends) (see Annex A7).

Only countries and economies with data from at least five PISA reading assessments are included. Not all countries and economies can compare their students' performance over the same period. For each country/economy, the base year, starting from which reading results can be compared, is indicated in parentheses next to the country's/economy's name ("00" = 2000, "01" = 2001, etc.). Both the overall direction and the change in the direction may be affected by the period considered. OECD average-23 refers to the average of all OECD countries with valid data in all seven assessments; Austria, Chile, Estonia, Israel, Luxembourg, the Netherlands, the Slovak Republic, Slovenia, Spain, Turkey, the United Kingdom and the United States are not included in this average.

Source: OECD, PISA 2018 Database, Table I.B1.10.

research-based knowledge originates in countries, such as Canada and the United States, in which there has been relatively little change in student learning outcomes as assessed in PISA over the last two decades. Arguably, this could help understand why some scholars of the process of educational change in those settings have concluded that reform at scale is more likely to fail than to succeed at changing the basic grammar of schooling (Elmore, 1996; Olson, 2003; Tyack & Cuban, 1997; Tyack & Tobin, 1994).

In other countries which have been well represented in the educational research literature, such as Australia or Finland, the student learning outcomes of students in PISA shows a pattern of consistent decline over the last two decades, albeit from relatively high levels of performance.

In contrast, relatively little educational research has focused on the approaches followed to improve school in countries where students show improvement in PISA scores over these two decades such as Jordan, Macao, Russia, Estonia, Portugal, or countries where students showed improvement during part of that period such as Albania, Chile, Colombia, Germany, Israel, Montenegro, Peru, Poland, Qatar or Romania.

It is therefore necessary to keep in mind that the prevailing conventional wisdom emerging from educational research may be biased by the nature of the educational systems where such research has been conducted in. The world is a much richer laboratory of educational ideas and practices than is covered by existing educational scholarship, much of which focuses in countries where improvement is elusive, while countries where improvement is observed are understudied.

In addition to the limitations of the existing knowledge base stemming from the relatively few countries covered by such literature, transferring ideas about 'what works' in system level change, teacher education and professional development across contexts should be done with great care. There are differences across systems in the rules and norms that shape who practices the profession. In some settings, teachers have more limited general knowledge than in others, they vary in professional preparation, the characteristics of the schools in which they work differ, this variation is also a reason to be curious about what works in different settings.

It is especially important to build a knowledge base about how best to support teachers and system level improvement in the developing world because 90% of the world's children attend schools there. We should not assume that what has proven to work in countries where higher levels of resources are available to support teachers may easily transfer to or be sustainable in contexts where the levels of resources are more limited or where the nature of educational institutions differs. We should be agnostic as to whether the same practices to support teacher professionalism apply in contexts where the extent and nature of the politization of education differ, or about whether changes in requirements for teacher preparation have similar effects in countries where governments have vastly different authority over teacher preparation institutions.

An example from the field of sanitation will illustrate the point that sometimes an approach or a technology that addresses a problem in one setting does not transfer well to a different setting, particularly when resource constrains are critical to the ability to solve the problem at scale. In his efforts to improve sanitation in the developing world, Bill Gates concluded that the toilets and water treatment systems developed and in use in the early industrialized world were poor fits to developing countries because they were resource intensive and generated excessive waste. This caused him to undertake projects to stimulate innovation in the design of next-generation toilets that could operate without sewer systems (Brueck, 2019; D'Agostino, 2018). This approach shows that in order to achieve the same public health results, attempting to transfer a technology developed at a particular time for a particular context, with a given level of resources and institutional capacity, to a different context would be suboptimal to inventing a new technology, designed specifically to address the needs and constrains of those contexts.

Developing countries face different education challenges than early industrialized countries. Because of growing populations and limited institutional capacity in the education sector, often they must attend to expanding access, while also improving quality. This creates different demands and constrains than improving quality in a context in which the population of school children is stable or declining. An expanding system may have to appoint teachers with relatively limited knowledge and skills, simply because the demand for teachers exceeds the availability of qualified candidates. The challenges faced by teachers are very different in a context where parents have comparable levels of education to those of teachers, than in contexts where many parents have very low levels of education. Levels of financing are also likely to influence the conditions of schools, as well as the nature of the infrastructure and resources in schools. General conditions of development in the communities in which schools work also create demands on teachers, they influence how easy it is for them to access school, but also what challenges the students that they teach experience. In settings of great needs there are demands placed on teachers to fill roles which go beyond the instructional role, in service of their students, such as participating in vaccination campaigns or in nutritional programs. The level of institutionalization of education can also influence demands on teachers, for instance, in some settings national politics have more pervasive effects than in others on teacher appointments and translate into demands for teachers to participate in political activities.

As developing countries advance reforms to develop twenty-first century competencies, of deeper learning and educating the whole child, even as they still address twentieth century challenges of access and basic literacies, we need to better understand what it is like to implement ambitious curriculum reforms in a context with over-crowded classrooms, poorly paid teachers and underfunded systems, with weak institutional capacity, or in systems where there is political or economic instability, or where the education system has been captured by vested interests and where patronage and corruption are rampant. This comparative analysis might help us discern which features of the implementation of system level reforms are sufficiently robust to 'work' across contexts, approaches at least worth trying, and which approaches might necessitate more careful sequencing, in which certain preconditions are first established before some components of reform can be pursued.

In order to determine what might be the best way to implement twenty-first century education reforms across these various contexts, we need to study reforms across vastly different contexts, not just on a limited set of similar countries. This book is an effort in that direction. We examine system level reforms across a range of different national education systems. The main thrust of the book is descriptive, providing a careful account of the details of implementation in each of the six countries studied. We also characterize the system level reforms in terms of whether they address cultural, psychological, professional, institutional and political dimensions of the change process. Finally, the concluding chapter draws some lessons about the implementation of reforms based on a cross-case analysis of the six cases.

1.7   Methods of This Study

The six cases of reform examined in this book were initiated as part of a graduate course in education policy analysis I teach at the Harvard Graduate School of Education. The authors are all experienced educators with professional experience as teachers, coaches, providers of teacher professional development, education leaders, government staff, education consultants for governments and international organizations. Collectively they have worked in Afghanistan, Australia, Bhutan, Burkina Faso, Canada, Central African Republic, Colombia, Cote D'Ivoire, Denmark, Djibouti, France, Guinea, India, Israel, Latvia, Malaysia, Maldives, Mali, Mexico, Niger, Pakistan, Panama, Rwanda, Syria, Switzerland, Tanzania, Thailand, Turkey, UAE, Uganda, United Kingdom, United States, and Zimbabwe.

To conduct these studies, the authors accessed published documents, statistical information, results from comparative studies, and interviewed education officials and researchers in the countries they were studying. Some of the teams also travelled to the countries they were studying for several weeks, after producing a first draft of the study, to collect additional data. Each chapter was then discussed by the entire team involved in studying the six cases, leading to several rounds of revisions to achieve coherence and comparability across chapters.

Upon completion of the course, the findings were presented to various audiences familiar with the contexts studied, including at a conference on global education at which senior leaders of practice discussed the reports and provided feedback. Subsequently each research team revised their chapter to achieve greater integration and coherence within the structure of this book. A final set of revisions followed helpful suggestions from the three anonymous reviewers engaged by Springer to peer review the manuscript.

The studies were informed by the content of the course, which reviewed literature on twenty-first century skills, deeper learning, system level change, curriculum and teacher education policy reform. The course readings included also some of the publications of the Global Education Innovation Initiative, a research and practice consortium I lead with the goal of supporting the transformation of public education systems towards greater relevance. The following guiding questions, which I developed to guide two previous studies of the Global Education Innovation Initiative, were used to frame the case studies:

1. What was the reform about, what time frame was covered by the reform?
2. What sources of evidence were used to conduct the study?
3. What Context preceded and gave rise to the reform? Was this reform part of the agenda of a new government? A response to an economic crisis? What were the educational antecedents of this reform? What were the factors which gave impetus to a reform agenda? Where there international influences of any sort? Did international evidence or ideas influence the context?
4. Description of the reform: what were the intended goals, what were the key components of this reform (change in law, budget, curriculum, assessment, etc.), what was the underlying theory of change of the reform? Who participated in the design of the reform and in implementation?
5. In what way did the educational goals of the country's reform relate to the idea of twenty-first century skills or breadth of skills or cognitive and socio-emotional development? Which specific outcomes and skills were emphasized in the reform?
6. Which specific components of the reform are directly related with the development of twenty-first century skills in students? How are they implemented? Description of specific programs that develop twenty-first century skills. (Curriculum, assessment, school autonomy, partnerships, specific programs in schools such as project based learning or specific programs of teacher professional development)
7. What were the various stages of implementation of the reform? Who participated? How are governments (federal/local) coordinating with other stakeholders?
8. What is known about the politics of the reform? Which factors supported implementation? Which impeded it?
9. What do we know about the results of the reform achieved so far? Have they been evaluated? What are the challenges?

1.8   Five Perspectives on Educational Change

Implementing educational policies depends greatly on communication and collaboration across a large number of stakeholders in the education system. They include those who initiate change, as well as those who implement change, they involve people at different levels of the system: in classrooms, school districts, various administrative levels, and senior leadership roles. Each of these actors makes sense of the change process through one or multiple frameworks, whether they are aware of it or not. I believe that deliberate attention to these frameworks, to what each of them reveals and to what they conceal, can help each actor better discern how to implement educational change, as well as better understand other stakeholders involved in the change process, and communicate with them.

To characterize these frameworks, I have developed a conceptual model that analyzes education reforms through five complementary lenses: **cultural, psychological, professional, institutional, or political**. (Reimers, 2020c). A cultural frame highlights the correspondence between societal demands and values and the proposed educational change; a psychological frame focuses on the use of the science of learning and teaching in the design of the change process; a professional frame reflects the creation of norms and processes designed to align professional practice with expertise; an institutional frame focuses on the process of educational change as the result of a system of interdependent processes and a political frame focuses on the role played by various interest groups in advancing or impeding educational change.

These frames serve as analytic tools to conceptualize change. In practice, any reform effort may reflect the reliance on strategies that are best understood through more than one frame. I applied those frames in a comparative study of curriculum reforms in Brazil, Finland, Japan, Mexico, Peru, Poland, Portugal, and Russia, and found that all of them reflected the use of strategies that illustrated more than one frame, but that none of them reflected strategies illustrating a comprehensive use of all five of them (Reimers, 2020b). Furthermore, I also found that institutional and political perspectives were more commonly used by reformers than cultural or psychological perspectives. Increasingly, professional perspectives are also in use as the importance of teacher expertise is recognized as critical to implementing ambitious reform efforts.

Another study of the Global Education Innovation Initiative, a compilation of reflections from system level leaders who had attempted ambitious education reform designed to make visible their theories of action, showed that institutional and political perspectives were dominant in their accounts (Reimers, 2019).

One of the contributors to that compilation, a former secretary of education of the city of Rio de Janeiro, in Brazil, summarizes her approach in a way that illustrates reliance on a professional and institutional perspective:

> Thus, two efforts had to be undertaken simultaneously: starting to build a culture of excellence and of high expectations for every student, and implementing affirmative action to ensure that the most challenged schools received additional support. The approach taken was inspired by Michael Fullan's recommendation of a systemic transformation when reforming the education in a city, so as to avoid fragmentation or the improvement of just some areas in a complex setting [....] With this approach in mind, my team and I developed a program based on the following principles:
>
> - Schools should collaborate with one another, in an ecosystem of learning;
> - Teachers should participate in the design of the curriculum, in the preparation of the textbooks to be used to support their practice, in the elaboration of the digital classes that were to be inserted in a platform to make teaching and learning more interesting, in the assessments, and in the elaboration of a remedial education course for the students who were not learning;
> - We would open the system for experimentation, trying to find scalable good practices;
> - Formative assessment would be incentivized and a unified test would be implemented in all schools every 2 months, with questions prepared collectively by teachers from different schools, to ensure that students were progressing as expected;

- Good teaching would be made visible, not only to the system, but to the whole city; and
- Equity and inclusion would be our most valued principles, alongside excellence. (Costin, 2019, 39–40).

Another contributor to that book, a former minister of education of Colombia, summarizes her approach through an institutional frame, and maintaining strategic focus as a way to prevent the capture of the change effort by various political interests:

we developed a program that increased enrollment at all educational levels, we developed a quality improvement system, and we modernized the management of the sector." (Velez, 2019, 51). "We had the strong conviction that it was crucial to undertake an institutional change that allowed the sector to obtain the results that were set in the plan and to make the change sustainable. An important chapter of our plan was focused on aligning institutions to their objectives. The parallel structures (that may be necessary to start a project) are ephemeral and do not guarantee long-term actions, which is the work needed in education. (Ibid, 54).

Several of these system level leaders use political frameworks to analyze their efforts, as is the case with a former Minister of Education of Mexico:

Unlike economic or financial markets, where you are always looking to increase and save your own resources, the opposite should be done in politics: you must spend your political capital at the beginning of your term, when this capital is possibly at its highest, to make difficult –but important– decisions, even if they are unpopular. The explanation is simple: your political power will vanish quickly, your incumbents will be cruel and brutal, and political circumstances will likely change. (Granados, 2019, 85).

Recognizing that education reforms can be used to advance personal political aims he advises future ministers to forget their political ambitions and stop campaigning.

Also relying on a political framework, a former Minister of Education of Peru, begins his reflection in this way:

If there is no political alignment behind education, you will have to fight to position education so that these constituencies understand its importance. Education is about giving the right quality service to all children and youth, and as such, it is a long-run endeavor that requires the full political commitment of the executive, of parliament, and of society in general. (Saavedra, 2019, 108).

1.9 Content of This Book

This book examines six system level reforms which all intended to improve instruction by expanding the depth and breadth of the curriculum. All of them addressed teacher professional preparation as part of the strategy of implementing the new curriculum, although they did it in different ways and with different results. In addition, some of them also enacted institutional reforms as a way to support the implementation of more ambitious curricula and to support increased teacher capacity, as with teacher professional preparation, there were important differences in the details of those reforms.

In Ontario, the provincial government developed and implemented a reform designed to improve the quality of instruction depending largely on providing teachers opportunities to co-construct the improvement process, and in promoting accountability and coherence across various levels of the system through the use of information. This reform took place in a context in which a new political administration attempted to create more collaborative approaches with teachers and teacher unions, following a contentious period. The focus of the reform was on the improvement of literacy, numeracy, and high school graduation rates. The main drivers of the reform were capacity building and accountability.

The reform adopted a learning orientation, of refining and adapting implementation as a result of the observed results of the actions undertaken. While these were not original goals of the reform, partway through the reform process, the development of twenty-first century skills became a goal in some provinces, as a result of a growing movement of deep learning, however there was no explicit emphasis on twenty-first century skills in policy, curriculum, or assessment. This reform illustrates the use primarily of political, professional and institutional perspectives in that it sought to align key stakeholders and to construct collaborative relationships between teachers and administrators, it sought to empower teachers as professionals and build on their professionalism and it sought to develop institutional capacity and coherence through the use of information. There is also some evidence of reliance on a psychological perspective.

In Singapore, the Government redesigned teacher initial preparation in line with a capacious vision for education which emphasized twenty-first century skills. The reform emphasized the holistic development of the teacher during their initial preparation, so they could in turn educate whole students. Because teachers are initially prepared in a single institution, the National Institute of Education, Nanyang Technological University, Singapore (NIE NTU, Singapore) it was possible to implement this new teacher preparation curriculum with great fidelity and coherence. The emphasis of this reform reflects a professional perspective, enhanced by an institutional perspective as there were other changes ongoing that supported the reform of teacher education, such as a curriculum reform. The chapter highlights how Singapore leveraged emerging ideas from international education organizations and think tanks on education for the twenty-first century to shape its own education strategy.

In Mexico, as part of a comprehensive set of structural reforms that sought to increase the competitiveness of Mexico's economy and to address inequality, the government advanced a comprehensive education reform which included a clear focus on a broad set of competencies. A key element of that reform included taking control over teacher appointments and careers away from the teacher union, which generated predictable opposition from the teacher union. The reform was approached primarily through a political and an institutional perspective. The sequence of reform, and the short tenure of the administration, limited effective use of a cultural, psychological or professional perspective, furthering the political opposition to the reform. While the reform included also a program of teacher evaluation and preparation, and repurposed an institute of educational evaluation to undertake the core functions of teacher support, these components of the reform strategy came too late in the tenure of the government advancing the reform to be fully or effectively implemented.

In Pakistan, the Punjab Education Reform was, essentially, an institutional capacity building strategy aimed at overhauling the delivery and monitoring systems in the province. The reform did not address breadth of skills, or curriculum, but rather increased the capacity of schools to deliver the existing curriculum strengthening capacity and accountability for access, literacy and numeracy. Following the approach to whole system reform used in the United Kingdom during the Tony Blair administration, the Punjab Education Reform established a delivery unit to maintain focus on the implementation of a limited set of reforms. The reform built management capacity as a way to strengthen the delivery chain to implement the reform goals, it also built teacher capacity, reflecting elements of a professional perspective. A decade into implementation of this reform, it was still not explicitly addressing twenty-first century skills.

In Kenya, the government implemented a competency-based national curriculum reform in 2017 intending to develop a broader range of competencies in line with supporting Kenya's greater competitiveness. It piloted the reform in 470 schools, for broader roll out subsequently. They also used a train-the-trainer (ToT) model for teachers' training and preparation. Part of the reform included a structural change to education, from 8 years of primary and 4 years of secondary education to 6 years of primary, 3 of middle, and 3 of tertiary education, to provide greater focus on technical and vocational education. The strategy adopted by the reform reflects a cultural and a political perspective. While the reform aimed at building teacher capacity, those efforts have been insufficient to equip teachers to teach the more ambitious competency-based curriculum.

In Zimbabwe, the government developed a new set of standards and curriculum frameworks with the aim of better equipping students for the evolving needs of the twenty-first century. To support the implementation of the new curriculum, the Ministry distributed school packages which included the curriculum framework, the syllabi and assessment resources. Challenges with the delivery of those packages, however, have limited the broad dissemination of the curriculum among teachers. The reform contemplates professional development for teachers, which is currently being implemented, as well as preparation and distribution of instructional materials and assessment, which have not yet taken place. The reform illustrates the use of an institutional and a professional perspective, roles for teachers and school administrators were redesigned to align them to the new curriculum goals.

To sum up, while an ambitious set of education goals guides reforms in Singapore, Mexico, Kenya and Zimbabwe, only in Singapore a relatively small system in which there is great institutional coherence and significant educational investment in education, is there evidence that teacher preparation programs are aligned with those ambitions. In Mexico, the sequencing of the reform prioritized the establishment of professional norms for teacher appointments and promotions. The contention generated by those changes, and a political transition, aborted the full implementation of the planned supports to build teacher capacity. In Kenya and Zimbabwe, the ambitious of the curriculum reforms greatly exceed the supports put in place to build institutional capacity.

If implementation of twenty-first century education was elusive in these four countries were policy declared the intent to pursue it, things were not much different in the two jurisdictions which chose first to build system capacity focused on the basic literacies: Ontario and Punjab. After a long period of building capacity, those systems had improved in the goals they had set out to improve, but they had not transitioned to pursue the breadth of skills advocated by the various organizations discussed in this chapter.

Which leaves us in a difficult place, concluding that twenty-first century education remains an elusive goal, one embraced rhetorically by reforms of education systems at various stages of implementation, but not yet reflected in implementation strategies which could possibly match those ambitions. In the chapters that follow we examine the details of the implementation of those reforms.

References

Branswell, H., & Joseph, A. (2020). *WHO declares the coronavirus outbreak a pandemic.* https://www.statnews.com/2020/03/11/who-declares-the-coronavirus-outbreak-a-pandemic/. Accessed 20 June 2020.

Brueck, H. (2019). A $350 toilet powered by worms may be the ingenious future of sanitation that Bill Gates has been dreaming about. *Business Insider.* https://www.businessinsider.com/bill-gates-foundation-helps-invent-tiger-toilets-powered-by-worms-2019-1. Accessed 8 Jan 2019

Care, E., Kim, H., Anderson, K., & Gustafsson-Wright, E. (2017). *Skills for a changing world: National perspectives and the global movement.* Washington, DC: Brookings.

CASEL. (2020). https://casel.org/. Accessed 29 Feb 2020.

Costin, C. (2019). How to ensure quality education in a very unequal city. In F. Reimers (Ed.), *Letters to a New Minister of Education* (pp. 37–49). Middletown, DE: CreateSpace.

D'Agostino, R. (2018). *How does Bill Gates's ingenious, waterless, life-saving toilet work?* https://www.popularmechanics.com/science/health/a24747871/bill-gates-life-saving-toilet/. Accessed 8 Jan 2019.

Delors, J. (1996). *Learning: The treasure within, report to UNESCO of the international commission on education for the twenty-first century.* Paris: UNESCO.

Deming, D. (2017). *The growing importance of social skills in the labor market* (National Bureau of Economic Research, Working paper 21473).

Elfert, M. (2015). UNESCO, the Faure Report, the Delors Report, and the political Utopia of lifelong learning. *European Journal of Education, 50*(1), 88–100.

Elmore, R. (1996). Getting to scale with good educational practice. *Harvard Educational Review, 66*(1), 1–27.

Global Partnership for Education. (2020). 21st century skills: What potential role for the Global Partnership for Education? *A Landscape Review.* https://www.globalpartnership.org/sites/default/files/document/file/2020-01-GPE-21-century-skills-report.pdf. Accessed 24 Feb 2020

Granados, O. (2019). Reflections from a secretary of education to his successor at the end of his tenure. In F. Reimers (Ed.), *Letters to a New Minister of Education* (pp. 83–90). Middletown, DE: CreateSpace.

National Research Council. (2012). *Education for life and work: Developing transferable knowledge and skills in the 21st century*. Washington, DC: The National Academies Press.

OECD. (2019a). *TALIS – The OECD teaching and learning international survey*. http://www.oecd.org/education/talis/. Accessed 3 Dec 2019.

OECD. (2019b). *PISA 2018 results. What students know and can do* (Vol. 1). https://www.oecd.org/pisa/. Accessed 6 Dec 2019

OECD. (2019c). *PISA 2018 results. Where all students can succeed* (Vol. 2). https://www.oecd.org/pisa/. Accessed 6 Dec 2019.

OECD. (2020). *Learning compass 2030*. http://www.oecd.org/education/2030-project/teaching-and-learning/learning/learning-compass-2030/OECD_Learning_Compass_2030_concept_note.pdf. Accessed 29 Feb 2020.

Olson, D. (2003). *Psychological theory and educational reform*. Cambridge, UK: Cambridge University Press.

Papay, J. P., Mantil, A., Murnane, R. J., An, L., Donohue, K., & McDonough, A. (2020). *Lifting all boats? Accomplishments and challenges from 20 years of education reform in Massachusetts*. Providence, RI: Educational Opportunity in MA, Brown University. https://annenberg.brown.edu/sites/default/files/LiftingAllBoats_FINAL.pdf. Accessed 28 June 2020.

Ravitch, D. (2010). *The death and live of the great American school system*. New York: Basic Books.

Reimers, F. (2017). *One student at a time*. Middletown, DE: CreateSpace.

Reimers, F. (Ed.). (2019). *Letters to a new minister of education*. Middletown, DE: CreateSpace.

Reimers, F. (Ed.). (2020a). *Empowering teachers to build a better world. How six nations support teachers for 21st century education*. Singapore: Springer.

Reimers, F. (Ed.). (2020b). *Audatious education purposes. How governments transform the goals of education systems*. Cham, Switzerland: Springer.

Reimers, F. (Ed.). (2020c). *Educating students to improve the world*. Singapore: Springer.

Reimers, F., & Chung, C. (Eds.). (2016). *Teaching and learning in the twenty first century*. Cambridge, MA: Harvard Education Publishing.

Reimers, F., & Chung, C. (Eds.). (2018). *Preparing teachers to educate whole students*. Cambridge, MA: Harvard Education Publishing.

Reimers, F., & Schleicher, A. (2020a). *A framework to guide an education response to the COVID-19 Pandemic of 2020*. Paris: OECD. https://read.oecd-ilibrary.org/view/?ref=126_126988-t63lxosohs&title=A-framework-to-guide-an-education-response-to-the-Covid-19-Pandemic-of-2020

Reimers, F., & Schleicher, A. (2020b). *Schooling disrupted, schooling rethought. How the COVID-19 Pandemic is changing education*. Paris: OECD. https://read.oecd-ilibrary.org/view/?ref=133_133390-1rtuknc0hi&title=Schooling-disrupted-schooling-rethought-How-the-Covid-19-pandemic-is-changing-education

Roser, M., & Ortiz-Ospina, E. (2013). *Primary and secondary education*. Published online at OurWorldInData.org. Retrieved from https://ourworldindata.org/primary-and-secondary-education

Saavedra, J. (2019). Letter to a new Minister of Education. In F. Reimers (Ed.), *Letters to a new Minister of Education* (pp. 109–120). Middletown, DE: CreateSpace.

Taylor, R. D., et al. (2017). Promoting positive youth development through school-based social and emotional learning interventions: A meta-analysis of follow-up effects. *Child Development, 88*(4), 1156–1171.

Tyack, D., & Cuban, L. (1997). *Tinkering towards Utopia. A century of public school reform*. Cambridge, MA: Harvard University Press.

Tyack, D., & Tobin, W. (1994). The 'grammar' of schooling: Why has it been so hard to change? *American Educational Research Journal, 31*(3), 452–479.

UNESCO. (1974). *Recommendation concerning education for international understanding, co-operation and peace and education relating to human rights and fundamental freedoms*. http://portal.unesco.org/en/ev.php-URL_ID=13088&URL_DO=DO_TOPIC&URL_SECTION=201.html. Accessed 28 June 2020.

UNESCO. (2018). *Progress on education for sustainable development and global citizenship education: Findings of the 6th consultation on the implementation of the 1974 recommendation concerning education for international understanding.* https://unesdoc.unesco.org/ark:/48223/pf0000266176. Accessed 28 June 2020.

UNESCO. (2019). *Educational content up close.* Paris.

UNICEF. (2017). Reimagining life skills and citizenship education in the Middle East and North Africa a four-dimensional and systems approach to 21st century skills conceptual and programmatic framework. https://www.unicef.org/mena/media/6151/file/LSCE%20Conceptual%20and%20Programmatic%20Framework_EN.pdf%20.pdf

UNICEF. (2020). *Child friendly schools.* https://www.unicef.org/lifeskills/index_7260.html. Accessed 28 Feb 2020.

United Nations. (1948). *Universal declaration of human rights.* https://www.un.org/en/universal-declaration-human-rights/

United Nations. (2020). *Sustainable development Goal 4.* https://sustainabledevelopment.un.org/sdg4. Accessed 24 Feb 2020.

Velez, C. (2019). Letter to a new Minister. In F. Reimers (Ed.), *Letters to a new Minister of Education* (pp. 51–56). Middletown, DE: CreateSpace.

Villegas-Reimers, E. (2003). *Teacher professional development. An international review of the literature.* Paris: UNESCO. International Institute for Educational Planning.

World Bank. (2018). *World development report. Learning to realize education's promise.* Washington, DC: International Bank for Reconstruction and Development/The World Bank.

World Bank. (2019). *Ending learning poverty. A target to galvanize action on early literacy.* https://www.worldbank.org/en/news/immersive-story/2019/11/06/a-learning-target-for-a-learning-revolution. Accessed 24 Feb 2020.

World Economic Forum. (2020). *Schools of the future defining new models of education for the fourth industrial revolution.* http://www3.weforum.org/docs/WEF_Schools_of_the_Future_Report_2019.pdf. Accessed 29 Feb 2020.

World Health Organization. (1999). *Partners in life skills education conclusions from a United Nations Inter-Agency meeting.* Geneva. https://www.who.int/mental_health/media/en/30.pdf. Accessed 28 Feb 2020.

Fernando M. Reimers is the Ford Foundation Professor of the Practice of International Education and Director of the Global Education Innovation Initiative and of the International Education Policy Masters Program at Harvard University. An expert in the field of Global Education, Reform and System Level Change, his research and teaching focus on understanding how to educate children and youth so they can thrive in the twenty-first century. He is a member of UNESCO's high level commission on the Futures of Education.

He has written or edited thirty-three books, of which the most recent include: *Educating Students to Improve the World, Audacious Education Purposes. How governments transform the goals of education systems, Empowering teachers to build a better world. How six nations support teachers for 21st century education, Letters to a New Minister of Education, Teaching and Learning for the 21st Century, Preparing Teachers to Educate Whole Students: An International Comparative Study, Learning to Improve the World, Empowering Global Citizens, Empowering Students to Improve the World in Sixty Lessons. Version 1.0, Learning to Collaborate for the Global Common Good, Fifteen Letters on Education in Singapore, Empowering All Students at Scale,* and *One Student at a Time. Leading the Global Education Movement.*

Chapter 2
Education Reform in Ontario: Building Capacity Through Collaboration

Taylor Boyd

2.1 Introduction

Ontario's educational performance preceding the reform was not lagging according to international standards. Students were consistently achieving top-quartile scores in math and top-decile scores in reading in PISA (Mourshed, Chijioke, & Barber, 2010). Ontario also had the largest proportion of immigrants in the country: as of 2018, these students represented 44% of the student population (O'Grady et al., 2019) and has seen higher performance of students of immigrant background compared to the Organisation for Economic Co-operation and Development (OECD) average (OECD, 2019). Yet by the province's standards, students were not performing well in literacy and numeracy. The Literacy and Numeracy Strategy was launched in 2004 to improve student reading, writing and math. The aim of the strategy was to have 75% of 6th graders able to read, write and do math by spring 2008 at the expected level. Only 55% of students had met this goal in 2003. Additionally, only 60% of students were graduating high school within 4 years. The target was to have 85% of Grade 9 students graduate within 4 years by 2010 (Levin, Glaze, & Fullan, 2008).

Just as troubling as student underperformance were the tensions which had risen among teachers and the Ministry of Education during the Conservative government of Premier Mike Harris from 1995 to 2002. The Ontario education system had faced major reforms starting in 1993 when the Royal Commission on Learning was initiated by the previous New Democratic Party (NDP) government. The Harris government acted on some of the recommendations of the reports by this commission and became the first administration to introduce full-scale testing by establishing the Education Quality and Accountability Office (EQAO). The EQAO was created as an independent agency which administers and evaluates standardized provincial

T. Boyd (✉)
Harvard Graduate School of Education, Cambridge, MA, USA

© The Author(s) 2021
F. M. Reimers (ed.), *Implementing Deeper Learning and 21st Century Education Reforms*, https://doi.org/10.1007/978-3-030-57039-2_2

tests – and as well as a College of Teachers to oversee accreditation and professional standards for teachers and teacher training institutions. The Harris government also introduced a new funding model in which municipal education taxes were replaced with province-level taxes. Other changes included amalgamating school boards, moving taxation, establishing a district aggregate average class size, reducing teachers' preparation time by as much as 50%, and increasing the time students and teachers spend in class each year (Earl, Freeman, Lasky, Sutherland, & Torrance, 2002).

Many of these changes were disempowering for teachers and ultimately detrimental for students. The Harris government passed an education bill (Bill 160) which restricted strike actions and mandated requirements for staff, class size, preparation time and established a minimum amount of instructional time. These were previously established by local school boards. Placing these aspects under provincial purview and classifying principals and vice-principals as management excluded them from teacher unions and alienated many teachers (Earl et al., 2002). The Harris administration was widely perceived by educators as being disrespectful to teachers by requiring teachers to implement a hurried curriculum without a full understanding of the standards which had a negative impact on teacher collaboration. The administration's relationship with educators further deteriorated in 1995 when Minister of Education John Snobelen was inadvertently caught on camera saying the government needed to "create a crisis in education to generate support for change" (Parker, 2017). This comment had little impact on the momentum for change that had been generated by the report by the Royal Commission and creation of the EQAO but it represented the manipulation of the government in taking a "brand-building" approach to reform (Parker, 2017).

Initiatives introduced under Premier Harris such as Teacher Adviser Program (TAP) increased teachers' workload which contributed to increased pressure and higher fatigue. As a result, teachers took on fewer extracurricular commitments in protest which negatively impacted their relationships with students. This loss of motivation often occurs when teachers feel reforms are politically mandated rather than student-centered (Hargreaves, 1998 as cited by Earl et al., 2002) and the mounting frustration experienced by many teachers resulted in a province-wide walkout by teachers in October 1997. Over the previous 4 years, 26 million student days had been lost due to strikes (Mourshed et al., 2010), leading many families to exit the public system altogether. Public confidence in education, which had been declining in the late 1990s, hit a low point at 43% in 2002 (Hart & Kempf, 2018).

2.2   British Influence

McGuinty's first priority was to "stabilize the patient" by changing the tone of conflict that had characterized the previous administration (D. McGuinty, personal communication, December 11, 2019). Inspired by the results-oriented approach of a 1997 literacy and numeracy reform in Britain, McGuinty committed to a few specific deliverables which were maintained across his tenure. This was an important act of accountability which helped rebuild trust with the public and teachers. The work of Special Advisor Michael Fullan provided the theoretical framework for the Ontario education reform, which was modeled on the education reform under British Prime Minister Tony Blair and chief strategist Michael Barber. Fullan had examined this reform while working at the Ontario Institute for Studies in Education (OISE). The Ontario strategy borrowed some elements from the British reform, including their focus on using professional development to build system capacity (Levin, 2008). Yet the British model was considered by many to be "too top-down, too target driven, and too punitive" (Fullan, 2010). Reform leaders in Ontario gave schools and boards more autonomy and flexibility on how they achieved priorities and how they responded to failure to achieve goals – with support rather than punishment (Levin, 2008). In addition, Britain's gains in education leveled off (Fullan, 2010); Ontario sought to design a reform whose impact would endure.

2.3 Strong Leadership

One of the most significant successes of the Ontario reform was the ability of policymakers and educators to link the external structure of the school, which includes standards, assessments, and accountability, with the internal structure of teaching, learning and instruction organization (Cohen & Mehta, 2017), by investing in teacher education, funding, system organization and leadership. The strength of the reform was a united effort across all levels of the education system to build capacity and accountability. A key part of the strategy was creating a Literacy and Numeracy Secretariat (LNS) to build leadership capacity at the provincial, district and community levels. The LNS was created to build teaching and leadership capacity and directly target improvement of student outcomes without bureaucratic constraints (Levin, 2008). Approximately forty Student Achievement Officers (SAO) were hired to design and implement improvement strategies in support of this initiative. SAO's and Ministry of Education staff in the Secondary Schools Programs Branch worked with district staff on a local basis to push districts "in a supportive and collegial way, which assisted and motivated districts, rather than in a commanding or punitive way" (Levin, 2008, p. 33). Every school was required to create a team to lead their success initiative.

The commitment to a collaborative and problem-solving approach at all three levels of government was essential to the design and implementation of school-level initiatives and was reflected in the design of leadership infrastructure and initiatives in the Ministry of Education. At the highest level, Canada's Council of Ministers of Education provides a forum for other provincial Ministers of Education to meet and discuss ideas and practices to implement (OECD, 2011). In 2007, the Leadership Alliance Network for Student Achievement (LANSA) was initiated to partner directors from the five highest-achieving districts with those from the 18 lowest-achieving districts in a professional learning community to share knowledge about how to implement strategies for literacy and numeracy. Directors, managers, and education officers often work through External Student Success Education Officers (ESSEOs) in regional offices. At the school level, Student Success teams are comprised of administration, student services, special education, co-op and classroom teachers to identify students at risk of not graduating and to coordinate a strategy and support transition from elementary to secondary schools. These 'Student Success Leaders' were also given the initiative to plan how funding is allocated to programs (Directions Evidence and Policy Research Group, 2014). Thus, there was initiative and accountability for educators at all levels of the system.

The selection of leaders in Ontario's education system was critical in preserving the continuous focus of reform goals. Strategic reform leader Ben Levin was a former deputy minister of education for the province of Manitoba and arrived with practical experience in the field. Premier McGuinty made a novel decision to bring Michael Fullan – former dean of OISE at the University of Toronto – into the cabinet room as an outside expert who became his Special Advisor on Education. In terms of political leadership, Ontario maintained a pattern of selecting leaders from within their ranks. Mary-Jean Gallagher was the director of the Greater Essex County school board term before taking on the role of the Assistant Deputy Minister of Student Achievement, during which she led the literacy and numeracy initiative. One of Gallagher's priorities was incorporating the LNS into the Ministry of Education, making it a core function of the ministry rather than a reform strategy. Expanding the scope of initiatives by incorporating them into the ministry was a key strategy in ensuring the reforms were sustainable. Kathleen Wynne assumed the role of Minister of Education from 2006 to 2010 following her role as Parliamentary Assistant to former Minister of Education Gerard Kennedy from 2004 to 2006. Minister Wynne had a Master of Education and was previously a school trustee. She assumed the role as Premier after McGuinty's resignation in 2013, serving for 5 years. Her experience in education made her well-positioned to maintain the administration's educational priorities (Mourshed et al., 2010), most importantly her role as Minister of Education from 2006 to 2010. Her file on parent involvement as Parliamentary Assistant which involved dealing with parent organizations and representativeness meant she had a working relationship with parents entering her role as Minister (K. Wynne, personal communication, November 5, 2019).

2.4 Student Success Strategy

Reform was implemented at the ministry, district and school levels. Programming at secondary schools was designed to improve student outcomes by increasing engagement with courses and staff. The Student Success/Learning to 18 strategy (SS/L18) launched in 2003 was designed to help secondary students graduate and reach their educational and career goals. The Ministry of Education provided approximately $130 million to school boards for student success initiatives in 2010/11 and raised funding to about $150 million in 2012/13 (Office of the Auditor General of Ontario,

2011). The strategy had five key goals: to increase the provincial graduation rate and decrease the drop-out rate, support positive outcomes for all students, provide students with new learning opportunities, build on students' strengths and interests, and provide students with an effective elementary-to-secondary school transition (Directions Evidence and Policy Research Group, 2014). The two prongs of this approach included innovative programs and instruction aimed at literacy and numeracy such as dual credits and experiential learning, as well as more personalized support from Student Success Teams (Ontario Ministry of Education, 2008b).

Efforts to support students were focused on building a relationship between students and teachers. Related initiatives included the Supervised Alternative Learning for Excused Pupils (SALEP) which was aimed at re-engaging students who were not on track to graduate and preparing them to reach their post-graduation goals. Staff were required to make formal transition plans, monitor students and promote their engagement as a "caring adult" (Directions Evidence and Policy Research Group, 2014). In further efforts to re-engage students, Ontario introduced legislation in 2005 requiring all students who had not graduated from high school to continue in a school or another appropriate learning program until they were 18 years of age (Levin, 2008).

One of the central tenets of helping secondary students graduate and reach their educational and career goals was providing personalized support for students. Leaders were established in schools to coordinate success initiatives and "to combat the anonymity that many students experience in high schools" (Levin, 2008, p. 35). Initiatives included the Grade 8–9 Transition Planning Initiative launched in 2005, which involved a collaboration between elementary and secondary schools to provide an adult to partner with students to facilitate the transition from elementary to secondary school. As this transition marks one of students' "perilous points in their educational trajectory" (Lee & Burkam, 2003) during which they are at a particularly high risk of dropping out, the narrow targeting of this strategy was instrumental in supporting student retention. Furthermore, the strong relationship between academic background and dropping out (Lee & Burkam, 2003) suggests that gains in student test scores may have contributed to lower dropout rates, thus advancing multiple goals of the reform.

Programming targeted at fostering relationships between students and a caring adult are supported by research showing that high quality student-teacher relationships are a better predictor of achievement in young children than students' relationships with their peers, and in some cases even a better predictor than their relationship with their mother (O'Connor & McCartney, 2007). In high school, students' relationships with their teachers are a critical protective factor. Students are less likely to drop out of school when they perceive positive relationships between themselves and their teachers (Lee & Burkam, 2003). This effect persists even once student background and school characteristics are considered, which suggests teachers can play a formative role in student retention across many contexts.

Another key partner in providing individualized support for students were parents. Parents Reaching Out (PRO) was started in 2006 to allow parents on school councils to identify barriers to parental involvement and act to address it. A review of these parent initiatives revealed that in Ontario's large urban areas, parents emphasized partnerships between homes, schools and communities, as well as language support and feedback from the parent community. The focus in primary schools was on literacy and numeracy, whereas in secondary schools, parents emphasized mental health (Hamlin & Flessa, 2018). The priorities identified by parents in this program can be used as a source of valuable feedback for the development of a larger program or strategy by the ministry.

In their 2006–2007 evaluation of the Student Success Strategy, the non-profit corporation Canadian Council on Learning found that there was a shift from an implied focus on the learner to a "highly intentional focus" on the learner for school programming, including flexibility, choice and monitoring, and that these measures led to improved academic and social outcomes including smoother transition into secondary school, better test scores and graduation rates (Directions Evidence and Policy Research Group, 2014). The council identified key factors which contributed to student success, including targeted funding, designation of student success staff in schools and leaders in boards, improved scheduling and funding flexibility, professional development opportunities, increased focus at points of student transition within and between schools, and innovative projects.

An area of reform in which Ontario excelled was the specific targeted programming toward student achievement. Professor Alan King performed research over 4 years tracking two cohorts and found that between 2003 and 2004, graduation rates for students going through the new programming was only 68%. Specifically, he found that credit accumulation in Grades 9 and 10 were significant predictors of graduation (King, 2002, 2003; King, 2004 as cited by Directions Evidence and Policy Research Group, 2014). Insights from this research were used in designing initiatives for students between Grade 7 and 12. Changes to the Education Act in 2009 increased school board responsibility for student achievement as well as Student Achievement Officers who facilitate professional learning communities for principals (Mourshed et al., 2010). In order to sustain student engagement and bolster course completion rates, a credit recovery initiative was introduced, in which students who failed a course must only repeat the parts which they failed, as opposed to repeating the whole course. Similarly, in credit rescue, schools provide additional assistance to students outside of class who were in danger of failing a course. This design was aimed at mitigating the negative emotional consequences of failure and improving retention rates.

Other initiatives to bolster student achievement included the Specialist High Skills Majors, which allows students to focus their studies in a certain area, and Dual Credit programs, in which students can enroll in courses which would count both towards their secondary school diploma and a post-secondary qualification. In addition, the School-College-Work initiative, aimed at improving the transition from high school to post-secondary pathways, was expanded across the province. The Cooperative Education and Apprenticeship program was also updated to include more scaffolding preceding a coop placement, more flexible course scheduling and tailored course design to allow students to participate in apprenticeships (Directions Evidence and Policy Research Group, 2014).

In addition to evaluations and research studies, a vital source of feedback for programming was students. In the Student Voice initiative established in 2008, students were encouraged to share their ideas about improving the Ontario school system and strengthen their sense of belonging. Students were also able to voice their opinions on the Minister's Student Advisory Council and apply for grants for leading projects on student engagement (Directions Evidence and Policy Research Group, 2014).

2.5   Capacity Through Collaboration

I believe that teachers and principals and district leaders are not unlike students in that some are strong, some are weak, but they can all improve. – Former Ontario Premier Dalton McGuinty

Following a troubled relationship with teachers under the previous administration, it became apparent to McGuinty's government that they "cannot afford to be at war with our teachers" (D. McGuinty, personal communication, December 11, 2019). They recognized teachers as critical partners in leading reform and took action to rebuild a trusting relationship with them. The government abolished some policies such as paper-and-pencil testing of new teachers and the professional development requirement, which had been perceived by many teachers as punitive, and replaced them with an induction program for new teachers and simpler system of teacher performance evaluation (Levin, 2008). Although the original reform design was top-down, reform leaders began to realize the need to develop capacity in districts and schools so that the drive for change did not only originate from the highest levels of leadership (M. Fullan, personal communication, December 9, 2019).

Demonstrating gains in student outcomes made by reform efforts was instrumental in securing funding to support programming. Over the course of the reform, the sustained focus on outcomes contributed to a rise in the education budget from $10 billion to $21 billion (D. McGuinty, personal communication, December 11, 2019). Equally important was fostering meaningful relationships with teachers and principals to maintain an understanding of what was happening in the classroom. A critical part of McGuinty's "resolute" leadership was combining his persistence in pursuing reform goals with his demonstration of empathy towards educators (Fullan, 2010). McGuinty held a roundtable with principals once every couple of months to learn about how the reform was being perceived (D. McGuinty, personal communication, December 11, 2019). Furthermore, the Ministry put in place a Partnership Table which brings the Minister of Education together with all major stakeholders on a regular basis. Most policy issues are discussed at these meetings before finalization and announcement (Levin, 2008).

A significant part of creating an environment for progress involved removing "distractors" which were preventing teachers from reaching their potential in the classroom and rebuilding a healthy relationship with teachers (D. McGuinty, personal communication, December 11, 2019). One of the most important developments in freeing teachers from their extracurricular obligations was the signing of a 4-year collective bargaining agreement (OECD, 2011). Previously, teachers were involved in labour negotiations for agreements which lasted only 2 years. Inspired by the cross-sector cooperation in Ireland which fueled rapid economic growth in the late 1990s and early 2000s, McGuinty helped to extend the term of agreements to allow teacher to devote their resources toward the classroom. Reducing class size was another strategy to remove distractors from the table. Although the research did not offer unanimous support for smaller class size, teachers had expressed concern at having to teach too many students (D. McGuinty, personal communication, December 11, 2019). As part of the collective agreement signed in 2005, the government supported 200 min of weekly preparation time for all elementary teachers which led to creation of about 2,000 new teaching positions for specialists. By 2007, 90% of the province's primary classes (K-3) had twenty or fewer students and about 5,000 new teachers were introduced into the elementary school system (Levin, 2008).

The system of support provided to principals and teachers was based on their conception as "lead learners" who, like their students, needed access to expertise from professionals and peers. In fostering a more collaborative teaching culture to raise student achievement, teachers were provided with strong individual classroom support. They were encouraged to take an "assessment for learning and as learning" approach to their professional learning, which involves specifying goals and implementation strategies, working with peers and engaging in pedagogical reflection (Ontario Ministry of Education, 2010). Learning involves not only teachers' peers but also their students as a vital source of feedback in their personal and professional development.

In an analysis of teaching culture in Ontario school boards, Hargreaves, Shirley, Wangia, Bacon, and D'Angelo (2018) noted a transition from professional collaboration, which is a descriptive approach that refers to how teachers collaborate and emphasizes the equality of all teachers, to the more prescriptive approach of collaborative professionalism, which involves professionals working together to improve student achievement and wellbeing. This approach emphasizes a sense of shared responsibility and values all voices in contributing to a collaborative and equitable learning culture. Key elements of this approach also include regular feedback in professional learning and development as well as collective responsibility among students, defined by "a moral responsibility and a central professional obligation" to student success (Hargreaves et al., 2018). In contrast to the culture of collaboration during the previous administration, once "distractors" had been removed from their workload, teachers were able to focus on developing their teaching skills and be more intentional in their collaboration with their colleagues and students.

Collaborative inquiry, which is an integral part of collaborative professionalism, played a significant role in Ontario educational policy starting in 2010 based on its ability to enhance teacher and student learning by engaging educators as researchers. Consultants and coaches worked with schools to encourage educators to reflect on their practice in collaborative inquiry, not as an expert but as a partner in learning. "Coaching at the elbow" gave teachers the assistance from instructional coaches as they attempted and practiced new strategies in literacy (Hargreaves & O'Connor, 2018). Evidence suggests that opportunities for teachers to receive this kind of support and coaching during implementation is a feature of effective programs internationally (Ingvarson, Meiers, & Beavis, 2005). Furthermore, research has found that the level of school support emerges as an 'enabling condition' for professional development as it influences the extent of active learning, follow-up and feedback and significant effects on program outcomes.

Another key strategy in providing support for students was resourcing parents to create their own improvement plans. The Parents Reaching Out (PRO) fund allowed school councils and parent organizations to apply for grants to start activities designed to support student learning at school ($1,000 for parent projects), regional or provincial level (up to $30,000). The province made significant investments in education and ensured these funds were distributed among schools and dedicated towards programming which empowered teachers and parents. This initiative was significant because it was an investment in innovation and an act of trust. Ontario funded over 5,500 school council PRO projects and over 200 regional projects with a budget of over $10 million (Mourshed et al., 2010). This program embodied another key component of the reform which was implementing policies and practices that increased individual and collective capacity to achieve accountability via shared responsibility, achieving both internal and external accountability.

Although equity was not an explicit goal of the reform, supports were put in place to narrow the achievement gap among schools. The "turnaround schools" program offered additional support to a small number of low-achieving schools who opted in voluntarily. The number of these schools had been reduced by 75% by 2006 (Levin, 2008), at which point these schools were put under the administration of the LNS and the Ontario Focused Intervention Partnership (OFIP) was established. OFIP is an equity strategy which identifies high needs schools and addresses them with a non-stigmatizing attitude and targeted support by working with educators and stakeholders to plan school improvement strategies. The OFIP School Strategy provides support to OFIP 1 schools, in which under 34% of students are underachieving in reading, and OFIP 2 schools, in which up to 50% of students were demonstrating low performance (Audet et al., 2007).

2.6 Professional Development

Professional development initiatives at Ontario schools combined many elements of the organization partnership model for professional development (Villegas-Reimers, 2003). For instance, the faculty of education at the University of Toronto OISE established a partnership with four school boards in Toronto called the 'Learning Consortium' which was aimed at improving teacher development. A planning committee organized formal and informal professional development activities, including in-service and pre-service programs, conferences, and reflective and monitoring practices. The Teacher Apprenticeship Program was another professional development initiative based in Toronto which helped provide teaching practice to students who wanted to enter teacher training programs but lacked the experience. Apprentices were assigned mentor teachers, and both participated in regular workshops and discussion groups (Villegas-Reimers, 2003). Partnerships were formed even at the course level: "Innovation, Creativity and Entrepreneurship" – a course designed by the Ministry of Education and Rotman School of Management at the University of Toronto – was offered as part of Specialist High Skills Major program for about 25 students in each district school board (Ontario Ministry of Education, 2016).

Another key aspect of the organization partnership model which was central to Ontario education reform was forming school and teacher networks. LANSA was aimed at forming partnerships among directors and building capacity to maximize instructional leadership and strategies to improve student outcomes. Directors from the highest-achieving districts formed a professional learning community with directors of the lowest-achieving boards to share strategies about how to implement numeracy and literacy strategies. This provided a framework for professional development around the School Effectiveness Framework and mentorship was implemented at all levels of leadership.

The Teacher Leadership and Learning Program (TLLP) was launched in 2007 as a joint initiative between the Ontario Teachers' Federation (OTF) and Ontario Ministry of Education (OME) with the goals of supporting experienced teachers in self-directed professional development. Each year, experienced teachers could apply to conduct a TLLP project. A research report found that over 95% of teachers participating in TLLP Summits from 2008 to 2012 reported being satisfied (Campbell, Lieberman, & Yashkina, 2013). Similarly, positive responses were observed for additional unpaid training opportunities which were provided for teachers to build their literacy and numeracy skills over the summer. Over 25,000 teachers attended this programming (D. McGuinty, personal communication, December 11, 2019), suggesting that teachers were intrinsically motivated to improve their classrooms. Although more research is required on the impact of this professional development on student outcomes, the high teacher satisfaction and engagement levels observed in these initiatives is promising for innovation in the classroom.

2.7   Data-Driven Accountability

The reform involved features of American standards-based reforms (SBR's) such as No Child Left Behind and Race to the Top which were aimed at reducing educational inequality and improving educational quality (Cohen & Mehta, 2017). The province used many instruments of SBR's including high academic standards, accountability for school outcomes, and support for school improvement. Examples of these instruments included a high pass rate of 70% on province-wide testing, benchmarks for student achievement on standardized tests, transparency in reporting of results, and investment in developing the skills and collaboration of teachers and administrators, respectively.

By using an independent agency (EQAO) to measure progress on student test scores, the government maintained accountability and transparency to educators and the public. Although the testing standard is determined by the Minister of Education, EQAO administers curriculum-based testing which results report on strengths and weaknesses of the curriculum and are used to inform curriculum improvements, compared to standardized testing which places results on a bell curve (D. Cooke, personal communication, November 8, 2019). Critically, results include more than test scores; teachers are surveyed on their school culture and students are surveyed on their attitudes towards test content (EQAO, 2017a, 2017b). EQAO results are used by a majority of teachers surveyed to identify if their students are meeting curriculum expectations, and by nearly all principals surveyed to inform school improvement plans and changes in teaching practice. Results are also used to guide school board improvement plans and at the ministry level to establish initiatives such as OFIP (EQAO, 2013).

Many teachers were distrustful and unsupportive of the EQAO because it was used by the administration for accountability and competition (Campbell & Levin, 2009). The Ontario Statistical Neighbours system which was established by the LNS and Information Management Branch was important in making the data-driven approach to reform accessible and individualized to schools. This program allowed schools and districts to compare their performance to that of other schools with similar demographics (Levin, 2008). This service included several indicators including EQAO results, demographic information from Statistics Canada, school programs, and information about programs related to literacy and numeracy initiatives. An important feature of this instrument was that it could be used by non-experts to make inquiries on an ad hoc basis and make searches based on individual schools and any combination of indicators (Campbell & Levin, 2009). Analyses revealed the most powerful predictors of student achievement were socioeconomic status, parental education and student mobility. Furthermore, the amount of low-achieving schools had dropped significantly by 2008, although schools that were performing in the middle of the range were not demonstrating improvement over time, which prompted the LNS to focus on these schools (Campbell & Levin, 2009). Data from this program informed Secretariat decisions and development of programs such as OFIP. Furthermore, this data was used to connect principals to share best practices as a method to "share and care and to support one another through the system" (D. McGuinty, personal communication, December 11, 2019).

2.8 Results

The success of the reform was reflected in both the dramatic improvement in student achievement and positive feedback from teachers. Literacy and numeracy rates improved from 54% to 70% on average for EQAO. 125,000 students achieved higher proficiency in reading and writing than without such a strategy; 93,000 more students graduated from high school (Ontario Ministry of Education & Fullan, 2013). Over 90% of teachers reported that the board had provided them with opportunities to improve their teaching practice and knowledge in literacy and numeracy, and at least 75% of teachers believed they had gained moderately or significantly improved understanding of effective techniques for teaching literacy and numeracy over the past three years (Audet et al., 2007). Public satisfaction with the school system and teacher performance rose to an all-time high of 65% in 2012 (Hart & Kempf, 2018).

Although the reform was considered successful in achieving the desired outcomes, student performance often fell just short of the benchmarks. A proficiency rate of 70%, just short of the original goal of 75%, was achieved for literacy and numeracy, and 82%, not 85%, was reached for high school graduation rates (Ontario Ministry of Education & Fullan, 2013). Furthermore, math scores faced stagnation in the years following the reform. In 2017, 62% of primary students met provincial standards for math compared to 67% in 2013, and 50% of junior students met this standard in 2017 compared to 57% in 2013. In contrast, scores for reading have improved: 74% of primary students meet provincial reading standards in 2017 compared to 68% in 2013, and this percentage rose from 77% to 81% in junior students (Hargreaves et al., 2018). In the context of Canadian performance, Ontario has scored below the national average on math since 2012 and above average on reading since 2009 (O'Grady et al., 2019). Thus, a critical challenge for Ontario lies in changing the trajectory of its math scores.

2.9   Criticisms

One of the limitations of reform outcomes analyses is that they are mostly described by those closely involved in its design and implementation as opposed to external evaluators. The McKinsey report which analyzed and helped popularize the reform success has been criticized for citing little psychological and sociological research on learning and teaching in their analysis of nations' educational attainment (Coffield, 2012). While academic expertise was a critical part of the reform strategy and implementation, buy-in from teachers and parents was a significant motivator in starting reform efforts. Often, the practitioner was valued over the researcher for driving change in school communities (M. Fullan, personal communication, December 9, 2019).

Despite gains in achieving more equitable student performance, particularly for English Language Learners (Campbell & Levin, 2009), the reform strategy has been criticized for raising general test performance rather than narrowing the achievement gap (Hargreaves & Braun, 2013). Many student subgroups, especially indigenous students, underperformed compared to their peers (Ontario Ministry of Education & Fullan, 2013). In addition, analysis of the reform has revealed the possibility that educators may have focused on students who were scoring just below the standard at the cost of ignoring students who struggled at much lower levels of achievement (Hargreaves et al., 2018). It is speculated that problems with school leadership and ministry staff may have led to pressures for teachers to focus on these "bubble kids" who were scoring just below target proficiency levels. Instead of raising the bar to narrow the gap, some have proposed the alternative strategy of narrowing the gap to raise the bar by addressing equity in order to improve overall quality (Hargreaves & Braun, 2013). Between 2009 and 2018, more rapid declines in math and reading among low-achieving students compared to their higher-achieving peers has contributed to increasing performance gaps (OECD, 2019).

Examining the reform beyond the classroom reveals barriers to access that may be a consequence of lending a high degree of autonomy to stakeholders. For instance, to receive a grant from the PRO initiative, parents must describe how the project will enhance parent engagement in support of improved student achievement, human rights and equity, and well-being (Ontario Ministry of Education, 2018). The pathway to school involvement, though, is not equally accessible to all parents. Families who do not speak English demonstrate lower participation in school-based involvement strategies. In contrast, higher family socioeconomic status is related to a broader range of school-based parent involvement and higher student outcomes in reading and numeracy (Daniel, Wang, & Berthelsen, 2016). School-based parent involvement positively predicts children's self-regulation which is linked to higher reading scores. Addressing these barriers in the classroom may be difficult for teachers who report having an especially difficult time engaging with disadvantaged families.

A review of parent initiatives revealed that in Ontario's large urban areas, parents emphasized partnerships between homes, schools and communities, as well as language support and feedback from the parent community. The focus in primary schools was on literacy and numeracy, whereas in secondary schools parents emphasized mental health (Hamlin & Flessa, 2018). There is evidence suggesting that the extent to which parents communicate their expectations about schoolwork and work with their children to make plans to reach educational and career goals not only positively impacts adolescent academic achievement but also mental health in high school (Wang & Sheikh-Khalil, 2014). Although there is no evidence that school-based involvement is directly related to improved academic performance, this was considered a critical strategy in helping families undergoing transitions feel a part of the community which was instrumental in effecting change in these communities in the years following the reform (K. Wynne, personal communication, November 5, 2019).

2.10 Defining and Assessing Twenty-First Century Competencies

While the original intent of the reform was limited to improving literacy and numeracy, partway through the reform these academic skills were conceptualized as being a foundation for the development of interpersonal skills for the twenty-first century (e.g. Ontario Ministry of Education, 2008a, 2008b; Canadians for 21st Century Learning and Innovation, 2012). Furthermore, the definition of literacy and numeracy started to shift to encompass a broader range of skills than basic competency as the reform progressed. Literacy was described as a tool for connection and personal growth which involves critical thinking, imagination, problem-solving, and a sense of social justice. Numeracy was defined as a framework for reasoning, problem-solving, learning and expression (Ontario Ministry of Education, 2008b).

A 2013 analysis revealed that the use of twenty-first century learning competencies was not formally discussed in Ontario policy documents. The framework, rather than including skills related to character development, instead focused on 'hard skills' which would prepare students for the workforce (Action Canada Task Force, 2013). Furthermore, the documents were identified as being unclear on how media and digital literacy - which are components of twenty-first century learning - would be incorporated into curriculum. Analysis revealed an emphasis in policy documents on critical thinking and character, which was accompanied by a lack of attention to computer and digital technologies, and a minimal focus on creativity, entrepreneurship and innovation.

2.11 Twenty-First Century Skills in the Curriculum

A critical challenge currently faced by Ontario educators is how to define and assess twenty-first century skills in the classroom. The U.S. National Research Council study "Education for Life and Work" identified four key challenges in order to develop assessments for twenty-first century competencies, including the need to consider choosing one subset of competencies from a range of competency frameworks to define student expectations; developing appropriate psychometric tools; considering the pressure of accountability that may bias people to standardized tests over more holistic assessments; and understanding the need to train teachers on strategies to promote deep learning (Ontario Ministry of Education, 2016). In Canada, twenty-first century skills are conceptualized as global competencies that are built on literacy and numeracy (O'Grady et al., 2019). Ministers have endorsed the competencies of critical thinking and problem solving, innovation, creativity, and entrepreneurship, learning to learn/self-awareness and self-direction, collaboration, communication, and global citizenship and sustainability. Although there is a range of frameworks for twenty-first century competencies in Canadian provinces and internationally, they are not necessarily priorities operationally and the lack of pedagogical methodology poses challenges for implementing them in the classroom (M. Fullan, personal communication, December 9, 2019).

In a survey of teachers from across Canada, those from Ontario indicated their curriculum placed a lower stress on character development of all the provinces surveyed, even though ministry documents in Ontario had the most references to character development (Action Canada Task Force, 2013). Ontario cites the Grade 10 Civics and Citizenship course as evidence of curriculum which fosters twenty-first century competencies (Ontario Ministry of Education, 2016). "Innovation, Creativity and Entrepreneurship" was a unique collaboration between OME and the University of Toronto but was only available to a select number of students in each district school board (Ontario Ministry of Education, 2016). Thus, "creative" content is not formally integrated throughout the curriculum and has generally limited representation even in elective courses. In most other countries, twenty-first century competencies are embedded across the curriculum as opposed to being taught as separate subjects (Kane & Ng-A-Fook, as cited by Ontario Ministry of Education, 2016). Presently, few of the frameworks and curricula for Ontario provide clearly elaborated standards or describe the impact of such a curriculum on learners.

The last major curriculum changes for elementary and secondary schools occurred under the Harris administration. Curriculum reform was not the major focus of the reform in 2003; although there was an increase in the focus and resources for literacy and numeracy in the high school curriculum, only minor revisions were made to the applied math curriculum, teacher resources and assessment strategies as part of the numeracy initiative (Directions Evidence and Policy Research Group, 2014). The Ministry of Education later performed consultations with school boards, built awareness of the Character Development Initiative, established resource teams and incentive funding to assist schools in implementing and expanding their Character Development initiatives, and conducted regional forums to engage with and foster a sense of shared responsibility among and engage parents, educators and the wider community (Ontario Ministry of Education, 2008a). Yet there was still a weak presence of interpersonal skills in the Ontario curriculum.

The intended successor of the reform for literacy and numeracy was a soft skills reform, but with the election of a new government, this change is occurring as part of deep learning. The deep learning movement in Ontario which began around 2015 provided the operational definitions of soft skills and the methodology for teachers to implement them. The 6 C's framework for deep learning (Fullan & Scott, 2014) includes character, citizenship, collaboration, communication, creativity and critical thinking as learning outcomes for new pedagogies. Classroom activities, learning progressions and rubrics are designed as a lens for teaching which can be applied to subject-specific content. These tools are explicitly aimed at building capacity in students by making learning intrinsically motivating by fostering autonomy and belongingness (Quinn, McEachen, Fullan, Gardner, & Drummy, 2019). Teachers have access to detailed rubrics for various stages of development for a range of interpersonal competencies, as well as frameworks for evaluating and reflecting on parallel curriculum standards and deep learning competencies. To build capacity at the school and district levels, Quinn et al. (2019) encourage establishing transparency in practice, creating common language for using and sharing research-based instruction, and providing sustained opportunities for teacher feedback and learning.

2.12 Moving Forward

The election of a new government in 2018 resulted in a shift to a "back to basics" approach to education which included proposals for a new math curriculum and a focus on STEM. This approach echoes the mandate of the McGuinty government in targeting foundational academic skills, with a renewed focus on math. Yet recent tensions at the time of writing between the government and teachers have culminated in the first major province-wide strike of the main Ontario education unions since 1997 (Canadian Broadcasting Corporation, 2020). These actions are in response to proposed increased class sizes and the introduction of mandatory online courses that signals a regression from the changes enacted under the McGuinty administration. Although twenty-first century skills are not part of the new administration's priorities, the capacity developed in schools and districts during the literacy and numeracy reform set the foundation for districts to take their own initiative to adopt deep learning. Although skilled leadership was central to introducing reform for academic skills, the gains in building capacity made during the tenure of McGuinty and later Wynne contributed to the ability of districts to innovate independently and find their own methods of implementing soft skills reform (M. Fullan, personal communication, December 9, 2019).

2.13 Conclusion

The reform in Ontario elementary and secondary schools beginning in 2003 under Dalton McGuinty's administration was successful in accomplishing its goals of significantly improving literacy and numeracy performance and improving secondary school graduation rates. A critical component of reform was improving teacher culture to foster a sense of shared responsibility and granting a high level of autonomy to teachers and administration in implementing reform in classrooms. Results were observed not only in improved standardized test scores from students but also in increased new teacher retention rates since the 1990s (Ontario Ministry of Education, 2008b). The supportive and continuous political leadership of the Ontario Premier's office for ten years and interdisciplinary leadership including experts experienced in education reform contributed to a unique environment for change that is not likely to be replicated in other provinces. An emphasis on relationship-building, mobilization of data and collaboration with stakeholders as part of a reform in professional norms may hold promise for other contexts. The Ontario reform shows that changes in teacher performance can be motivated by investing resources in professional development and supporting the structure rather than the size of the incentive.

As other countries develop strategies for educational improvement, Ontario must consider its role in the global context. Canada has demonstrated a stagnant trend in reading performance since 2000 and declining performance in math since 2003 (OECD, 2019). Concerningly, a faster decline in scores for the lowest-achieving students compared to highest-achieving students contributed to a greater performance gap (OECD, 2019). Throughout the country, the disparity between high- and low-achievers in math and science scores is greater than the OECD average (O'Grady et al., 2019). Therefore, Canadian provinces and territories including and beyond Ontario must develop strategies for boosting math scores. More broadly, educators must look beyond Canadian borders and continue contributing to the international mission of making progress towards the fourth United Nations Sustainable Development Goal of providing inclusive and equitable education for all learners.

In future years, collecting a broader range of data, including behavioural indicators such as absentee rates and rates of violent incidents (D. Cooke, personal communication, November 8, 2019), would give educators access to more detailed information to use in designing improvement strategies. It is essential that new tools of measurement are developed to assess outcomes of new pedagogies and that educators and researchers determine how to adapt the EQAO to measure soft skills. Continuing to integrate research and practitioner knowledge to inform curriculum for twenty-first century skills may forecast Ontario's move from being a great education system to an excellent one.

Acknowledgements I would like to thank Dave Cooke, Michael Fullan, Dalton McGuinty, and Kathleen Wynne for sharing their insights and experiences working in Ontario education, in aid of this project. Their insights have contributed to an array of perspectives that have richened the exploration of the reform in this chapter.

References

Action Canada Task Force. (2013). *Future tense: Adapting Canadian education systems for the 21st century.* Retrieved from http://www.actioncanada.ca/wp-content/uploads/2014/04/TF2-Report_Future-Tense_EN.pdf

Audet, W., Barnes, M., Clegg, M., Jaimeson, D., Klinger, D., & Levine, M. (2007). *The impact of the literacy and numeracy secretariat: Changes in Ontario's education system.* Unpublished report, Canadian Language and Literacy Research Network. Retrieved from http://www.edu.gov.on.ca/eng/document/reports/OME_Report09_EN.pdf

Campbell, C., & Levin, B. (2009). Using data to support educational improvement. *Educational Assessment, Evaluation and Accountability, 21(1)*, 47. https://doi.org/10.1007/s11092-008-9063-x

Campbell, C., Lieberman, A., & Yashkina, A. (2013). *The Teacher Learning and Leadership Program: Research Project.* Retrieved from https://www.otffeo.on.ca/en/wp-content/uploads/sites/2/2013/09/tllp_full_report-.pdf

Canadian Broadcasting Corporation. (2020, February 21). *Special coverage of Ontario education strikes as teachers rally at Queen's Park.* https://www.cbc.ca/news/canada/toronto/ontario-teachers-provincewide-strike-1.5470980

Canadians for 21st Century Learning and Innovation. (2012). *Shifting minds: A 21st century vision of public education for Canada.* Retrieved from https://www.c21canada.org/wp-content/uploads/2012/11/Shifting-Minds-Revised.pdf

Coffield, F. (2012). Why the McKinsey reports will not improve school systems. *Journal of Education Policy, 27*(1), 131–149. https://doi.org/10.1080/02680939.2011.623243

Cohen, D., & Mehta, J. (2017). Why reform sometimes succeeds: Understanding the conditions that produce reforms that last. *American Educational Research Journal, 54*(4), 644–690. https://doi.org/10.3102/0002831217700078

Daniel, G., Wang, C., & Berthelsen, D. (2016). Early school-based parent involvement, children's self-regulated learning and academic achievement: An Australian longitudinal study. *Early Childhood Research Quarterly, 36*, 168–177. https://doi.org/10.1016/j.ecresq.2015.12.016

Directions Evidence and Policy Research Group. (2014). *The Ontario student achievement division student success strategy evidence of improvement study.* Retrieved from http://www.edu.gov.on.ca/eng/research/EvidenceOfImprovementStudy.pdf

Earl, L., Freeman, S., Lasky, S., Sutherland, S., & Torrance, N. (2002). *Policy, politics, pedagogy, and people: Early perceptions and challenges of large-scale reform in Ontario secondary schools.* Toronto, ON: Report commissioned by The Ontario Secondary Teachers' Federation. Retrieved from https://www.researchgate.net/publication/242044410_Policy_Politics_Pedagogy_and_People_Early_Perceptions_and_Challenges_of_Large-scale_Reform_in_Ontario_Secondary_Schools1

Education Quality and Accountability Office. (2013). *EQAO: Ontario's provincial assessment program: its history and influence.* Retrieved from https://collections.ola.org/mon/27009/324062.pdf

Education Quality and Accountability Office. (2017a). *Student demographic data and questionnaire responses.* https://www.eqao.com/en/research_data/Data_Portal_for_Researchers/Pages/student-demographic-responses.aspx

Education Quality and Accountability Office. (2017b). *Teacher and principal questionnaire responses.* https://www.eqao.com/en/research_data/Data_Portal_for_Researchers/Pages/teacher-and-principal-questionaire-responses.aspx

Fullan, M. (2010). The big ideas behind whole system reform. *Education Canada, 50*(3), 24–27. Retrieved from http://michaelfullan.ca/wp-content/uploads/2016/06/13396082070.pdf

Fullan, M., & Scott, G. (2014). *New pedagogies for deep learning whitepaper: Education PLUS.* Retrieved from https://michaelfullan.ca/wp-content/uploads/2014/09/Education-Plus-A-Whitepaper-July-2014-1.pdf

Hamlin, D., & Flessa, J. (2018). Parental involvement initiatives: An analysis. *Educational Policy, 32*(5), 697–727. https://doi.org/10.1177/0895904816673739

Hargreaves, A., & Braun, H. (2013). *Data-driven improvement and accountability.* Retrieved from http://scholar.google.com/scholar_url?url=https://nepc.colorado.edu/sites/default/files/pb-lb-ddia-policy.pdf&hl=en&sa=X&scisig=AAGBfm1i5JJiyXu1tFx84pZdMy63fdUR-Q&nossl=1&oi=scholarr

Hargreaves, A., & O'Connor, M. T. (2018). *Leading collaborative professionalism.* Retrieved from http://www.andyhargreaves.com/uploads/5/2/9/2/5292616/seminar_series_274-april2018.pdf

Hargreaves, A., Shirley, D., Wangia, S., Bacon, C., & D'Angelo, M. (2018). *Leading from the middle: Spreading learning, well-being, and identity across Ontario.* Toronto, ON: Council of Ontario Directors of Education.

Hart, D., & Kempf, A. (2018). *Public attitudes toward education in Ontario 2018: The 20th OISE survey of educational issues.* Retrieved from https://www.oise.utoronto.ca/oise/UserFiles/Media/Media_Relations/OISE-Public-Attitudes-Report-2018_final.pdf

Ingvarson, L., Meiers, M., & Beavis, A. (2005). Factors affecting the impact of professional development programs on teachers' knowledge, practice, student outcomes & efficacy. *Education Policy Analysis Archives, 13*(10), 28.

Lee, V., & Burkam, D. (2003). Dropping out of high school: The role of school organization and structure. *American Educational Research Journal, 40*(2), 353–393. https://doi.org/10.3102/00028312040002353

Levin, B. (2008). *How to change 5000 schools: A practical and positive approach for leading change at every level.* Cambridge, MA: Harvard Education Press.

Levin, B., Glaze, A., & Fullan, M. (2008). Results without rancor or ranking Ontario's success story. *Phi Delta Kappan, 90*(4), 273–280. https://doi.org/10.1177/003172170809000408

Mourshed, M., Chijioke, C., & Barber, M. (2010). *How the world's most improved school systems keep getting better, a report McKinsey & Company.* Retrieved from https://www.mckinsey.com/industries/social-sector/our-insights/how-the-worlds-most-improved-school-systems-keep-getting-better

O'Connor, E., & McCartney, K. (2007). Examining teacher–child relationships and achievement as part of an ecological model of development. *American Educational Research Journal, 44*(2), 340–369. https://doi.org/10.3102/0002831207302172

O'Grady, K., Deussing, M., Scerbina, T., Tao, Y., Fung, K., Elez, V., & Monk, J. (2019). *Measuring up: Canadian results of the OECD PISA 2018 study: The performance of Canadian 15-year-olds.* Canada: Council of Ministers of Education.

Ontario Ministry of Education. (2008a). *Finding common ground: Character development in Ontario schools, K–12.* Retrieved from http://www.edu.gov.on.ca/eng/policyfunding/memos/june2008/FindingCommonGroundEng.pdf

Ontario Ministry of Education. (2008b). *Reaching every student: Energizing Ontario education.* Retrieved from https://michaelfullan.ca/wp-content/uploads/2016/06/13396078200.pdf

Ontario Ministry of Education. (2010). *Growing success: Assessment evaluation and reporting in Ontario schools.* Retrieved from http://www.edu.gov.on.ca/eng/policyfunding/growsuccess.pdf

Ontario Ministry of Education. (2016). *21st century competencies: Foundation document for discussion.* Retrieved from http://www.edugains.ca/resources21CL/About21stCentury/21CL_21stCenturyCompetencies.pdf

Ontario Ministry of Education. (2018). *Parents reaching out grants.* Retrieved from http://www.edu.gov.on.ca/eng/parents/faqRegion.html

Ontario. Ministry of Education, & Fullan, M. (2013). *Great to excellent: Launching the next stage of Ontario's education agenda.* Ministry of Education. Retrieved from http://www.michaelfullan.ca/wp-content/uploads/2013/09/13_Fullan_Great-to-Excellent.pdf

Organisation for Economic Co-operation and Development. (2011). Ontario, Canada: Reform to support high achievement in a diverse context. In *Lessons from PISA for the United States, Strong Performers and Successful Reformers in Education,* OECD Publishing. https://doi.org/10.1787/9789264096660-en

Organisation for Economic Co-operation and Development. (2019). *Canada – Country Note – PISA 2018 Results.* Retrieved from https://www.oecd.org/pisa/publications/PISA2018_CN_CAN.pdf

Parker, L. (2017). Creating a crisis: Selling neoliberal policy through the rebranding of education. *Canadian Journal of Educational Administration and Policy,* (183), 44–60.

Quinn, J., McEachen, J., Fullan, M., Gardner, M., & Drummy, M. (2019). *Dive into deep learning: Tools for engagement.* Thousand Oaks, CA: Corwin Press.

Villegas-Reimers, E. (2003). *Teacher professional development: An international review of the literature.* Paris: International Institute for Educational Planning. Retrieved from: http://unesdoc.unesco.org/images/0013/001330/133010e.pdf

Wang, M., & Sheikh-Khalil, S. (2014). Does parental involvement matter for student achievement and mental health in high school? *Child Development, 85*(2), 610–625. https://doi.org/10.1111/cdev.12153

Taylor Boyd is an Ed.M. graduate of the Human Development and Psychology program at the Harvard Graduate School of Education. She holds a B.A. in Psychology from Western University in Ontario, Canada. Her research examines creativity, motivation and autonomy in early childhood settings and elementary classrooms, including cross-cultural differences in teaching and learning in Ontario and Norway. Taylor has worked in recreation programming in immigrant and refugee communities in her hometown of Toronto and is interested in exploring child development in diverse populations.

Chapter 3
Singapore's Teacher Education Model for the 21st Century (TE21)

Durgesh Rajandiran

3.1 Introduction

The innovative and transformative Teacher Education Model for the 21st Century (TE21) was introduced in Singapore by the National Institute of Education, Nanyang Technological University, Singapore (NIE NTU, Singapore) in 2009. Frequently called revolutionary, this model is seen as the pinnacle of 21st century teacher education because it revamped the existing teacher education system to include 21st century values, skills, research, assessments, and professional development into a teacher's trajectory. This framework has catalyzed the implementation of a variety of reforms in initial teacher preparation programs and lifelong teacher professional development initiatives that still exist today.

A recap of Singapore's history will tell us that the country was initially struggling to stand on its feet after gaining independence from Malaysia in 1965. With no natural resources to fuel the economy, its leaders saw education as a sustainable investment towards its growth (Reimers & Chung, 2019). Since then, Singapore has gradually and continually paved a stable path towards developing a 21st century education system through four distinct phases over four decades: (1) survival-driven, (2) efficiency-driven, (3) ability-driven, and (4) values-driven, student-centric phases (Reimers & Chung, 2019). Coupled with political and economic stability, this nation now enjoys the luxury of continuity and high performance in its education system.

Despite Singapore's success in building an exemplary 21st century education system over four decades, there is a gap in the literature about the external influences on the development of Singapore's education system. For example, it remains unclear how Singapore's developmental trajectory compares to international conversations about the future of education, such as the UNESCO reports *Learning to*

D. Rajandiran (✉)
Harvard Graduate School of Education, Cambridge, MA, USA

© The Author(s) 2021
F. M. Reimers (ed.), *Implementing Deeper Learning and 21st Century Education Reforms*, https://doi.org/10.1007/978-3-030-57039-2_3

Be headed by Edgar Faure in 1972 and *Learning: The Treasure Within* headed by Jacques Delors in 1996 (see Chap. 1 for more details). Even within the specific literature of Singapore's 21st century teacher education system, they extensively discuss the conceptualization and the implementation of TE21 from the point of view of NIE NTU, Singapore (Saravanan & Ponnusamy, 2011; Tan, 2012; Tan, Liu, & Low, 2017), but relatively few of them have included external influences and responses from the most important stakeholder, the teachers.

Hence, there are two main objectives for this chapter. First, it aims to analyze the sequence of events and strategies employed by Singapore towards building a 21st century education system in tandem with international conversations surrounding the future of education over the four decades since Singapore's independence. Second, this chapter will scrutinize the recommendations of TE21 and two specific reforms catalyzed by TE21 within the initial teacher education program while including individual opinions and experiences of teachers. We find that Singapore's phases of education over four decades incorporated suggestions from international literature and evidence from local and global events to design a uniquely-Singaporean education system that leave teachers and students largely satisfied with the reforms brought about by TE21. However, despite Singapore's meticulously-planned four decades and its institutional strength, we find that a cultural shift towards exemplifying 21st century competencies demands more than merely incorporating 21st century skills into the curriculum for students. A cultural reform is unfortunately challenging and appears to persist in systems regardless of their developmental stages (see Chap. 6 on Kenya for a cultural reform in a different context).

Information for this project was sourced from interviews with Prof. Tan Oon Seng, the immediate past Director of NIE Singapore and Prof. Low Ee-Ling, Dean of Teacher Education at NIE Singapore, one Principal, two Head of Departments, and three teachers from the Singaporean education system. Additional data was obtained from the NIE repository, the Ministry of Education (MOE) repository, the National Archive of Singapore, official Government of Singapore webpages, reports from the Organization of Economic Cooperation (OECD), peer-reviewed journal articles, and books written by the NIE members.

3.2 Marking the "Little Red Dot" by Its Phases of Education

Singapore is a densely populated land area of 719 square kilometers with a current estimated population of 5.7 million (World Development Indicators, 2020). Fondly referred to as the "Little Red Dot" by local politicians and international observers alike, this tiny and diverse island finds itself the subject of many conversations in the world, often for topping human development measures, including outcomes in education. Singapore's commitment towards a good education system, including teacher preparation, began immediately after gaining independence from Malaysia in 1965.

In this post-independence era, dubbed the survival-driven phase, the main priority was economic survival using local talent. Teacher preparation and education opportunities were revamped while prioritizing basic literacy and mathematics skills in the curriculum (Reimers & Chung, 2019). The Teachers' Training College launched its first set of degrees in education in 1971, a move which indirectly tagged prestige on the teaching profession while demonstrating a dedication towards building a strong and selective teacher body in the country (National Institute of Education Singapore [NIE], 2009). Not only that, the teacher education campus was prioritized for renovations to attract the best and the brightest into the field (Reimers & Chung, 2019). The country was satisfied with its average acquisition of literacy and mathematical skills from this survival-driven phase, but the generalized and basic education curriculum meant that disadvantaged students were left in the lurch and were often dropping out of schools. The next efficiency-driven phase was then introduced to provide high-quality alternative options for these students.

In the efficiency-driven phase from 1979 to 1996, differentiated streams were introduced to match students' previous knowledge and ability to their academic trajectory. Thus, teachers with a variety of specializations beyond literacy and mathematical skills were needed, including expertise in technical and vocational skills and the arts. Unlike the survival-driven phase where quantity was prioritized, the quality of mass education in the efficiency-driven system was also deemed important. Accordingly, teacher preparation saw many specializations introduced within the broader field of education, including administrative, research, and leadership degree programs (NIE, 2009). Singapore's system of streaming students based on their knowledge and ability in this efficiency-driven phase was an effective solution for the domestic economy; however, in mid-1990s, the nation began realizing that the education system was failing to bridge the gap between academic and non-academic social skills to remain a competitive force in the global economy (Reimers & Chung, 2019).

After the long and arduous efficiency-driven phase to improve mass education in Singapore, the country was prepared to move into an ability-driven phase where the main priority in education was the development of individual potential. The ability-driven phase, starting from 1997 to 2011, marked the wide and deliberate introduction of 21st century competencies in Singapore's education system, including the initial teacher preparation program. While the goals of the ability-driven phase still resonate strongly within the education system, Singapore formally shifted to a values-driven, student-centric phase in 2011 that places character development at the core of the system (National Archives of Singapore, 2011). In this phase, teachers have the added responsibilities of instilling values in each student and reaching out to the community with the aim of producing a holistic ecology for learning (Reimers & Chung, 2019). The ability-driven and values-driven, student-centric phases underscore TE21's recommendations and will be elaborated in great detail in the subsequent sections.

These four, well-planned phases that build from previous phases' successes and shortcomings while taking present domestic and global challenges into account demonstrate the gradual growth of Singapore's education system to be among the best in the world. The country and its different leaders over the course of four decades constantly prioritized education because building human capacity was the only way to propel the country's economy forward. Not only did the country prioritize educational outcomes for students, they also realized that teachers are the driving force behind student outcomes, and this theory of change will be discussed in Sects. 3.3 and 3.4.

3.3   Local and International Context

In order to comprehend how and when Singapore started with its teacher education reform, we first need to understand the local and global landscapes that shaped Singapore's agenda. This section will explore international conversations surrounding 21st century skills and teacher education, and conduct a comparative analysis between these conversations and Singapore's phases of education.

3.3.1   21st Century Skills

Approaching the turn of the millennium in the late 1990s, the world witnessed an unprecedented rapid increase in technological changes and innovation. Due to the quickly-evolving technological landscape, Bransford (2007) notes that innovation cycles start and end within a short frame, and that education systems are often unable to adapt to meet the demands of a field. Hence, the training provided at educational institutions may be nugatory by the time students enter the workforce. These changes were foreseen by some visionaries even in the 1970s and they gradually laid the foundations for conversations surrounding 21st century teaching and learning to take place. The United Nations Educational, Scientific, and Cultural Organization (UNESCO) was instrumental in leading the discussion surrounding the future of education. The organization published two foundational reports on adaptive and lifelong learning, *Learning to Be* headed by Edgar Faure in 1972 and *Learning: The Treasure Within* headed by Jacques Delors in 1996 (see Chap. 1 for more details). While there is a lack of evidence to support Singapore's references of these specific UNESCO reports to inform its curriculum and teacher preparation programs, Prof. Tan Oon Seng, the immediate past Director of NIE Singapore and Prof. Low Ee-Ling, Dean of Teacher Education at NIE Singapore recognize that "the publications from world bodies and think tanks have always been part of [their] literature review and global environment scan, whether they be from international academic colleagues or global organizations, such as UNESCO, OECD" (Low & Tan, 2020). The comparison of the timelines of these two formative UNESCO reports to that of the Singaporean education system is illuminating because it demonstrates how quickly Singapore, which only gained independence in 1965 with no natural resources to fuel the economy, was able to mobilize its talents to be among the best within a short time. In 1972, Singapore was still in its post-independence survival-driven phase when The Faure Report argued for progressive lifelong education in the world. Remarkably, in 1996, Singapore was wrapping up with its efficiency-driven phase and preparing to move on to an ability-driven phase that will respond to economic, social, and technological change in the country and globally—all of which align with pillars of education found in The Delors Report.

By the end of the millennium, governments, education scholars, and organizations were forced to confront the nimbleness of the global innovative space and to find a common ground for the future of education. Singapore was no exception—the increasing income gap approaching the 1997 Asian financial crisis meant that wealthier families could afford private tuition to assist their children achieve excellent grades while the rest of the students were struggling to even pass (Lee & Low, 2014). A country that largely relies on its human capital cannot afford such a disparity in its educational outcomes, especially when the world is rapidly innovating. Shortly before the Asian financial crisis beset Southeast Asians nations in July 1997, Singapore's Prime Minister at the time, Goh Chok Tong, announced the government's new vision for the Ministry of Education (MOE) "Thinking Schools, Learning Nation" (TSLN) in June 1997. This vision, which launched two decades of major structural overhaul in four broad areas—namely, infrastructure of the education system, curricula and assessment, training and development, and school environments—was initiated to prepare citizens who are committed and capable of meeting future challenges using 21st century skills (Ministry of Education, 2019).

At the start of the 21st century, the Organisation for Economic Co-operation and Development (OECD) has also led two initiatives for its member nations to define and assess 21st century competencies: The Definition and Selection of Competencies (DeSeCo) project and the Program for International Student Assessment (PISA) for mathematical, scientific, and reading literacies. DeSeCo and PISA go hand-in-hand because the former, which was published in 2003, provides a framework for the latter that also began in 2003. DeSeCo's framework is grounded in three broad competencies for individuals, which are abilities to use tools interactively, to interact in heterogeneous groups, and to act autonomously (Rychen & Salganik, 2003). No representatives from Singapore were involved in the conception of DeSeCo or PISA, and yet, within the last two decades, Singapore, an OECD member, has been consistently ranked among the top five in the 70-nation PISA test. What these numbers mean relative to other participating countries is astounding: "90 percent of Singaporean students scored above the international average in mathematics and science, and Singapore's fifteen-year-olds outperformed those of every country in reading, mathematics, and science" (National Center on Education and The Economy: Empower Educators, 2017, p. 1). These consistent results speak volumes about Singapore's ability as a nation to reach its educational potential as defined by the DeSeCo Project and PISA through its successful implementation of 21st century competencies in its education system.

Within the two decades of the 21st century, several scholars and organizations have proposed their definitions of 21st century skills. While many reports to date that propose 21st century skills have been the product of evaluations based on the economic demands and skill gaps of the global landscape, an influential report that incorporated scientific evidence from the social sciences is the National Research Council report (2012), *Education for Life and Work: Developing Transferable Knowledge and Skills in the 21st century*, commonly known as the Hilton and Pellegrino report. The authors not only included proposals for the development of human capital as supported by psychological research, but they also posed evidence-based consequences for individuals in the short- and long-run based on the development of their competencies. By synthesizing scientific research in the field of human development, Hilton and Pellegrino propose a 21st century framework that covers cognitive, intrapersonal, and interpersonal competencies in detail. Singapore, in actuality, had developed a 21st Century Competencies (21CC) framework for its national curriculum in 2010, shortly before the Hilton and Pellegrino report was released. Singapore's 21CC framework has a set of core values that are self-oriented, and broader sets of values that signify socio-emotional and global competencies. While Singapore developed its framework using locally-generated evidence-based educational review and research, the contrasting of Singapore's 21CC framework to the Hilton and Pellegrino report reveals striking similarities. In a very recent comparison done between the two frameworks, Reimers and Chung (2019) finds that Singapore's competencies fit well into the three broad categories proposed by Hilton and Pellegrino; hence, it demonstrates that Singapore's 21CC framework is grounded in a universal psychological framework for the 21st century despite being based on locally-sourced evidence.

3.3.2   21st Century Teacher Education

Teacher education programs have been around since the nineteenth century, but how and why teacher education impacts students is not self-evident to many; therefore, teacher education is often the subject of criticism for being ineffective despite being a prerequisite to teach. In fact, even in developed education systems, changes to the teacher education system happen much later or less rigorously. To dispel the myth that anyone can be a teacher and that teacher education systems are unnecessary and ineffective, Darling-Hammond (2000) published an article discussing evidence supporting the claim that teacher education results in teacher effectiveness, which in turn improves student outcomes. This article—aptly produced at the turn of the millennium—found that "teaching for problem solving, invention, and application of knowledge requires teachers with deep and flexible knowledge of subject matter who understand how to represent ideas in powerful ways and organize a productive learning process for students who start with different levels and kinds of prior knowledge, assess how and what students are learning, and adapt instruction to different learning approaches" (Darling-Hammond, 2000, p. 166–7). The idea that teachers require "deep and flexible knowledge" from Darling-Hammond is central to teaching and learning in the 21st century if students are expected to possess the 21st century skills discussed in the previous section. A similar logic is found to be the impetus for Singapore's teacher education reform. TE21 is the product of a prevalent notion when TSLN was introduced, which is the realization that '21st century learners call for 21st century teachers' (NIE, 2009).

Over the following years, several articles and books were published proposing the incorporation of 21st century competencies into teacher education programs, and these writings collectively carved the definition of 21st century teacher education. Darling-Hammond and Bransford (2007) published a formative report commissioned by the National Academy for Education titled *Preparing Teachers for a Changing World: What Teachers Should Learn and Be Able To Do,* which provides common elements that should be part of a teacher education curriculum. The authors propose a framework that recommends new teachers in the 21st century to have a basic understanding of learning sciences, language acquisition, diversity in learning, classroom management, innovative assessments, the use of technology in classrooms—all of these in addition to deep and flexible subject matter knowledge (Darling-Hammond & Bransford, 2007). With Darling-Hammond and Bransford (2007) providing a framework for teacher education curriculum, Korthagen, Loughran and Russell (2006) attempted to identify common fundamental principles that should be inculcated in teacher education programs to produce teachers who are responsive in a dynamic manner for the 21st century. The authors provide seven simple yet thought-provoking principles about learning that shifts the mindset of teachers to continuously strive for their students' successes while embodying 21st century skills themselves. The principles are: learning about teaching involves continuously conflicting and competing demands, requires a view of knowledge as a subject to be created rather than as a created subject, requires a shift in focus from the curriculum to the learner, is enhanced through student-teacher research, requires an emphasis on those learning to teach working closely with their peers, requires meaningful relationship between schools, universities and student teachers, and is enhanced when the teaching and learning approaches advocated in the program are modelled by the teacher educators in their own practice (Korthagen et al., 2006). Parallels in the types of innovative student assessment methods can be drawn between Darling-Hammond and Bransford (2007), (Korthagen et al., 2006) and the teacher education reform in Singapore, specifically on how to teach the differences between formative and summative assessments that are viable options for the 21st century. A combination of the different types of assessments bode well with the goal of building students' unique characters in the values-driven, student-centric phase because students will be forced to reflect on their progress and the final outcome simultaneously. In an education system that has singularly focused on final examinations as the only method of assessment, innovative formative components, such as wholesome learner's portfolios, can shift the culture in schools and instil new values.

Further adding to the repertoire of teacher education models is Hoban (2007)'s book, *The Missing Links in Teacher Education Design: Developing a Multi-linked Conceptual Framework.* This book focuses on the common gaps across teacher education programs, specifically in university curriculum, the theory-practice links between schools and university, the diversity in teacher education programs, and the personal narratives of teachers and teacher educators that shape their identities. The content of each chapter zooms into a particular teacher education program and the link that they were trying to make between stakeholders in their context. The authors for each case also briefly discuss the challenges they face, which include issues with securing buy-ins from various organizations and teaching bodies to realize the program. In Singapore's teacher education reform, it is evident that the challenges within these different contexts were thoroughly studied as a unique tripartite relationship was proposed to bring the equal weight of the MOE, the NIE and schools together in order to minimize friction between different entities while strengthening the theory-practice link within the local context (NIE, 2009).

While the surveyed literature was written about and for the Western context, Prof. Tan and Prof. Low explained how useful the key findings and recommendations were when the NIE was adapting and contextualizing them for Singapore with an Asian perspective in mind:

> We acknowledge that a large part of research literature is still today primarily Western in orientation. But we have never shied from looking at best international ideas and asking how they can be applied to our local context. Singapore is unique from many other countries, especially Western ones, and so it is by necessity that we need to contextualize any of the international best practices and literature to our circumstances. When we contextualize, we do not change our Asian philosophy. For example, the goal of education in the Western context is freedom through individual rights. In the Asian context, the goal of education is freedom through group, family and societal cohesiveness. We are more inclined towards community harmony and the societal good as a whole. We keep to this core value of the collective welfare of all (Low & Tan, 2020).

3.4 Goals in 21st Century Teacher Education and the Theory of Action

After the announcement of TSLN in 1997, a number of initiatives were systematically implemented to include 21st century skills into the national curriculum; but the realization that '21st century learners call for 21st century teachers' (NIE, 2009) called for the MOE in collaboration with the NIE to perform an extensive review of the initial teacher preparation program, known as the Programme Review and Enhancement 2008–2009 (PRE).

3.4.1 Program Review and Enhancement 2008–2009 (PRE)

The PRE committee consisted of NIE professors and researchers led by the Director of the NIE at the time, Dr. Lee Sing Kong (NIE, 2009). The underpinning philosophy that guided the PRE committee was the purpose of education as outlined by the MOE: "to nurture the whole child –morally, intellectually, physically, socially, and aesthetically" (NIE, 2009, p. 28). The PRE committee's theory of change assumes that students' development of 21st century skills emerges as a result of competent 21st century educators. Therefore, the PRE committee first charted the intended student outcomes in a 21CC instructional setting. The outcomes included (1) learning and innovation skills, (2) knowledge, information, media and technology literacy skills, (3) life skills, and (4) citizenship skills (NIE, 2009). To match these student skillsets to teacher competencies, the PRE committee designated three areas within 21CC that teachers need to develop: (1) expertise at the intersection of information, media, and multicultural literacy, (2) knowledge in supporting learning communities that allow students to integrate 21CC into classroom practice and real world contexts, and (3) effective instruction of 21CC that support innovative pedagogies and high order thinking skills. A tangential but laudable outcome of the PRE is the beginning of systematic incorporation of evidence-based educational practices that were tested and proven in Singapore into any changes of their teacher preparation programs. For effectiveness of educational policies, Singapore's theory of action included an Enhanced Partnership Model that places equal importance on three primary bodies of education, namely MOE, NIE, and schools (NIE, 2009). Based on the understanding of existing and emerging trends using rigorous data collection and analysis through the PRE process, the Teacher Education Model for the 21st Century (TE21) framework was introduced in 2009.

3.4.2   The Teacher Education Model for the 21st Century (TE21)

The key takeaways from the PRE process were mapped into six recommendations by the PRE committee that were deemed crucial to the holistic development of teachers, which in turn serves as an investment towards equipping young Singaporeans with 21st century competencies. To support the implementation of these recommendations, the budget for education increased by 11% in 2010; hence, bringing the total amount allocated for education from 8.70 billion Singaporean dollars (S\$) to S\$9.66 billion for the year following the introduction of TE21 (Tan et al., 2017; Singapore Budget, 2010, 2011).

3.4.2.1   Recommendation 1

The New V³SK Model aligns well with Singapore's newest phase in education starting in 2011, which is the values-driven, student-centric phase. Initially introduced as the ASK Model (Attitudes, Skills and Knowledge) then the VSK Model (Values, Skills and Knowledge), the New V³SK Model prioritizes the child, individual identity, and the community within important values that will "permeate the programmes and curricula" (NIE, 2009, p. 45). The derivation of this new model demonstrates the fluidity of the Singaporean education system as it has undergone three variations in one decade to meet the rapidly changing needs of the global landscape. The attributes of a 21st century teaching professional under the New V³SK Model are formalized as having the **V**alues of learner-centeredness, teacher identity, and service to the profession and community, the **S**kills required by an educator, and in-depth subject-matter **K**nowledge. Even though the focus of this model is to understand every child's individual learning profile, teachers need to have high standards to maximize the child's potential and a drive to learn to adapt accordingly to each individual learner. At the core of this symbiotic teacher-child relationship is believing that every child can learn and contribute as an outstanding member of society.

3.4.2.2 Recommendation 2

The PRE committee recommends that the NIE's Initial Teacher Preparation (ITP) and Postgraduate Diploma in Education (PGDE) programs incorporate Singaporean context-specific 21st century teacher competencies in their graduation criteria. The list of guidelines for the criteria is known as the Graduand Teacher Competencies (GTCs), and it is reflected in the GTC Framework (GTCF) for trainee teachers. While there is no one-to-one mapping between the New V³SK Model and GTCs, the values, skills, and knowledge inform the three performance dimensions that support 21st century instruction in classrooms. The dimensions identified by the PRE committee are professional practice, leadership and management, and personal effectiveness (NIE, 2009). A crucial point to note about the GTCs is that these competencies should be demonstrated at the point of graduation from ITP and PGDE programs, but some core competencies within each dimension cannot be realized until after the teacher is in the field. For example, the GTCF states that a teacher should take the initiative to improve their professional development throughout their teaching tenure, but the NIE is unable to measure this competency at the point of graduation. Therefore, the Enhanced Partnership Model will ensure continued mentoring after the teacher has graduated from the training programs. This example of post-graduation training to improve teacher skills aligns with the development of a teacher identity as outlined in the New V³SK Model while enforcing the receptiveness for adaptability in the teaching profession.

3.4.2.3 Recommendation 3

The PRE committee recommends bridging the gap between theory and practice within teacher education by strengthening the theory-practice nexus. This process is not at all simple as the gap between theory, policy, and practice is evident in many fields, especially in the social sciences and humanities. The NIE has proposed four approaches that encompass theory and practice within evidence-based teacher education, namely reflection, pedagogical tools that bring the classroom into the university, experiential learning, and school-based enquiry or research. The basis of this recommendation is that teachers utilize research in pedagogy to inform their classroom practices and use classrooms as a research ground to test teaching strategies that can be extrapolated to the larger education sector in the Singaporean context. The Enhanced Partnership Model that brings the equal weight of MOE, NIE and schools together is pertinent for the success of this recommendation. Ideally, the NIE would provide the theoretical expertise via teacher education programs, the MOE act as policymakers, and schools would provide the research ground during their teacher preparation programs to develop evidence-based teaching practices.

3.4.2.4 Recommendation 4

The PRE committee recommends program refinement and an extended pedagogical repertoire as TE21's fourth goal. Following on from TSLN, academic curriculum and co-curricular activities for students have been revamped to account for the incorporation of 21CC. Similarly, teachers need a framework that will inculcate 21CC instruction in teacher trainees through the NIE ITP and PGDE curricula. A powerful and observable culture in Singapore, for example, is the obsession with grades and academic excellence bar none, as suggested by Reimers and Chung (2019). An innovative and collaborative change within an academic system that has solely relied on grades at every level of instruction is no easy task. Therefore, teachers need to be equipped to propel a cultural shift to change the mindset of parents and students despite being the result of a previous examination-oriented system. The PRE committee proposes establishing a strategy and framework for 21st century teaching and learning that will uphold the following principles within the Singaporean education system: (1) a pedagogy curriculum must be discipline-appropriate as the basis of multi-disciplinary learning; and (2) these pedagogies must be learner-centered (NIE, 2009). Some examples of teaching practices that move further away from examinations include facilitating blended learning, role playing, experiential learning, and problem-based learning within classrooms.

3.4.2.5 Recommendation 5

Establishing an assessment framework for 21st century teaching and learning is necessary to measure the success of initiatives in Singapore. Assessments typically manifest as examinations in Singapore. Nonetheless, with the changes to include 21st century competencies in the education system, assessment methods need to evolve to meet the needs of the 21CC curriculum for students. The PRE committee recommends an assessment framework that "will enable [Singapore] to produce teachers who have high assessment literacy levels and able to adopt the best practices to effectively evaluate student outcomes" (NIE, 2009, p. 95). The NIE wants to move away from examination grades as the only means of assessment and they believe that the training starts at the ITP and PGDE programs. In fact, a wholesome portfolio assessment that covers multiple perspectives and a range of platforms is recommended for teacher training assessment too. The hope is that teachers will learn how individual learners' portfolio assessment works on a multifaceted dimension to productively benefit a student's holistic development instead of merely developing an excellent test-taker.

3.4.2.6 Recommendation 6

The PRE committee recommends establishing enhanced pathways for professional development. Given that fluidity and adaptability to challenges are part of the TSLN vision, this recommendation proposes the provision of alternative accelerated pathways for professional upgrading that will instill a lifelong learning experience for teachers. A feature that Singapore has observed in other high-performing countries such as Finland is the high baseline academic qualification for teachers (NIE, 2009). A lifelong professional development opportunity with high standards not only attracts the best to the teaching profession, but it also goes hand-in-hand with almost all of the other recommendations, including bridging the theory-practice gap by continuously informing themselves of the latest developments. The PRE committee recommends altering the bachelors program in teaching to include an accelerated masters program for qualified teacher trainees so that they benefit from additional evidence-based training through school attachments and research experience.

3.5 Implementation of TE21 Recommendations in the Teacher Preparation Program

A slew of programs and initiatives were introduced by the NIE, the MOE, schools after the introduction of TE21. As this chapter focuses on the initial teacher preparation reform in Singapore, this section will sample the implementation of two selected initiatives that encompass the first five recommendations from Sect. 3.4.

3.5.1 Learning e-Portfolio

As part of the revamp of the ITP and PGDE programs, the NIE introduced a new course called the Professional Practice and Inquiry (PPI) course to allow pre-service teachers to formulate their own teaching philosophies. The PPI course was first introduced to junior college trainee teachers in July 2010 before being introduced to all trainee teachers by July 2012 (Tan et al., 2017). This course was introduced with the goal of tying together Recommendations 1, 2, and 3; specifically, the PPI intends to provide a space for pre-service teachers to identify and reflect on the values of teaching and learning that will scaffold their future classroom experiences while meeting the set of competencies established by the GTCs. A huge motivation for this effort was also to ensure continuity for teachers to aggregate their learning and modify their philosophical models as they see fit throughout their pre-service training and careers. To meet all these goals, the NIE introduced the e-Portfolio, which is an electronic platform for teachers through the PPI course to reflect and track their knowledge while maintaining a collection of artefacts that align with the requirements of the GTCs (Tan et al., 2017).

The e-Portfolio is not merely a diary of theoretical philosophy developed by trainee teachers; it is in fact used simultaneously as pre-service teachers undergo their practicum experience. Trainee teachers have multiple opportunities to revise their teaching identity and philosophy using locally-generated, evidence-based results. The interweaving of theory and practice through the e-Portfolio is especially valuable in the final practicum experience as teachers are often placed in schools that will be their post-training permanent working environment. Just as trainee teachers are taught to develop these portfolios, they are instructed to guide their future students to develop similar learning portfolios for formative assessments. A current biology teacher in a junior college who underwent teacher training via the PGDE program in 2013–2014 reflected on her e-Portfolio experience and was thrilled that the methods introduced at the NIE were viable options for her future students in classrooms too. Linking her e-Portfolio experience to her practicum, she said that the feedback loop between theory in lectures and application during her practicum gave her plenty of opportunities to learn about values that were integral to herself and to craft her personalized e-Portfolio (Biology Teacher 1, 2019).

3.5.2 Experiential Learning

Recommendation 4 and 5 of TE21 highlight the need to develop learner-centered pedagogy curriculums with the potential for holistic assessments. One such initiative is the mandatory requirement of experiential learning in a variety of subjects in secondary schools and junior colleges. Examining the secondary school and junior college geography curricula specifically, the MOE previously recommended fieldwork whenever possible, but it was not mandatory. These excursions and field trips were not necessarily reflective or illuminating for the students; in fact, Chew (2008) claims that assessments for such excursions typically involve regurgitation of information provided by teachers and tour facilitators (Tan et al., 2017).

In the spirit of providing teacher trainees with similar curriculum and assessment methods as expected for their future students, the NIE introduced experiential learning and assessment in the PGDE program in 2010 for geography pre-service teachers. These trainee teachers were given access to leading experts in fieldwork and extensive training on how to critically conduct fieldwork. At the end of the program, they were expected to create an experiential learning package using fieldwork for secondary schools or junior colleges. Tan, Liu, and Low (2017) found that these trainee teachers had a renewed appreciation for critical and analytic fieldwork which was drastically different from their personal experiences with field trips.

One secondary school geography teacher who participated in the PGDE program from 2016–2017 was so excited about the experiential learning reform that he began designing his experiential learning package during his undergraduate degree. He never had the luxury of travelling much when he was younger; when he got a teaching scholarship to get his undergraduate degree in California, he knew he had the make the best of the opportunity not just for himself, but for his career as a geography teacher too. He planned trips to national parks and searched for study abroad opportunities to see the world and think about potential ways he could use his travel experiences as inspiration for his future students. Using the activities from his college travel experiences as a guide, he planned a fieldwork trip to an island for his students to investigate the physical geography using hand-ons activities instead of passively observing on tours (Geography Teacher, 2019).

3.6 Success and Persistent Challenges

Given that a variety of programs and modules were introduced following from the TE21 framework, a thorough analysis of the combined effectiveness of all the programs is an impossible task. However, with quantitative data from global organizations and personal anecdotes from the teachers interviewed, we can infer the success and persistent challenges of these programs.

3.6.1 Teaching, Learning, and Research

The Teaching and Learning International Survey (TALIS) administered by the OECD is the largest international survey held every 5 years about educators' working conditions, learning environments, and teaching styles. Singapore unfortunately did not participate in the inaugural survey in 2008; hence, we do not have a baseline condition before TE21 was introduced in 2009. However, Singapore participated in the 2013 and 2018 surveys, and we can compare the results in those years to each other and to the OECD averages. Singapore stands out among other OECD countries in most of the parameters measured. One measure that is indicative of 21st century teaching style is the percentage of time teachers spend actively teaching, which implies more time for students to self-direct during a lesson. Singapore was at 71% in 2013 and 74% in 2018, when the OECD averages float around 80%. (OECD, 2014, 2019a). This measure provides evidence for the many opportunities of autonomous learning for students that not only allow them to reflect on their individual learning styles, but also inculcate curiosity and creativity that are central features of a 21st century education.

Changes to the teacher education program requires time to permeate the education system and produce visible results in student outcomes. The NIE has made recent efforts to develop 21st century skills assessment methods for the Singaporean context. In 2015, the NIE launched a new journal, *Learning: Research and Practice* to encourage and support "distinct and progressive research that responds to the problems of current educational practices and traditional views of learning" ("Learning: Research and Practice"). This journal tracks the research done in the Singaporean context that attempts to investigate 21st century pedagogical and assessment methods. While Singapore has not conducted large-scale studies to measure the effectiveness of its 21CC instruction, trial studies in selected schools and student populations have experimented with different methods of teaching and assessing 21CC skills in classrooms. Tan, Caleon, Ng, Poon, and Koh (2018), for example, have shed some light on how Singaporean students respond to collective creativity and collaborative problem solving in manipulated settings. Koh, Hong, and Tan (2018) has experimented with technology to assess self-awareness and teamwork-awareness in a pilot population. While none of these studies have conclusive evidence that can be extrapolated to all students in Singapore, they certainly pave the path towards larger experiments involving 21st century skills in the near future.

3.6.2 Institutional Strength

As evident from the comparison of Singapore's development in education to the two UNESCO reports, *Learning To Be* and *Learning: The Treasure Within*, Singapore caught up and overtook the rest of the world at an unprecedented rate. Reimers and Chung (2019) allude to two reasons for Singapore's rapid success in developing its education system: (1) the small size of Singapore and its centralized education system allow for quick and coherent nationwide implementations of policies and initiatives; and (2) the education system has been dynamic and adaptive to changes in the local and global landscape and accordingly aligns its goals to foreseeable challenges. While Singapore's physical size certainly promotes efficient implementation, we cannot discount the decades of calculated design of the entire education system. Singapore's size merely bolsters the strength of the educational programs and policies, including the implementations of the recommendations from TE21.

A Principal at a low-performing secondary school, who has been in the teaching force for two decades, observed that the more recent pre-service teachers who joined his school for their practicum bring in new ideas to engage students in different types of activities that they believe will boost students' interests in academics. One example that remains in his memory to this day is the creative idea proposed by a new chemistry teacher to use physical exercise as the medium to introduce chemical reactions to his students. The teacher's logic was simple: most of the students in his class were athletes and the best way for them to approach chemistry with less fear was to combine it with their activities of interest. The Principal was not well-versed with TE21 before our interview, but he was quick to note the connection between the introduction of TE21 and the point at which he started observing changes in pre-service teachers' enthusiasm for innovation, especially in thinking about addressing equity at a low-performing school. Witnessing the intended outcomes of reforms that follow from TE21 at schools in a relatively short time suggests that Singapore's education system is highly coordinated to disseminate and affect changes at multiple levels in a rapid manner (Principal, 2020).

3.6.3   Autonomy at Higher Levels

The changes brought about by TE21 heavily focus on improving pre-service training by the NIE and lifelong professional development by the MOE. These facets of development do not directly address how teachers in leadership positions, such as Head of Department or Principal, can assist the teachers under their purview to improve their 21st century skills. Due to the lack of specific instructions to teachers in leadership positions, there is a large variation in the types of activities that teachers can participate in. One teacher, who is also the Head of the Mathematics Department at his junior college, noted the similar profiles of pre-service teachers entering the school for their practicum who get vastly different opportunities within the same school depending on their departments. Every department gets the same set of broad guidelines for pre-service teachers' 3-week practicum that include the basics such as classroom observations and mentorship meetings, but each Head of the Department (HOD) has the freedom to plan how to execute them. The Mathematics HOD at the junior college observed that HODs, for example, interpret mentorship meetings differently. He typically performs 1-on-1 check-in sessions with pre-service teachers under his purview, but another HOD could count departmental meetings as mentorship meetings (Mathematics HOD, 2020). Another teacher, who is the Head of the Economics Department in her school, confirms that professional development sessions are subjective and that they vary drastically by department. She says that HODs have the autonomy to conduct the in-house departmental professional development sessions as they see fit; therefore, even teachers within the same school can have very different in-house professional development experiences (Economics HOD, 2019).

3.6.4   Resistance Towards a Cultural Reform and Its Effects on Students

Reimers and Chung (2019) have identified challenges within the education system that can be addressed with increased efforts to hear the voice of a key stakeholder, the parents, and clearer communication on expected student outcomes. A biology teacher at a high-performing junior college has a difficult time justifying her teaching methods to some parents. When she tells parents about the innovative projects that their children were involved in, most parents question the need for such activities when their children's A-Level results is the sole determinant for university entrance (Biology Teacher 2, 2019). While the tertiary education admittance system is an obstacle towards implementing 21st century teaching methods, the resistance by some stakeholders reflects the deeply ingrained belief that test-taking is the most important skill to be taught and learned in schools.

The most recent PISA assessment in 2018 included school climate and socio-emotional development, in which Singapore had conflicting findings that reflect the state of confusion of students regarding their expected outcomes. 68% of students in Singapore were reported to cooperate with their classmates when the OECD average is at 62%, yet 76% were reported to compete with their classmates when the OECD average is much lower at 50% (OECD, 2019b). Students in Singapore are bullied at a higher rate at 26% compared to the OECD average at 23%, yet 94% of students thought that it is good to help those who are unable to defend themselves when the OECD average is at 88% (OECD, 2019b). These results suggest a tension between the push from the education system towards embodying 21st century skills and the advise from parents and some teachers to compete with each other for academic excellence. From the outset, the findings appear to reflect the clash of ideologies and beliefs between two generations that have been and are a part of vastly different education cultures.

3.7 Conclusion

There are two main takeaways from this chapter. First, by examining the literature around the time of TE21's introduction, it is evident that Singapore extracted concepts from suggested 21st century teacher education designs and adapted them for a Singaporean context, which align with the psychological framework for reform. They not only incorporated these suggestions, but they also anticipated challenges based on other existing models and designed solutions that will make the revamp process as seamless as possible. Darling-Hammond (2006) calls for resisting the pressure against watering down teacher preparation programs simply because it is impossible to work around certain challenges, and Singapore has taken that very seriously to design a well-planned 21st century teacher education program. Second, Singapore's implementation of TE21 has many lessons to offer to other countries. It has adhered to the ingredients of a successful institutional reform, including the involvement and communication with the majority of key stakeholders, incorporation of evidence-based teaching practices, and enforcement of a nimble yet well-fortified system—there seems to be almost no anticipation of failure. Despite being close to perfection, it is important to also investigate the responses that the framework has generated from key stakeholders. While there are no major failures at this stage of the reform, unaddressed persistent challenges, such as the resistance towards a cultural shift in the society as a whole, will only be detrimental to the education system in the long run.

References

Biology Teacher 1, personal communication, November 27, 2019.

Biology Teacher 2, personal communication, December 6, 2019.

Bransford, J. (2007). Preparing people for rapidly changing environments. *Journal of Engineering Education, 96*(1), 1–3.

Chew, E. (2008). Views, values and perceptions in geographical fieldwork in Singapore schools. *International Research in Geographical and Environmental Education, 17*(4), 307–329.

Darling-Hammond, L. (2000). How teacher education matters. *Journal of Teacher Education, 51*(3), 166–173.

Darling-Hammond, L. (2006). Constructing 21st-century teacher education. *Journal of Teacher Education, 57*(3), 300–314.

Darling-Hammond, L., & Bransford, J. (Eds.). (2007). *Preparing teachers for a changing world: What teachers should learn and be able to do*. Hoboken, NJ: Wiley.

Delors, J. (1996). *Learning: The treasure within*. Paris: UNESCO.

Economics HOD, personal communication, December 2, 2019.

Faure, E. (1972). *Learning to be: The world of education today and tomorrow*. Paris: UNESCO.

Geography Teacher, personal communication, November 14, 2019.

Hoban, G. (Ed.). (2007). *The missing links in teacher education design: Developing a multi-linked conceptual framework* (Vol. 1). Berlin/Heidelberg, Germany/Dordrecht, The Netherlands: Springer.

Koh, E., Hong, H., & Tan, J. P.-L. (2018). Formatively assessing teamwork in technology enabled twenty-first century classrooms: Exploratory findings of a teamwork awareness programme in Singapore. *Asia Pacific Journal of Education, 38*(1), 129–144.

Korthagen, F., Loughran, J., & Russell, T. (2006). Developing fundamental principles for teacher education programs and practices. *Teaching and Teacher Education, 22*(8), 1020–1041.

Lee, S. K., & Low, E. L. (2014). Conceptualising teacher preparation for educational innovation: Singapore's approach. In *Educational policy innovations* (pp. 49–70). Singapore: Springer.

Low, E. L., & Tan O. S. (2020). email correspondence, February 11, 2020.

Mathematics HOD, personal communication, January 13, 2020.

Ministry of Education. (2019, August 22). Retrieved October 17, 2019, from http://www.moe.gov.sg/about

National Archives of Singapore. (2011, September 22). Retrieved February 1, 2012, from https://www.nas.gov.sg/archivesonline/data/pdfdoc/20110929001/wps_opening_address_(media)(checked).pdf

National Center on Education and The Economy: Empower Educators. (2017, February). Retrieved October 17, 2019, from http://ncee.org/wp-content/uploads/2017/02/SingaporeCountryBrief.pdf

National Institute of Education Singapore. (2009). *A teacher education model for the 21st century*. Retrieved from https://www.nie.edu.sg/docs/default-source/te21_docs/te21-online-version%2D%2D-updated.pdf?sfvrsn=2

National Institute of Education (NIE), Singapore. (n.d.). *Learning: Research and practice*. Retrieved August 29, 2020, from https://www.nie.edu.sg/research/publication/learning-research-and-practice

National Research Council. (2013). *Education for life and work: Developing transferable knowledge and skills in the 21st century*. Washington, DC: National Academies Press.

OECD. (2014). *TALIS 2013 results: An international perspective on teaching and learning*. Paris: OECD Publishing.

OECD. (2019a). *TALIS 2018 results (Volume I): Teachers and school leaders as lifelong learners*. Paris: OECD Publishing.

OECD. (2019b). *PISA 2018 results (Volume I, II, & III): Combined executive summary*. Paris: OECD Publishing.

Principal, personal communication, January 17, 2020.

Reimers, F. M., & Chung, C. K. (Eds.). (2019). *Teaching and learning for the twenty-first century: Educational goals, policies, and curricula from six nations.* Cambridge, MA: Harvard Education Press.

Rychen, D. S., & Salganik, L. H. (2003). *Key competencies for a successful life and well-functioning society.* Göttingen, Germany: Hogrefe Publishing.

Saravanan, G., & Ponnusamy, L. (2011). Teacher education in Singapore: Charting new directions. *Journal of Research, Policy & Practice of Teachers & Teacher Education (JRPPTTE), 1*(1), 16–29.

Singapore Budget. (2010). *Expenditure overview 2009: Ministry of education.* Retrieved from http://www.singaporebudget.gov.sg/budget_2009/2009/expenditure_overview/moe.html

Singapore Budget. (2011). *Expenditure overview 2010: Ministry of education.* Retrieved from http://www.singaporebudget.gov.sg/budget_2010/expenditure_overview/moe.html

Tan, J. P. L., Caleon, I., Ng, H. L., Poon, C. L., & Koh, E. (2018). Collective creativity competencies and collaborative problem-solving outcomes: Insights from the dialogic interactions of Singapore student teams. In *Assessment and teaching of 21st century skills* (pp. 95–118). Cham, Switzerland: Springer.

Tan, O. S. (2012). Fourth way in action: Teacher education in Singapore. *Educational Research for Policy and Practice, 11*(1), 35–41.

Tan, O. S., Liu, W. C., & Low, E. L. (Eds.). (2017). *Teacher education in the 21st century: Singapore's evolution and innovation.* Springer.

World Development Indicators. (2020). Retrieved February 1, 2020, from https://databank.worldbank.org/reports.aspx?source=2&country=SGP

Durgesh Rajandiran is a 2020 graduate from the Human Development and Psychology M.Ed. program at the Harvard Graduate School of Education (HGSE). She has a B.A. in Linguistics and English Literature from the University of California, Los Angeles (UCLA). Prior to HGSE, she was an academic researcher in language acquisition and language processing at the Department of Psychology at Harvard University. As an undergraduate at UCLA, she was a tutor in English and Computer Skills for immigrant employees with incomplete formal education. She also has several years of experience in educational innovation and social impact spaces in Malaysia and the US.

Chapter 4
2013 Mexico's Education Reform: A Multi-dimensional Analysis

Paul Moch Islas, Anne K. Calef, and Cristina Aparicio

4.1 Introduction

In February 2013, the Mexican Congress approved a constitutional change to shift education policy throughout the country. The new amendment sought to ensure a quality education for all students, equipping them with the skills needed to succeed in the twenty-first century, as recognized by organizations such as the World Bank, the OECD, and others (SEP, 2017a). The Mexican constitution previously guaranteed the right of all individuals to a free education, but the new language pushed this concept further - guaranteeing a "quality" universal education that included educational infrastructure, new school organization, and – most polemically – a "suitable" teacher (Mexico, 2016). Coupled with three administrative laws, the education reform that began in 2013 (hereafter referred to as the "Reform") sought a major cultural shift, first by reasserting federal control over the education sector, and later by promulgating a new pedagogical and curricular model through its "New Education Model" (*Nuevo Modelo Educativo,* "NME") (SEP, 2017a). However, such a sequencing limited initial stakeholder engagement, leading to political turmoil that ultimately hindered the Reform's implementation and lasting impact.

Collectively, the Reform had two main goals, one explicit, to improve the quality of education and one implicit, to allow the Federal government to retake control of the education sector, as over time much control had shifted to teacher unions. These changes aimed to fundamentally alter the power dynamics that had existed in Mexico's education sector and previously limited the state's capacity to conduct education policy. The architects of the Reform argued that without seizing control

P. M. Islas (✉) · C. Aparicio
Harvard Graduate School of Education, Cambridge, MA, USA
e-mail: paulmochislas@gse.harvard.edu; caparicio@gse.harvard.edu

A. K. Calef
Massachusetts Institute of Technology, Cambridge, MA, USA
e-mail: calef@mit.edu

© The Author(s) 2021
F. M. Reimers (ed.), *Implementing Deeper Learning and 21st Century Education Reforms,* https://doi.org/10.1007/978-3-030-57039-2_4

of the sector from teacher unions, it would be impossible to implement the shift towards twenty-first century competencies ("21CC") that they envisioned. As a result, the sequence that followed first prioritized institutional and political approaches before focusing on the pedagogical and curricular aspects that more directly affected teaching and learning. Reformers hoped that this succession would radically transform national education culture, however, when combined with the short political cycle in Mexico, this order resulted in a limited implementation of the pedagogic components.

The Reform process began before President Enrique Peña Nieto's inauguration as part of the structural reform proposed by the transition team and later named the *Pacto por Mexico* ("Agreement for Mexico"). The Reform was one of the first *Pacto* laws to take effect in February 2013, but its implementation took the Department of Education (*Secretaria de Educación Pública*, "SEP") longer than anticipated, beginning in 2015 and not reaching full implementation until 2017 (see Appendix A). In addition to creating a new legal and institutional framework, the Reform began by executing a set of teachers' evaluations that substituted political considerations with a merit-based system to appoint new teachers, promote them within a structured professional pathway, and determine who remained in the classroom. The Reform also transformed relations between schools, communities, local and state governments, and federal entities that make up Mexico's education sector. Finally, the Reform introduced new pedagogies and curricula to educate students to be twenty-first century global citizens. As mandated in the constitution, the new model contained a set of standards, guidelines and teaching practices that not only prioritized teacher autonomy and revalued teacher agency, but also guaranteed a new type of instruction capable of achieving the Reform's ambitious goals.

This paper will begin by analyzing Mexico in international and domestic contexts to understand the urgency of the Reform. It will then use Reimers (2020b, c) five perspectives on education change to analyze the Reform and evaluate the sequence in which it was implemented (See Appendix B). It also argues that an uneven commitment of state governments to implement the policies of the Reform hindered its adoption. The paper concludes by outlining the results of the Reform to date and summarizing the relationship between the five perspectives. Ultimately, we argue that the initial deprioritization of pedagogical aspects stymied the cultural shift towards a 21CC model that the Reform sought. When coupled with a limited political cycle, the Reform's sequence left little time for full implementation of its more pedagogical and popular aspects, such as the New Education Model (*Nuevo Modelo Educativo*, "NME"), and faced dramatic reprisal from the subsequent presidential administration.

4.2 International Context

The *Pacto* reforms passed at the beginning of the Peña Nieto administration were influenced by international policies and pressures. Scholar Carlos Elizondo Mayer-Serra explains that one factor leading to the broad support of the *Pacto* reforms was a growing consensus around the need for structural reforms to encourage economic growth, especially the reforms that had been suggested by international organizations, such as the OECD, for over a decade (Mayer-Serra, 2017, p. 28). Former Secretary of Education Aurelio Nuño Mayer echoed this sentiment, explaining that the *Pacto* sought a suite of reforms to facilitate greater integration into the global economy through increased economic competition, access to resources, and financial reform (A. Nuño Mayer, personal communication, January 29, Nuño Mayer, 2020).

Results from the OECD's Program for International Student Assessment (PISA) and Teaching and Learning International Survey (TALIS) that situated Mexico at the bottom of the international distribution of student learning outcomes also spurred action (OECD, 2014). A year before the introduction of the Reform, the OECD released a detailed assessment of each participating country's performance on the 2012 PISA exam. An analysis of Mexico's results revealed that, while the country's 2012 scores showed a stark improvement from its 2003 results, it still scored 16% below the OECD average, with a mean of 413 in mathematics that placed students on the second from the bottom of six possible levels of proficiency (OECD, 2013). Further, more than half of 15-year-olds in Mexico failed to meet the minimum achievement benchmark in mathematics, such that there was a 2 year gap in mathematical performance between the Mexican and OECD averages (Cabrera Hernández, 2018).

Analyses of the existing curriculum and Mexico's knowledge assessment, the National Plan for the Evaluation of Knowledge (PLANEA) exam, further demonstrated these gaps. More than 50% of the students did not meet minimum benchmarks in language and communication (INEE, 2015). Even worse, over 66% of Mexican learners did not score above the minimum benchmarks in mathematical knowledge (INEE, 2015). Additionally, the educational model failed to arm pupils with socioemotional skills, namely interpersonal and intrapersonal abilities, that are integral to achieving success in today's globalized world (Hrusa, Moch Islas, Schneider, & Vega, 2020). Global demand and advancement in technology put a premium on education and skilled labor, requiring that education reform experts focus on the development of 21CC (OECD, 2019).

Educator results were similarly discouraging. TALIS results from 2012 showed an important need to update pedagogical practices to better support students in their development of 21CC (Reimers, 2018). Reimers (2018) found that one in ten teachers, and two in five primary school teachers, had not received university training. Likewise, only three out of five teachers in Mexico had received specific training to be teachers, 33% had not received specialized training in the subjects they were teaching, and only three out of four teachers felt prepared to teach (OECD, 2014).

Although the majority of Mexican teachers reported having received some type of professional training, more than a quarter reported that the training they had received was not related to the subject they were teaching (Reimers, 2018).

OECD and PISA reports provide critical context for the Reform's emphasis on universal, 21CC, quality education. Reports from the TALIS and PISA increased international pressure on Mexico. Internally, PLANEA results spurred Mexican civil society to push for a deep pedagogical and political transformation that it viewed as fundamental for the country's integration into an everyday more global-ized world.

4.3 Domestic Context

Mexico was governed by a one-party hegemonic system from its revolution in 1910 until the defeat of the Institutional Revolutionary Party (*Partido Revolucionario Institucional,* PRI) in 2000. During this period, the PRI consolidated a corporatist governance structure in which political interest groups such as unions (*Confederación de Trabajadores de México*), farmers (*Conferencia Nacional Campesina*), the mili-tary (*Union Revolucionaria*), and others (i.e. *Confederación Nacional de Organizaciones Populares*) maintained representation in internal party organisms (Córdova, 2014). There was an understanding that economic and political benefits were granted only to those who aligned with the PRI's interests (Gindín, 2008). Under this corporatist model, it was expected that the government would ignore corrupt practices in exchange for electoral support (Audelo Cruz, 2005). Such prac-tices were common in the most powerful labor union in the education sector, the National Union of Education Workers (*Sindicato Nacional de Trabajadores de Educación,* "SNTE"), that was responsible for position assignments, promotion decisions, and salary allocations for teachers (Tuckman, 2013). As stated in the World Bank's, 2018 report "Learning to Realize Education's Promise," "evidence from...Mexico suggests that union behavior (and ability to resist reform) depends on the influence of partisan identities, organizational fragmentation, and the competi-tion for union leadership" (World Bank, 2018, p. 192).

The electoral victory of right-wing opposition candidate, Vicente Fox (from the *Partido Acción Nacional,* "PAN" - National Action Party), in the year 2000 began a new era of democratic plurality in Mexico (Woldenberg, 2012). This altered politi-cal landscape, however, did not translate into a new governance model. Fox contin-ued to rely on existing power structures, perpetuating the political alliance with teachers' unions. Despite largely perpetuating the status quo, President Fox did cre-ate a new, independent entity to evaluate the education system, increase transpar-ency, and heighten public accountability (SEP, 2002). The National Institute of Educational Evaluation (Instituto Nacional de Evaluación Educativa, "INEE") would be a critical actor in all successive education reforms, and signaled a larger shift towards a technical, research-based approach for assessing education policy and progress (Hrusa et al., 2020).

The political alliance that developed between President Fox and the SNTE was further solidified during Felipe Calderón's administration from 2006 to 2012. Calderón depended on a political alliance with the SNTE's newborn political party, the *Partido Nueva Alianza* ("PANAL") to narrowly defeat leftist candidate Andrés Manuel López Obrador by a margin of 0.56% in the 2006 presidential election (INE, 2014). Deeply linked to the SNTE, Calderón proceeded to grant SNTE leaders key administrative positions in the SEP, thus entrenching SNTE power over the education sector. In contrast, Enrique Peña Nieto's 2012 electoral victory relied on a coalition that included the PRI but not the PANAL.

Historically, Mexico's education system has been highly centralized under the SEP. With 36.4 million pupils, more than two million teachers and 260,000 schools, this level of centralization can present challenges (INEGI, 2016). On paper, hiring and salary decisions were jointly decided by the SEP and local education authorities ("*Autoridades Educativas Locales*," AELs) through split commissions, however, the SNTE often controlled government appointees and, in many cases, also had allies in key SEP and state-level positions. The only way to gain a public teaching position was by graduating from one of the "Escuelas Normales" (teacher colleges) which guaranteed a post for all graduates. Such a policy took agency away from school principals who had no control over hiring decisions. At a local level, promotions were sanctioned by the unions, and the criteria used were tied to demonstrated loyalty to the union and active participation in union strikes and marches (Muñoz Armenta, 2008).

In a country with stark economic inequality, teaching positions were considered a source of financial stability, which granted unions considerable power over their members, particularly in low-income and rural communities. A perception of the Reform as potentially threatening the livelihood of these communities was particularly true in Mexico's southern states (Chiapas, Oaxaca, Michoacán, Guerrero, and Veracruz), which had the lowest rankings on the Human Development Index (Permanyer & Smits, 2018) in Mexico and where the National Coordinator of Education Workers (*Coordinadora Nacional de Trabajadores de la Educación,* "CNTE"), the most radical section of the SNTE, maintained a larger presence. Educational policies that placed life-long teaching positions in jeopardy were perceived as major disruptors to the social fabric, causing significant uproar. This response helped reinforce the message asserted by radical members of the union that the Reform was meant to further marginalize the already excluded communities of these states (López Aguilar, 2013; Ahmed & Semple, 2016). Peña Nieto wanted to demonstrate the extent to which his administration would back the Reform, so soon after it was signed into law, he imprisoned SNTE president Elba Esther Gordillo on charges of embezzlement (Tuckman, 2013). Such an action was intended to show the government's commitment to ending corrupt and clientelistic practices that had become rampant within the education sector (Muñoz Armenta, 2008). Nonetheless, it fueled the narrative that the administration was targeting teachers (Gómez Zamarripa & Navarro Arredondo, 2018).

4.4 Analysis of the *Reforma Educativa* in a Five Dimensional Framework

Viewing the Reform through each of Reimers' five dimensions of the education system elucidates the logic, goals, strategies, successes, and shortcomings of the Reform. While the frameworks are in no way mutually exclusive, Reimers explains that an attention to each dimension allows for the examination of a reform's "internal coherence" and can also guide the sequencing of reform (Reimers, 2020b, p. 9) that emerge as governments set priorities due to limited economic and political resources. The sequence of these stages is important to the success of a reform's multidimensional goals, as is evident in Mexico's case.

The Reform was primarily a political and institutional reform that sought a national cultural shift through the promulgation of a new educational model. The genesis of the reform is most visible when focusing on the political aspects that foreground how "education affects the interests of many different groups, and that those vary within and across groups, and may be in conflict" (Reimers, 2020b, p. 39). An attention to this political dimension not only highlights the Reform's roots in Mexico's shifting political landscape but also its deep connection to Peña Nieto's other structural reforms. The early Reform actions that followed were aimed at institutional aspects of education, what Reimers' defines as "various structures, processes and resources that provide resiliency to the system of education" (Reimers, 2020c, p. 8). Constitutional changes fundamentally altered the legal framework governing Mexican education and necessitated political actions, namely the creation of teacher performance exams that then flared tensions between actors.

It was not until halfway through the Reform that actions emphasizing the psychological and professional dimensions of educational change emerged, such as a new educational model and a push for teacher professional development to promote 21CC. Reimers defines the psychological frame as concentrating on "theories of learning which undergird the learning and teaching process for students, teachers, administrators and parents" (Reimers, 2020c, p. 8). In the case of Mexico, the first clearly communicated focus on pedagogical and curricular best practices surfaced with the New Education Model (*Nuevo Modelo Educativo*, "NME"). Similarly, the professional aspects, those that seek to align current and required levels of professional capacity, did not crystallize until the broad stakeholder engagement during the NME's development. They were further developed in the last years of Peña Nieto's administration when the national strategies for teacher professional development were published.

Adopting Reimers' cultural framework focuses attention to the "broader set of external social expectations, norms, and values which define what are accepted education goals and practices" (Reimers, 2020c, p. 8) and it is here that we see the ultimate goals of the Reform. The Reform sought to induce three major changes to the educational landscape in Mexico: create a student-centered education model, increase educator accountability and professionalism, and shift power from unions to school communities and the SEP (Moch Islas & Schneider, 2018). Each change would represent a significant shift in the culture around education, and each was ultimately difficult to accomplish due to the limited temporal scope of the reform and the implementation challenges it faced at a subnational level. Arguably, had the dimensions of the reform been implemented in a different order, namely the NME and professional development prior to evaluations, it could have eased the political acceptability of the Reform and allowed for greater progress towards its cultural goals. The following sections will examine the Reform under each of Reimers' five dimensions, ultimately arguing that the sequence in which priorities were addressed led to the Reform's major setbacks, shortcomings, and, ultimately, its repeal. While each section focuses on a particular frame, the policy changes pursued by the Reform ultimately aligned behind two goals: the explicit (improved educational outcomes due to new pedagogical practices) and the implicit (reasserting federal control of the education sector).

4.4.1 Institutional

The Reform began with major institutional changes that outlined the mechanisms necessary to transform the education sector. Reimers (2020a) refers to the institutional frame as one that "focuses on the educational structures, norms, regulations, incentives, and organizational design which provide stability and meaning to the work of teaching and learning and to all social interactions designed to support them" (Reimers, 2020c, p. 18) The Reform sought to create a new legal and institutional framework, by first amending Article 3 of the Constitution and the General Law of Education (LGE) and then passing the General Law of the Professional Teacher Service (LGSPD), and the National Institute for Education Evaluation Law (LINEE) in September 2013 (Ramírez Raymundo et al., 2016). Rewriting Article 3 was a vital institutional driver of the Reform.

The LGSPD created the new Professional Teacher Service (*"Servicio Profesional Docente,"* SPD) to systematize regulations for the hiring, recognition of performance, and contract renewal of teachers, as well as the newly created pedagogical advisors position (*"Asesor Técnico Pedagógico,"* ATP). Teachers, ATP's, and school administrators were all evaluated under the new system (Moch Islas & Schneider, 2018). Working in conjunction with the INEE and local education authorities (*"Autoridades Educativas Locales,"* AELs), the National Coordination of the SPD was charged with organizing competitive hiring pools from which aspiring teachers would be selected based on clear, rigorous criteria (Mexicanos Primero, 2018). Under the SPD, there were two pathways to advance in the teacher profession, one vertical and one horizontal (LGSPD, 2013). The vertical pathway outlined how teachers could attain leadership positions, moving from roles as a teacher to that of supervisor, ATP, or principal, while the horizontal ladder was tied to one's performance within their given role (SNTE, 2015). Progress on the horizontal ladder, metered by the recognition exam, included salary increases that could add up to more than 122% of their base salary (LGSPD, 2013). Movement on both pathways was determined by one of four evaluations- hiring (*ingreso*), ability to keep a teaching position (*permanencia*), recognition of performance (*reconocimiento*), and career progression (*promoción*) (LGSPD, 2013). The LGSPD also outlined educators', ATPs' and school administrators' right to professional development and created several institutional mechanisms to provide that training (outlined in Sect. 3.3).

Another component of the legal framework created by the Reform was the LINEE that granted autonomy and new responsibilities to the INEE (INEE, 2018). In conjunction with the LGSPD and changes to the LGE, this entrusted the INEE with five primary tasks:

1. Design and implement assessments of the education system;
2. Coordinate the National System for Educational Evaluation (*Sistema Nacional de Evaluación Educativa,* "SNEE");
3. Create regulatory frameworks to guide the evaluations of teachers, administrators, policies, and programs;
4. Analyze and publicize evaluation results;
5. Issue recommendations that require a formal response from the SEP.

     (Hrusa et al., 2020)

This focused mission and newly granted status of an "autonomous constitutional body" (LINEE, 2013) allowed the INEE to become a technical entity that was independent from the political cycles, promoted research-based pedagogies, and served as a "counterweight" to the SEP (Reimers, 2018). The LINEE also positioned the National System for Educational Evaluation (*Sistema Nacional de Evaluación Educativa,* "SNEE"), which consisted of the executive branch of the federal government (President and SEP), the INEE, and the AELs, as the highest authority in education (Martínez Bordón, 2018).

The empowerment of the INEE was closely aligned with the Reform's goals to transition to a merit-based hiring and promotion system, improve student outcomes by empowering community participation in education, and broaden control of the educational sector (Schmelkes, 2018). The INEE fostered the transparency integral to merit-based employment systems and greater social participation by disseminating regulatory frameworks (*lineamientos*) and indicators, overseeing evaluation mechanisms, and publishing diagnostic and evaluative reports (LINEE, 2013). As scholars seek to understand the Reform, it is important to highlight the role of altering institutional and legal systems to shift control from teacher unions to the state. The architects of the Reform viewed these institutional changes as the foundation of this new system (Nuño, 2020). For them, it was a necessary first step to allow for transformations in other areas of the education sector. However, because it was the product of an agreement between the major political parties with limited stakeholder involvement it was perceived as a top-down strategy. This perception caused the more radical factions of the teachers' union to reject the reform and to block the buy-in of constituencies critical to its success: the teachers.

4.4.2 Political

Analyzing the reform from a political perspective focuses attention on the Reform's genesis as part of the *Pacto por Mexico* ("Agreement for Mexico") as well as the initial stages of implementation. This section looks first at the political context of the Reform, identifying the reassertion of state control, after decades of corporatist governance structures (Audelo Cruz, 2005; A. Nuño Mayer, personal communication, January 29, 2020), as a major goal of the Reform (Granados Roldán, 2018; Granados Roldán, 2018b; Hrusa et al., 2020; Martínez Bordón & Navarro Arredondo, 2018). Turning next to implementation, we analyze how the Reform sought to shift political and financial power through the sequence of its priorities and altering of governance structures. Finally, we examine how the Reform sought to empower third-party evaluative bodies in order to increase transparency and accountability of all actors.

Immediately after President Peña Nieto took office, an unprecedented agreement was signed by the leaders of all three major political parties in Congress. The *Pacto por Mexico* was a series of 95 agreements divided into five categories: democratic governance; transparency, accountability, and the fight against corruption; civil rights and liberties; security and justice; and economic growth, employment and competitiveness (Mayer-Serra, 2017). Together, the *Pacto* reforms sought major structural changes in the electoral, judicial, fiscal, economic, labor, telecommunications, energy, and education sectors (Echávarri & Peraaza, 2017). When considering the political aspects of the Reform, its emergence within the *Pacto* cannot be ignored. The Peña Nieto administration sought a broad series of policy goals that previous administrations had not succeeded in achieving (e.g. liberalization of the energy sector) (Mayer-Serra, 2017). During the 70 years of hegemonic PRI political control, a strong corporatist model of governance emerged in which the government empowered organized factions, such as labor unions or private business, in exchange for electoral power (Audelo Cruz, 2005). Both the Fox and Calderón administrations had attempted broad reforms after the PRI was defeated in the 2000 presidential election, but neither succeeded in enacting structural change that challenged established stakeholders (Mayer-Serra, 2017).

Like with other *Pacto* reforms, architects of the Reform viewed the disruption of existing power dynamics in the education sector as key to implementing structural reforms. Contact with other stakeholders was thus limited and initial implementation was swift to avoid pressure from interest groups (Mayer-Serra, 2017). Martínez Bordón and Navarro Arredondo (2018) note that while many of the topics addressed in the Reform had circulated in public debate and discussion for much time prior, there remained a lack of stakeholder engagement during the Reform design process. Given the polemic nature of each *Pacto* reform, it was feared that concessions for stakeholders in one *Pacto* agreement (e.g. inviting the SNTE into the design of the Reform) would lead to concessions for stakeholders in all, thus threatening the success of the *Pacto* (A. Nuño Mayer, personal communication, January 29, Nuño Mayer, 2020). The arrest of SNTE leader Esther Elba Gordillo at the beginning of the *Pacto* sent a clear message to all union leaders that opposition to reforms would not be accepted (Mayer-Serra, 2017).

The most controversial aspects of the Reform, teacher evaluations with negative consequences for failure, were established and implemented in the first phase of the Reform in order to assert governmental leadership of the education sector (Moch Islas & Schneider, 2018). By creating the SPD with its required exams and alternative pathways to entering the teacher profession (INEE, 2017), the Reform claimed control over functions that had historically been carried out by teacher unions. Rapidly enacting institutional changes without pause to involve other stakeholders was political by design, and had significant ramifications for future implementation.

The Peña Nieto administration decided to confront the teacher unions with all instruments at its disposal. When the SNTE retained members' paychecks, the government responded by redesigning the control of federal budget and teacher payroll through the creation of the Contribution Fund for Educational Payroll and Operating Expense (*Fondo de Aportaciones para la Nómina Educativa y Gasto Operativo,* "FONE") (Granados, 2020). When the SNTE paralyzed a state's economy by blocking highways and railroads, the government sent police to break picket lines (Animal Político, 2016). When the SNTE brought 3400 teachers cases before a judge, the court ruled in favor of the SEP in over 90% of the cases (Granados, 2020). After the SNTE walked out of schools to protest, the government amplified the voice of parents who demanded that teachers return to the classroom through press briefings, interviews, and media coverage (Chaca, García, & Martin, 2016). The SEP also asserted political control by redesigning state education agencies that had been heavily influenced by non-governmental stakeholders. In state governments, around 60 to 70% of the local secretaries of education, depending on the year, had some form of an affiliation with the SNTE (Granados, 2020). The most famous example of which is the State Institute for Oaxacan Public Education (*Instituto Estatal de Educación Pública de Oaxaca,* "IEEPO").

Responsible for the distribution of teacher positions and SEP-provided financial resources, the IEEPO's organization, members, processes, and operations were largely controlled by the National Coordinator of Education Workers (*Coordinadora Nacional de Trabajadores de la Educación,* "CNTE") (Briseño, 2015). On July 15, 2015, the Governor of Oaxaca dismantled the IEEPO and replaced it with governor-appointed public administrators in order to recuperate regional resources and governmental authority (Granados Roldán, 2018a; Granados Roldán, 2018b). This change was predicted to be so polemic that hundreds of state and local police were posted outside of the IEEPO prior to the announcement, demonstrating once again the political priorities and consequences of the Reform (Briseño, 2015). Political tensions came to a head in Nochixtlán on June 19, 2016 when CNTE protests and government forces clashed, leaving six dead and over 100 wounded (Partlow, 2016).

The Reform also created local, state, regional, and national level School Councils for Social Participation (nationally the *Consejo Nacional de Participación Social en la Educación* "CONAPASE" and locally the *Consejo Escolar de Participación Social,* "CEPS") to distribute the power it had gained and share best practices at different scales. At a regional level, the councils became forums where state governors and the SEP discussed and co-constructed the implementation of learning communities (Nuño, Nuño Mayer, 2020). At a local level, CEPS engaged citizens as key actors in the design, implementation and evaluation of education policy (Reyes, 2018). At a school level, the goal was to bring school leaders and families together to foster co-responsibility in student learning and holistic development. CONAPASE and the CEPS would provide insight into the design and implementation of school improvement plans that addressed school management, culture, and operations (LGE, 2013).

Acknowledging the political nature of the new policies, the architects of the Reform also sought to empower the INEE as a fiscally and politically autonomous body responsible for the evaluation of the education system as a whole. The INEE was given responsibility for supervising educator evaluations, analyzing their results, and issuing recommendations to the SEP and other involved parties. In addition to writing and disseminating the evaluation frameworks, the INEE's external position to the SEP allowed it to perform a certifying role – validating teacher appraisal mechanisms and supervising the appraisal processes (OECD, 2019). It is notable that, in response to criticism, the INEE recommended that the 2016 cycle of performance evaluations be optional to allow for a redesign of the test (OECD, 2019). The INEE played a critical role in not only attempting to quell political tensions generated by the Reform, but also to promote fidelity to the educational best practices laid out in the initial legislation and later the NME. The INEE was a powerful actor in encouraging pedagogical practices throughout the Reform.

4.4.3   Psychological and Professional

Reimers' psychological and professional lenses encourage an attention to the technical aspects of the reform- specifically the pedagogical best practices (psychological) and educators' current capacities and knowledge (professional) (Reimers, 2020c). Studying the Reform from these two perspectives, we see that the psychological and professional dimensions were not prioritized until later stages of the reform, first with the development and implementation of the New Education Model (*"Nuevo Modelo Educativo,"* NME) in 2015 and then with the published Professional Development Strategy in 2017. The latter was never fully implemented due to the end of the political cycle and a lack of participation from some state governments (Mexicanos Primero, 2018).

Changes to the LGE called for a revision of the education model to be developed with broad participation from stakeholders. In contrast to the top-down approach of the initial set of policies (i.e. the evaluation of teachers) the new model was to be crafted with input from AELs, teachers, unions, experts, and families. The result was an extensive consultation period from February 2014 to June 2014 before the NME was released in 2016 (Mexicanos Primero, 2018). Reimers (2020b) explains that the professional dimension of educational change demands that teachers are engaged as "subjects rather than objects of the reform" (Reimers, 2020b, p. 32), and the 2014 "National Consultation on the Educational Model' 'represents the first time that the Reform attempted to do so. Approximately 28,000 participants engaged in 18 regional and three national forums hosted by the SEP, resulting in 15,000 proposals (Nuño, 2018; Díaz-Barriga, 2018). The SEP also sought input and feedback from universities, CTE, and CTZ during this period (Nuño, 2018). The result of the forums was a robust educational model focused on five main topics: curriculum, centering schools, suitability of teachers, inclusion and equity, and governance (Martínez Bordón & Navarro Arredondo, 2018).

The NME succeeded in emphasizing 21CC development both in content, e.g. stressing both cognitive and social and emotional skills, and pedagogical practices, e.g. encouraging student collaboration and self-direction (Hrusa et al., 2020). Specifically, the NME highlighted 11 primary skills that fall under three categories: Fields of Academic Knowledge, Areas of Social and Personal Development, and Spheres for Curricular Autonomy. It asserted a novel approach to achieving these learning objectives by emphasizing questions, projects, and problems which consider student interest and promote personal research, collaborative learning, and inverted classroom models (SEP, 2017a).

Another feature of the NME was that it created space to contextualize relevant content for all learners, while ensuring equity principles. As cited in Bonilla (Bonilla-Rius, 2020), former Undersecretary of Education Tuirán stated that, "a quality education with equity and inclusion was defined by NME as one that: expands educational opportunities for all, without distinctions of any kind; favors the integration of heterogeneous school communities; recognizes that students have different abilities, tempos and learning styles; distributed equitably all resources (technical, physical and human) required for teaching and learning; and grants significant and comparable learning to all students" (Reimers, 2020b, p. 118). In seeking to educate the child as comprehensively as possible, the NME was divided into three components- Academic Knowledge, Social and Personal Development, and Curricular Autonomy (SEP, 2017a). It is worth highlighting that socio-emotional learning (SEL) was allocated a specific time in all K-12 grades to promote self-knowledge, self-regulation, autonomy, empathy and collaboration (Bonilla-Rius, 2019).

In addition, the NME asserted two major changes to how education was conceptualized in Mexico by highlighting the importance of early childhood education and "placing students at the center." (SEP, 2016) The early childhood education program was outlined in the SEP-released report "Start Out Right" (*Un buen comienzo*) (SEP, 2017f) and called for the coordination of different agencies that oversaw early childhood education with the goal of providing education and care from birth (Bonilla, 2020). By "placing students at its center," the NME defined clear learning outcomes and positioned teachers as facilitators of learning rather than transmitters of knowledge (SEP, 2017a). Respecting teachers' and administrators' professional abilities, the NME sought to ensure that teachers, teacher leaders, and principals had additional autonomy and opportunities for peer collaboration (Hrusa et al., 2020).

It was not until 2017 that the SEP published a set of strategies which aimed to transform pre-service teacher training by providing teacher colleges with the resources to innovate and change institutional practices. Outlined in the "Strategy for Strengthening and Transformation of the Teacher Colleges" (*Estrategia de Fortalecimiento y Transformación de las Escuelas Normales*), the SEP sought to steer teacher colleges towards a focus on research and multilingualism, without forgetting the varied cultural contexts of the country (SEP, 2017a, p. 8). The Strategy also demonstrated the NME's commitment to bilingualism, as can be seen in its innovative and inclusive proposals to strengthen indigenous and foreign language instruction (Granados Roldán, Puente de la Mora, & Betanzos Torres, 2019, Granados Roldán, 2018a, Granados Roldán, 2018b). These strategies targeting initial teacher training were published under the "National Program for English Instruction" (*Programa Nacional de Inglés* – PRONI), which mapped learning outcomes, instructional activities, and assessments to achieve proficient literacy in a second language (McCabe, Tamis-LeMonda, Bornstein, et al., 2013).

The Continuous Professional Development Strategy (*Formación Continua,* "FC") also proposed novel strategies for ongoing teacher training (SEP, 2017g). The FC recognized and outlined the complexities of implementing the NME and its new methods of instruction. It thus intended to catalyze real change in learning outcomes by identifying areas for teacher growth using performance assessments and personalized attention to ameliorate any gaps (SEP, 2017g).

In line with the Reform's goals of increasing school autonomy, a number of professional development opportunities were envisioned as school based. The School Technical Assistance Services ("*Servicio de Asistencia Técnica a la Escuela,*" SATE) was created to facilitate professional development within schools through collective learning and mentorship (Hrusa et al., 2020). Designed as spaces to collectively discuss, learn from, and address problems experienced at schools, Regional Technical Councils ("*Consejos Técnicos de Zona,*" CTZ) were established as an additional opportunity for the professional development of school leaders (Mexicanos Primero, 2018). Finally, the SEP devoted 1 day (4 h) every month to School Technical Councils ("*Consejo Técnico Escolar,*" CTE) for teacher collaboration and planning as well as school-based projects and professional development (Reyes, 2018). Despite these new institutions, the Reform struggled to provide the necessary professional development for educators and school leaders to adapt to these changes and truly shift school cultures (Reimers, 2018).

Finally, the NME contained grade level standards and benchmarks that considered different socio-learning environments (family & community; ludic & literary; and formative & academic) (SEP, 2018). Each standard was paired with a corresponding didactic communication activity as well as hands-on activities to help students develop language proficiency and conceptual understanding (Vega & Terada, 2013). For example, the design of the National English Strategy curriculum contained printed texts in their native and second languages to foster the ability to decode unfamiliar words and assist with reading comprehension (Castro et al., 2011).

The NME's brief implementation period greatly limited its scope and reach, as can be seen most clearly with professional development. Reimers (2018) identifies constructing a system for professional development as a primary challenge faced by any reform. Hrusa et al. (2020) argue that implementation of evaluations before a robust professional development system was established caused a radical faction of educators to view the Reform as punitive, despite reformers' best intentions. Professional development continues to be a challenge. In a 2018 INEE report, more than half of teachers sampled had not taken a course about discipline, student evaluation or social emotional learning in the last 2 years (INEE, 2018).

4.4.4 Cultural

As defined by Reimers (2020b), in order to analyze a reform through a cultural perspective, it is important to consider the "broader set of external societal hopes for schools, norms and values which define what are accepted educational goals and practices" (Reimers, 2020c, p. 8). Many times, these goals are not explicitly described by the authors of a reform, the legal framework, or the entity that is implementing it. In Mexico's case, the authors of the Reform understood the importance of underscoring the pedagogical ambitions, curricular goals, and learning outcomes, goals that the transformation aimed to achieve. They did so in three different documents: Article 3 of Mexico's Constitution (Mexico, 1917 as amended), the statement "Ends of Education in the 21st Century" (SEP 2017a), and in the documents compiled under the title "Key Learnings" (SEP, 2015). The Reform aimed to induce change in Mexico's education culture in four primary ways: building a student-centered system as defined by "Key Learning Outcomes" (2015), increasing accountability and restoring dignity to the teacher profession through the creation of the SPD, altering the school-community paradigm to focus on increased social participation, and shifting power from unions and into the newly created institutions like the INEE and the CONAPASE (Nuño, 2020). In order for the current inequality that prevails in our modern society to disappear, education is key (United Nations, 2015). In these policy documents, Mexico, aligned with the UN view, promoted education not only as a human right, but also as the key to access every other human right. Reform authors made clear the state's obligation and mandate to not only ensure educational access for all, but also guarantee that public education is high-quality and relevant, emphasizing the pedagogical importance of the Reform (Mexico, 2013).

The Mexican Constitution is a set of normative values that outline a collective vision for an ideal country. It recognizes education's role as a key element to shape society. Peña Nieto's administration changed Article 3 of the Constitution to state that education should be public, secular, free, and universal. Importantly, the new language in the Constitution went beyond guaranteeing access to education to define, in almost exhaustive detail, how the state understood quality education:

Title II: The criteria that will guide this education will be based on the results of scientific progress, the fight against ignorance and its effects: servitudes, fanaticism, and prejudice.

(a) It will be democratic, considering democracy not only as a legal structure and a political regime, but as a life system based on the constant economic, social, and cultural improvement of the people;

(b) It will be national, insofar as - without hostilities or exclusivism - it will attend to the understanding of our problems, to the use of our resources, to the defense of our political independence, to the assurance of our economic independence, and to the continuity and enhancement of our culture;

(c) Contribute to the best human coexistence, in order to strengthen the appreciation and respect for cultural diversity, the dignity of the person, the integrity of the family, the conviction of the general interest of society, the ideals of fraternity and equality of rights of all, avoiding the privileges of races, religion, groups, sexes or individuals, and;

(d) It will be of quality, based on the constant improvement and the maximum academic achievement of the learners;"

 (Mexico, 1917 as amended))

The most significant change to the Mexican Constitution which took place during the Peña Nieto administration, was the emphasis that education be of "quality." Further, the new amendment framed quality not as static but "based on the constant improvement and the maximum academic achievement of learners" (Mexico, 2017; Article 3, Title II).

To the Reformers, a "quality" education was based in twenty-first Century Competencies (21CC). Education scholars assert that in our fast-paced world 21CC must be taught with student-centered pedagogies to ensure "higher achieving" citizens fit for the challenges of a globalized world (Gebhard, 2014; NRC, 2012). The Reform sought to achieve learning outcomes, through new pedagogical strategies, that went beyond basic numeracy and literacy. For example, a focus on literacy that extended beyond the ability to decode. Reading comprehension, and the aptitudes to communicate in more than one language, are competences required for success in basic education and to understand the complexities of the world we live in (Gebhard, 2014). These ideals are also considered in the letter "The Ends of the Education in the 21st Century" in which the SEP states the mission of the Reform and the NME (SEP, 2017a).

To highlight and strengthen the fundamental role of schools as a catalyst of the transformation, the SEP promoted an infrastructure plan to improve schools called "Escuelas al cien" that aimed to strengthen schools and position them as the cornerstone of citizenship education. Alongside this strategy, the Reform also promoted greater school autonomy by awarding schools financial decision-making power and thus further weakening unions' control on education spending. The establishment of SATEs further empowered schools by promoting peer-to-peer learning. SATEs sought to improve school functioning and advance best practices for teachers and principals across regions through support, assessment, and monitoring of individualized professional development, knowledge, and capacities (Chapman & International Institute for Educational Planning, 2005). A key aspect of SATEs was a new mentorship program that paired veteran and beginning teachers (SEP, 2017b). Finally, CONAPASE aimed to create learning communities that included all stakeholders in education. School leaders and families came together to foster co-responsibility for student learning and holistic development. To do so, they participated in the design and implementation of the school improvement plan, development of a productive learning atmosphere, and vigilance of proper school management and operations.

The Reform sought to catalyze a major cultural shift in teaching and learning in Mexico by moving towards 21CC skills and pedagogies. To achieve that goal, the Reform included a variety of strategies that increased school autonomy and peer collaboration (Consejo Asesor, 2014). However, while the Reform claimed to value the role of the teacher, it neglected to engage them early-on in the decision process. Ultimately, there was not enough time to deploy teacher professional development strategies and fully actualize the Reformers' desired cultural shift. The narrative surrounding the Reform then became dominated by union leaders who decried their loss of privileges and later threw their political support behind opposition presidential candidate, Andrés López Obrador. The long term vision of the Reform to accomplish major cultural changes was disrupted by the presidential election in 2018, and the polarized policy changes that followed.

4.5   Results of the Reform

The Reform had two main objectives, one explicit and one implicit, that aimed to alter one of the world's largest educational systems. The explicit goal was to ensure a quality education for all Mexican students by promoting a shift in the school community paradigm, introducing new pedagogical strategies for teacher and student learning, closing the equity gap in educational access, and increasing social participation in the educational system (Hrusa et al., 2020). The implicit objective was to take federal control of the education system from teacher unions in order to break political ties that had allowed for corporatist practices.

Mexico is an important example of how large-scale reforms that require long time frames for implementation exceeding the duration of political cycles are susceptible to dismantling (Reimers, 2018). Cohen and Mehta (2017) assert that the education sector is particularly vulnerable to public opinion and political pressure and we see that clearly in this instance. It is thus difficult to assess the Reform's impact on student learning outcomes given its short and recent implementation. However, there are some conclusions and evidence that point to the Reform's impact. We begin this section by analyzing the results from the 2018 PISA and some of the results published by the CNSPD (*Consejo Nacional del Servicio Profesional Docente,* "CNSPD") regarding teachers' assessments. We then review two studies conducted by independent researchers and the World Bank that compare the performance of educators that were hired through merit-based systems and discretionary systems. Finally, we analyze other outcomes produced by the Reform, such as collaborative mechanisms for teachers and school communities as well as the backlash against the Reform at the end of Peña Nieto's administration.

With the release of the 2018 PISA results we find that average performance scores have remained stable in reading, mathematics and science (OECD Mexico,

2019). However, when comparing 2018 results to earlier PISA administrations, the greatest increases are between 2003 and 2009 and although some gains were made in the sciences from 2009 to 2018, math and reading results flatlined from 2009 to 2018 (OECD Mexico, 2019). The overall results remain below OECD averages. While this data largely reflects the trajectory set prior to the Reform, they are fundamental to measuring the education sector moving forward.

Despite resistance to the SPD exams, the majority of teachers still participated, with high levels of success. Throughout the country, more than 1.5 million teachers engaged in at least one aspect of the SPD, either for hiring/entrance (*ingreso)*, promotion (*promoción*) or performance recognition (*permanencia*) during the 6 years of the Peña Nieto administration (México, 2018). In addition, over 206,0000 teachers were hired through the entrance exam process (México, 2018). Out of the vast majority of elementary teachers only 11%, and 16% of secondary education teachers (see Tables 4.1 and 4.2), scored an unsatisfactory grade. It is also notable that 52% of elementary teachers and 54% of secondary teachers performed in the range of "good" to "outstanding," disproving the popular narrative that current teachers were not qualified for their positions (CNSPD, 2019).

Further there is evidence that teachers who entered the teaching profession through rules-based hiring practices are more effective than teachers hired through other mechanisms. Ricardo Estrada (2017) concludes in "Rules vs. Discretion in Public Service Teacher Hiring in Mexico" that students learn better from teachers who were selected through rules-based hiring, as was scaled up by the 2013 reform, than by teachers that were selected through a discretionary process, as was done prior to the Reform. Estrada analyzes school performance data from 2008 to 2013 when a pilot rules-based hiring program existed alongside traditional discretion-based practices (de Hoyos & Estrada, n.d.). Linking student achievement data from "*telesecundarias*," secondary schools in rural areas where students are taught all

Table 4.1 Elementary Teachers' Recognition Performance Assessment

School cycle	Assessed	Insufficient	Sufficient	Good	Outstanding
2015–2016	104,860	13,601	40,221	42,769	8269
2016–2017	24,005	2615	10,365	9151	1874
2017–2018	75,274	7046	23,614	32,925	11,689
Total	204,139	23,262	74,200	84,845	21,832

Source: Adapted by the authors with information of the CNSPD (2019)

Table 4.2 Secondary Teachers' Recognition Performance Assessment

School cycle	Assessed	Insufficient	Sufficient	Good	Outstanding	Excellent
2015–2016	27,704	4577	9015	11,705	1568	839
2016–2017	7608	1236	2597	3176	410	189
2017–2018	11,801	1809	2149	4064	3583	196
Total	47,113	7622	13,761	18,945	5561	1224

Source: Adapted by the authors with information of the CNSPD (2019)

subjects by one teacher and instruction relies heavily on IT support, to teacher hiring status, this study is able to establish causal effects of hiring models on student performance. This study finds that only 1 year after teachers started working with those students, they were able to improve the scores of their pupils by 0.52 and 0.31 standard deviations, which is a significant result in the context of educational interventions (Estrada, 2017). These results support the idea that the 206,000 teachers who earned their teaching position due to the rules-based hiring practices introduced by the SPD will be more effective than their peers hired through union nepotism. It is expected these new teachers will spearhead the transformation of teaching in Mexico from within the system and that their results will become evident in the upcoming years (Nuño Mayer, 2020).

The Reform also had significant financial implications. A SEP-conducted census of school infrastructure and personnel, combined with the centralization of the payroll, eliminated the practice of "double negotiation," in which the SNTE negotiated separately with local states and the federal government. As a result of this "double negotiation" unions were receiving benefits from two entities for the same positions, thus severely damaging the finances of many states (Otto Granados, 2020). The Reform also modified the Contribution Fund for Educational Payroll and Operating Expense (*Fondo de Aportaciones para la Nómina Educativa y Gasto Operativo*, FONE) so that all salary payments would be directly deposited into teachers' bank accounts, eliminating the union's control of payroll (Nuño Mayer, 2018). The FONE performed a payroll audit that removed 44,000 posts that were not used for teaching, with a value of five billion pesos (Nuño Mayer, 2018).

The Reform also saw gradual acceptance from teachers throughout the country. Aurelio Nuño Mayer explained in his article "Respuesta a nexos: La reforma educativa" that following the reassertion of state control the 2017 Teacher's Day celebrations occurred without teacher strikes for the first time in more than a decade (Nuño Mayer, 2018). In addition, evaluation processes were gradually normalized, including in the states where resistance was strongest, Chiapas, Guerrero, Michoacán and Oaxaca (Nuño Mayer, 2018). In all cases, participation rates above 90% were reached (Nuño Mayer, 2018). It is also interesting to review the high acceptance the Reform had among students in teacher colleges. In a face-to-face survey conducted in 2017, when asked about how they valued different components of the SPD over 94% of students stated that they thought it is "indispensable" or "were happy with" earning more according to a merit-based system, the promotion via an evaluation, and 74% thought the same of the permanence evaluation (Proyecto Educativo, 2017).

While many different mechanisms were used to promote dialogue throughout the Reform, the unnecessarily accelerated pace at which teacher evaluations proceeded reinforced the perception that the Reform was punitive. The intended positive outcomes of the assessment process were never properly explained, solidifying teacher opposition to the Reform (Hrusa et al., 2020), that is educators felt as if they were the targets of mandates and directives rather than collaborators in the development of the reform (Tirado, 2018). Further, while the evaluation framework was detailed in its expectations of teachers and principals, it was not aligned with teachers' existing knowledge. This misalignment only exacerbated the perception that evaluations were a form of punishment, rather than an avenue through which to improve (Hrusa et al., 2020). In fact, since the Reform implementation, the idea of evaluation has consistently been used by detractors to attack the Reform as disrespectful of teachers and to frame it as a labor reform rather than an educational one (Granados, 2018a, Granados, 2018b). Crucially, the INEE's framework never secured the backing of the CNTE or SNTE, and was in fact the target of substantial criticism and the subject of widespread resistance (Reimers, 2020a). This lack of acceptance clouded the perception of assessments, not just as a mechanism of the Reform, but in the sector as a whole and ultimately led to López-Obrador's decision to dismantle the INEE (Hrusa et al., 2020).

Former Secretary of Education Nuño Mayer believes that more time for implementation would have led to greater teacher support (A. Nuño Mayer, personal communication, January 29, 2020). The *Formación Continua* (2017) strategy was meant to "promote a profound cultural change, remove baseless beliefs, and begin a pathway through work grounded in trust of teachers" (SEP, 2017a, p. 8). However, the strategy was never fully implemented due to the shift of power in 2018. Its initial focus on implementing legal and political changes, rather than technical professional development strategies, failed to engage teachers. Ultimately, the Reform's attempts to recast teacher evaluations as formative were unsuccessful in combating the power of a narrative supported by teacher unions and the new President (Hrusa et al., 2020). As of February 2020, the Reform has been overruled by a new constitutional amendment to Article 3 now known as the "New Education Reform" 'proposed and accepted by the Morena majority in Congress and the Senate in 2019 (Gaceta Parlamentaria, 2019).

Even with the new amendment, many of the changes still follow the same spirit of the past Reform. Although the concept of "education of quality," perceived as controversial by some allies to President López Obrador, has been removed, it was replaced by conceptually similar but semantically different, "excellence in education" (Gaceta Parlamentaria, 2019). Along those same lines, President López Obrador had publicly accused the INEE of being used to "humiliate and degrade" teachers, echoing the narrative put forth by educator unions that the evaluations were purely punitive (Hrusa et al., 2020). President López Obrador then dismantled the INEE and created a similar entity, the National Commission for the Continued Improvement of the Education (*Comisión Nacional para la Mejora Continua de la Educación*, "MejorEDU"). MejorEDU was absorbed by the SEP and its president was appointed by the Secretary of Education but appointments still required approval by Congress (SEP, 2020). Even though MejorEDU lacks the constitutional legal and financial autonomy that the INEE possessed, it remains a technically autonomous entity. However, in one of the two commissions that oversee MejorEDU, most of the members have an explicit political affiliation with Morena. On the other hand, each member of the political commission has teaching experience, most in K-12 grades, and the technical council members all have strong academic records in education policy and research (SEP, 2020). Even though the secondary laws of the "New Education Reform" have not been presented, it is expected that the full day schools program (*Escuelas de tiempo Completo*) will remain, albeit with a reduced budget (Animal Político, 2019). Similarly, it is anticipated that the entrance and promotion evaluations included in the SPD will continue but under a new name, the Unit of the Career System for Teachers (*Unidad del Sistema para la Carrera de las Maestras y los Maestros* "USICAMM") (USICAMM, 2020). However, other aspects of the Reform such as the National English strategy have been completely defunded and eliminated.

4.6 Conclusion

Analyzing the Reform through different lenses allows for a nuanced understanding that moves beyond the contrasting narratives that dominated media coverage (Hrusa et al., 2020). When seen from an institutional perspective, the Reform achieved a new legal and governance framework. If analyzed from the psychological perspective, the technical foundations, and their translation into programs and policies, had strong foundations in international best practices and were widely supported by Mexican education experts. How these two aspects would interact was dependent on the success of the political transformation- which was also the locus of most controversies. President Peña Nieto's administration had to counter the narrative, prominent in Mexico's collective psyche, that the teacher union was able to elect or defeat presidents, as was the case in the 2006 election. This necessitated a firm power grab by the Mexican government beginning with the imprisonment of Elba Esther Gordillo, the SNTE leader, and continuing with the systematic weakening of the CNTE and the SNTE. This caused a major uproar, and union leadership fiercely fought back. Nonetheless, reclaimed political power was given to the newly installed regional, state and municipal CEPS, where the unions became one voice of many in the decision making processes. Despite changing political tides, the Reform had a lasting impact on the relationship between the SNTE and the government.

However, the fact that professional aspects of the reform were used to weaken unions rather than support teachers undermined the effectiveness of Reform strategies. From a political perspective, by establishing a merit-based educator career pathway without the support necessary to ensure teacher growth, the Reform lost major support and was viewed as punitive, rather than generative. As stated by the Reform's architects, there was not enough time to deploy the set of professional development policies that would have enhanced and solidified the Reform among teachers. Even though the Reform had widespread support among the general public, and most of the policies (aside from the performance recognition exam) were also popular with teachers, the narrative deployed by López Obrador and teacher union leadership was one of conflict.

From a technical standpoint, also referred to as the psychological perspective, the Reform appears robust. The Reform followed international best practices for a comprehensive system-level change that integrated all the different elements of the education sector to generate a student-centered transformation to foster global citizenship and 21CC competencies. The autonomy granted to the INEE ensured that education statistics would remain independent from politics and that any unforeseen consequences of the Reform's implementation would be corrected, as was the case when the SEP and the INEE paused evaluations for a year in order to adjust and improve them. The NME was further proof of the comprehensive plan to achieve ambitious learning outcomes that not only emphasized content knowledge and student-centered pedagogies, but also addressed socio-emotional skills and promoted well-rounded students with strong interpersonal, intrapersonal, and cultural competencies.

Analyzed through the cultural perspective, the ultimate goal of the Reform was to radically change the education culture in Mexico and create a system based on accountability and autonomy. The late implementation of the NME, only beginning a year before the start of López Obrador's administration, did not allow for the full results of the Reform to emerge. However, the idea and importance of teachers' evaluations as well as the shift of paradigm seem to have been internalized by a new generation of teachers (Proyecto Educativo, 2017). Additionally, the Reform elevated the role of early childhood education, as well as of socio-emotional learning by making them a central component of the NME. Both topics have continued to occupy a prominent role in López Obrador's own education reform.

In 2018, the teacher unions became a key ally of López Obrador's coalition. López Obrador's campaign promise to repeal and replace anything done by the previous administration fit perfectly with the desires of the teacher union leadership who hoped to overturn the Reform (Olmos, 2019). Just months after his inauguration, the new administration released Elba Esther Gordillo, stripped the INEE of their autonomy, reinstalled all teachers removed from the classroom during the previous administration (regardless of why they had been released), and appointed union members in key positions within the SEP and AELs.

Appendices

Appendix A: Timeline of Mexico's Education Reform

December 2012	The president formally announced the launching of the educational reform and sent three education bills to Congress.
Mirth–September 2013	Legislative process that amended the constitution –to include the responsibility of the state to provide quality education and the organization of teachers' appraisals, associated to quality education– And the enaction of three new education acts.
January–June 2014	First public consultation with the purpose of defining the education goals and the educational priorities for developing the curriculum (basic education, upper secondary & teacher training colleges).

(continued)

February 2016	The National Board of directors of the strategy *School at the Centre of the System* was formally established, with education officials from SFP and the 32 states governments as its members.
July 2016:	The first drafts of the NME, Mexico's twenty first century goals, and the curriculum (PreK-9) & (10–12) were published.
July– December 2016	Second public consultation and debate on the recently published documents.
March 2017	The final versions of NME and *Goals for Twenty First century Education* and *Route for the implementation of the New Educational Model* were published.
June 2017	Publication of the final version* of the curriculum (PreK-9) & (10–12).
July 2017	Started NME's implementation route.
August 2017–August 2018:	Several implementation actions to disseminate the national curriculum (PreK-9) in all schools: Pilot project (phase 0) of curricular autonomy implemented in 1027 schools; online in-service training for one million plus teachers, and several other academic activities, at the national, regional and school levels.
December 2017	The final version of the curriculum for early childhood (0 to 3) was published.
July 2018	Presidential election.
August 2018	Application of the national curriculum (PreK-9) started in schools.
December 2018	A new federal government takes office.

Source: Elisa Bonilla in Reimers (2020b, p. 133)

Appendix B: Glossary

AEL	*Autoridades Educativas Locales)* Local Education Authorities
ATP	*Asesor Técnico Pedadgógico)* Pedagogical Technical Advisor
CEPS	*(Consejo Escolar de Participación Social)*
CNSPD	*(Consejo Nacional del Servicio Profesional Docente)* National Council of the Professional
CNTE	*(Coordinadora Nacional de Trabajadores de la Educación)* National Coordinator of
CONAPASE	*(Consejo Nacional de Participación Social en la Educación)* National School Councils for Continued Improvement of the Education
CTE	*(Consejo Técnico Escolar)* School Technical Councils
CTZ	*(Consejos Técnicos de Zona)* Regional Technical Councils

Education	Educational Payroll and Operating Expense
Education Workers	Evaluation Law
FC	*(Formación Continua)* Continuous Professional Development Strategy
FONE	*(Fondo de Aportaciones para la Nómina Educativa y Gasto Operativo)* Contribution Fund for
IEEPO	*(Instituto Estatal de Educación Pública de Oaxaca)* State Institute for Oaxacan Public
INEE	*(Instituto Nacional de Evaluación Educativa)* National Institute of Educational Evaluation
LGE	*(Ley General de Educación)* General Law of Education
LGSPD	*(Ley General del Servicio Profesional Docente)* General Law of the Professional Teacher
LINEE	(Ley *Instituto Nacional de Evaluación Educativa*) National Institute for Education
MejorEDU	*(Comisión Nacional para la Mejora Continua de la Educación)* National Commission for the
NME	*(Nuevo Modelo Educativo)* New Education Model of Knowledge
PAN	*(Partido Acción Nacional)* National Action Party)
PANAL	*(Partido Nueva Alianza)* New Alliance Party
PLANEA	*(Plan Nacional para la Evaluación de los Aprendizajes)* National Plan for the Evaluation
PRI	*(Partido Revolucionario Institucional)* Institutional Revolutionary Party
PRONI	*(Programa Nacional de Inglés)* National Program for English Instruction
SATE	*(Servicio de Asistencia Técnica a la Escuela)* The School Technical Assistance Services
SEL	*(Aprendizaje Socio-Emocional)* Socio Emotional Learning
SEP	*(Secretaria de Educación Pública)* Department of Education Service
SNEE	*(Sistema Nacional de Evaluación Educativa)* National System for Educational Evaluation

SNTE	(*Sindicato Nacional de Trabajadores de Educación*) National Union of Education Workers Social Participation
SPD	(*Servicio Profesional Docente*) Professional Teacher Service System for Teachers Teaching Service
USICAMM	(*Unidad del Sistema para la Carrera de las Maestras y los Maestros*) Unit of the Career

References

Ahmed, A., & Semple, K. (2016). Por qué la Reforma Educativa en México ha causado oposición y violencia. *New York Times*. Retrieved from: https://www.nytimes.com/es/2016/06/30/espanol/america-latina/por-que-la-reforma-educativa-en-mexico-ha-desatado-oposicion-y-violencia.html

Animal Político, Redacción. (2016). *Maestros de la CNTE cierran autopista del Sol en Guerrero y retienen camiones en Oaxaca*. Animal Político. Retrieved from: https://www.animalpolitico.com/2016/07/maestros-de-la-cnte-cierran-autopista-del-sol-en-guerrero-y-retiene-camiones-en-oaxaca/

Animal Político, Redacción. (2019). *Escuelas de tiempo completo tendrán 56% menos para equipo*. Retrieved from: https://www.animalpolitico.com/2019/12/2020-escuelas-tiempo-completo-tendran-56-menos-para-equipamiento/

Audelo Cruz, J. M. (2005). Sobre el concepto de corporativismo: Una revisión en el contexto político mexicano actual. In M. A. L. Olvera & D. C. Salgado (Eds.), *Estudios en homenaje a don Jorge Fernández Ruiz: Derecho constitucional y política* (p. 24). Universidad Autónoma de México. https://archivos.juridicas.unam.mx/www/bjv/libros/4/1627/5.pdf

Bonilla-Rius, E. (2019). *Former director-general for curriculum development*. Mexican Ministry of Education.

Bonilla-Rius, E. (2020). Education truly matters: Key Lessons from Mexico's educational reform for educating the whole child. In F. Reimers (Ed.), *Audacious education purposes: How governments transform the role of education systems* (pp. 105–152). Cham: Springer.

Briseño, P. (2015, July 22). Asestan golpe a la CNTE; quitan control a la disidencia magisterial. *Excélsior*. https://www.excelsior.com.mx/nacional/2015/07/22/1035928

Cabrera Hernández, F. (2018). Efectos del Programa Escuelas de Tiempo Completo en la reducción de brechas educativas: un avance hacia la equidad. In A. Martínez Bordón & A. Navarro Arredondo (Eds.), *La Reforma Educativa a Revisión: Apuntes y reflexiones para la elaboración de una agenda educativa* (pp. 2018–2024). Mexico: Instituto Belisario Domínguez, Cámara de Senadores.

Centro de Investigación y Docencia Económicas (CIDE). (2016). *Consulta Sobre El Modelo Educativo 2016*. Mexico: CIDE. https://Framework-Gb.Cdn.Gob.Mx/Happenings/Modelo-Educativo-Sep/05_Informe_Me2016.Pdf

Chaca, R., García, I., & Martin, F. (2016). *Padres de familia exigen regreso a clases en Oaxaca y Chiapas*. El Universal. Retrieved from: https://www.eluniversal.com.mx/articulo/nacion/politica/2016/09/6/padres-de-familia-exigen-clases-en-oaxaca-y-chiapas

Chapman, J. D., & International Institute for Educational Planning. (2005). *Recruitment, retention, and development of school principals*. International Institute for Educational Planning.

Cohen, D. K., & Mehta, J. D. (2017). Why Reform Sometimes Succeeds: Understanding the Conditions That Produce Reforms That Last. *American Educational Research Journal, 54*(4), 644–690. https://doi.org/10.3102/0002831217700078

Consejo Asesor. (2014). *Foro nacional para la revisión del Modelo de Educación Normal.Versión preliminar de la síntesis y recomendaciones*. La Paz: Consejo Asesor. https://evaluaryaprender. files.wordpress.com/2015/02/conclusiones-del-foronacional.pdf

Consejo Nacional del Servicio Profesional Docente (CNSPD). (2019). *Datos Evaluaciones Reforma Educativa*. Retrieved from: https://servicioprofesionaldocente.sep.gob.mx/

Constitución Política de los Estados Unidos Mexicanos, Diario Oficial de la Federación, Ciudad de México, México, 5 de febrero de 1917. *Article 3*. Last Reform, 29 of February 2016. Translated by the authors.

Cordero, G., Alfonso Jiménez, J., Navarro-Corona, C., & Vázquez, M. A. (2017). *Diagnóstico de la política pública de formación y desarrollo profesional del personal educativo de educación básica de la reforma educativa*. México: INEE.

Córdova, A. (2014). *La ideología de la Revolución Mexicana*. Ediciones Era.

de Educación, L. G. (LGE). (2013). *Ley General de Educación. Última Publicación 20/05/2014*. México: Cámara de Diputados del H. Congreso de la Unión. Retrieved from: http://www. ordenjuridico.gob.mx/Documentos/Federal/pdf/wo39036.pdf

de Hoyos, R., & Estrada, R. (n.d.). *¿Los docentes mejoraron? ¡Sí!* [Nexos]. Retrieved February 8, 2020, from https://www.nexos.com.mx/?p=39531

de la Federación, D. O. (LGSPD) (2013). Ley General del Servicio Profesional Docente. In *México, Cámara de Diputados del H. Congreso de la Unión, Secretaría General Secretaría de Servicios Parlamentarios* (Vol. 11). Retrieved from https://www.sep.gob.mx/work/models/ sep1/Resource/558c2c24-0b12-4676-ad90-8ab78086b184/ley_general_servicio_profesional_ docente.pdf

de la Federación, Diario Oficial (INEE). (2017). *Criterios técnicos y de procedimiento para el análisis de los instrumentos de evaluación, el proceso de calificación y la emisión de resultados para llevar a cabo la evaluación del desempeño del personal con funciones de dirección y supervisión en Educación Básica en el ciclo escolar 2017–2018*. http://www.dof.gob.mx/ nota_detalle.php?codigo=5502106&fecha=23/10/2017

de la Federación, Diario Oficial (INEE). (2018). *Criterios técnicos y de procedimiento para el análisis de los instrumentos de evaluación, el proceso de calificación y la emisión de resultados para llevar a cabo la evaluación del desempeño del personal docente y técnico docente en Educación Básica, para el ciclo escolar 2018–2019*.

de la Federación, Diario Oficial (LGSPD). (2013). Ley General del Servicio Profesional Docente. In *México, Cámara de Diputados del H. Congreso de la Unión, Secretaría General Secretaría de Servicios Parlamentarios* (Vol. 11).

de la Federación, Diario Oficial (LINEE). (2013). *Ley del Instituto Nacional para la Evaluación de la Educación*. Publicado en el Diario Oficial de la Federación el 11.

López Aguilar, M.J. de (2013). Una reforma "educativa" contra los maestros y el derecho a la educación. *El Cotidiano, 179*, 55–76.[fecha de Consulta 23 de Febrero de 2020]. ISSN: 0186-1840. Retrieved from: https://www.redalyc.org/articulo.oa?id=325/32527012005

Díaz-Barriga, A. (2018). *El que mucho abarca... La reforma educativa al pie del patíbulo*. Nexos. Retrieved from: https://www.nexos.com.mx/?p=39535

Echávarri, J., & Peraaza, C. (2017). Modernizing schools in Mexico: The rise of teacher assessment and school-based management policies. *Education Policy Analysis Archives, 25*, 90. https://doi.org/10.14507/epaa.25.2771

Estrada, R. (2017). *Rules vs. Discretion in public service: Teacher hiring in Mexico*. CAF. Development bank of Latin America. Retrieved from: https://pdfs.semanticscholar. org/825b/21bb734259aa8c334fdb8443f8b3dc243e41.pdf

Gaceta Parlamentaria. (2019). *Iniciativa del Ejecutivo federal. Con proyecto de decreto, por el que se reforman los artículos 3o., 31 y 73 de la Constitución Política de los Estados Unidos Mexicanos*. http://gaceta.diputados.gob.mx/PDF/64/2018/dic/20181213-II.pdf

Gindín, J. (2008). Sindicalismo docente en México, Brasil y Argentina: una hipótesis explicativa de su estructuración diferenciada. *Revista mexicana de investigación educativa, 13*(37), 351–375. Retrieved from http://www.scielo.org.mx/scielo.php?script=sci_arttext&pid=S1405-66662008000200003

Gómez Zamarripa, E., & Navarro Arredondo, A. (2018). Para entender mejor la Reforma Educativa: estabilidad y cambio en el sistema educativo mexicano. In A. Martínez Bordón & A. Navarro Arredondo (Eds.), *La Reforma Educativa a Revisión: Apuntes y reflexiones para la elaboración de una agenda educativa 2018–2024.* Mexico: Instituto Belisario Domínguez, Cámara de Senadores.

Granados Roldán, O. (2018a). *Reforma educativa* (Primera edición). Fondo de Cultura Económica.

Granados Roldán, O. (2018b). *Reforma Educativa Mexicana: Balance, perspectivas y desafíos.* PowerPoint presentation, 2018. Retrieved via private e-mail from the office of the Secretary of Education.

Granados Roldán, O. (2020). *The Mexican education reform, 2013-2018: Results, challenges and lessons learned.* Presented at the Harvard Graduate School of Education on February 24, 2020.

Granados Roldán, O., Puente de la Mora, X., & Betanzos Torres, E. O. (2019). *Fortalecimiento de derechos, ampliación de libertades, I.* Mexico: Fondo de Cultura Economica.

Guevara, S., & Paul Moch, I. (2018). *La Reforma Educativa de la Cuarta Transformación.* Animal Politico. https://www.animalpolitico.com/blogueros-blog-invitado/2018/12/13/la-reforma-educativa-de-la-cuarta-transformacion/

Hernández Navarro, L. (2013, February 28). Elba Esther Gordillo's downfall in Mexico is political, and personal. *The Guardian.* https://www.theguardian.com/commentisfree/2013/feb/28/elba-esther-gordillo-mexico-embezzlement

Hrusa, N. A., Moch Islas, P., Schneider, J. A., & Vega, I. J. (2020). Policies for teacher professionalization in Mexico's education reform. In *Empowering teachers to build a better world: how six nations support teachers for 21st century education.* Springer.

Instituto Nacional de Geografía y Estadística (INEGI). (2016). *Encuesta Intercensal 2015: Principales Resultados* [PDF File]. Retrieved from https://www.inegi.org.mx/contenidos/programas/intercensal/2015/doc/eic_2015_presentcion.pdf

Instituto Nacional Electoral (INE). (2014). *Reforma Educativa 2012–2013.* Mexico: INE. https://pac.ife.org.mx/debate_democratico/descargas/Reforma-Educativa-2012-2013.pdf

Instituto Nacional para la Evaluación de la Educación. (2018). *Práctica educativa y trayectoria profesional en docentes de primaria. Reporte Nacional* (p. 117). Instituto Nacional para la Evaluación de la Educación. https://www.inee.edu.mx/publicaciones/practica-educativa-y-trayectoria-profesional-en-docentes-de-primaria-reporte-nacional/

Instituto Nacional para la Evaluación de la Educación (INEE). (2018). *Acerca del INEE.* https://www.inee.edu.mx

Instituto Nacional para la Evaluación Educación (INEE). (2015). *Plan Nacional para la Evaluación los aprendizajes (PLANEA): Resultados nacionales 2015.* Mexico: INEE. https://www.inee.edu.mx/images/stories/2015/planea/final/fasciculos finales/resultadosPlanea-3011.pdf

Kemmerer, F. (1994). *Utilizing education and human resource sector analyses.* UNESCO International Institute for Educational Planning.

López Obrador, A. M. (2018). *Mensaje de AMLO en el Zócalo de la Ciudad de México.* https://lopezobrador.org.mx/2018/07/02/mensaje-de-amlo-n-el-zocalo-de-la-ciudad-demexico/

Majgaard, K., & Mingat, A. (2012). *Education in sub-Saharan Africa: A comparative analysis.* The World Bank. Retrieved from https://documents.worldbank.org/en/publication/documents-reports/documentdetail/892631468003571777/education-in-sub-saharan-africa-a-comparative-analysis

Martínez Bordón, A. (2018). El INEE: un nuevo actor en la política educativa. In A. Martínez Bordón & Navarro Arredondo, Alejandro (Eds.), *La Reforma Educativa a revisión: Apuntes y reflexiones para la elaboración de una agenda educativa 2018-2024* (pp. 197–220). Mexico City: Instituto Belisario Domínguez, Senado de la República.

Martínez Bordón, A., & Navarro Arredondo, A. (Eds.). (2018). *La Reforma Educativa a revisión: Apuntes y reflexiones para la elaboración de una agenda educativa 2018–2024* (pp. 11–16). Mexico City: Instituto Belisario Domínguez, Senado de la República.

Martínez Bordón, A., & Navarro Arredondo, Alejandro. (2018). Introducción. In A. Martínez Bordón & Navarro Arredondo, Alejandro (Eds.), La Reforma Educativa a revisión: Apuntes y reflexiones para la elaboración de una agenda educativa 2018-2024 . Mexico City: Instituto Belisario Domínguez, Senado de la República.

Mayer-Serra, C. E. (2017). Reforma de la Constitución: La economía política del Pacto por México. *Revista Mexicana de Ciencias Políticas y Sociales, 62*(230), 21–49. https://doi.org/10.1016/ S0185-1918(17)30016-8

Mexicanos Primero. (2018). *La Escuela Que Queremos: Estado de la educación en México.* Mexico [PDF File]. Retrieved from: http://mexicanosprimero.org/images/recursos/estudios/ LEQQ/LEQQ28Feb.pdf

Mexico, (2017, as amended). Constitución Política de los Estados Unidos Mexicanos. *Constitución publicada en el Diario Oficial de la Federación el, 5*(2014) http://www.ordenjuridico.gob.mx/ constitucion.php

Moch Islas, P., & Schneider, J. A. (2018). *Reforming Education in Mexico (Case Studies in Education Policy Reform: Teaching Case).* Harvard Graduate School of Education.

Muñoz Armenta, A. (2008). Escenarios e identidades del SNTE: entre el sistema educativo y el sistema político. *Revista mexicana de investigación educativa, 13*(37), 377–417. Retrieved the February 29, 2020, from http://www.scielo.org.mx/scielo. php?script=sci_arttext&pid=S1405-66662008000200004&lng=es&tlng=es

National Research Council. (2012). *Education for life and work: Developing transferable knowledge and skills in the 21st century.* National Academies Press.

Nuño Mayer, A. (2018, November 1). *Respuesta a nexos.* La reforma educativa. Nexos. Retrieved from: https://www.nexos.com.mx/?p=39966

Nuño Mayer, A. (2020, January 29). *Interview with Aurelio Nuño Mayer.* Personal communication.

OECD. (2014). *TALIS 2013 Results: An International Perspective on Teaching and Learning (TALIS).* OECD Publishing. Retrieved from: https://doi.org/10.1787/23129638

Olmos, J. G. (2019, September 12). Asignación automática de plazas y capacitaciones voluntarias, pacta la CNTE con el gobierno de AMLO. *Proceso.* https://www.proceso.com. mx/599479/asignacion-automatica-de-plazas-y-capacitaciones-voluntarias-pacta-la-cnte-con-el-gobierno-de-amlo

Organisation for Economic Co-operation and Development (OECD). (2013). *PISA 2012 results in focus: What 15-year-olds know and what they can do with what they know.* Washington, DC: Author.

Organisation for Economic Co-operation and Development (OECD). (2019). *Strong foundations for quality and equity in Mexican schools.* OECD. https://doi.org/10.1787/9789264312548-en.

Partlow, J. (2016, June 20). At least 6 dead in Mexico as education protesters clash with police. *Washington Post.* https://www.washingtonpost.com/world/the_americas/at-least-six-dead-as-education-protesters-clash-with-police/2016/06/20/41e6e8fc-3705-11e6-af02-1df55f0c77ff_ story.html

Permanyer, I., & Smits, J. (2018). *Moving beyond country level averages.* United Nations Development Program. Retrieved from: http://hdr.undp.org/en/content/ subnational-human-development-index-moving-beyond-country-level-averages

Presidencia de la República., Sexto Informe de Gobierno, México, p. 300

Proyecto Educativo. (2017, May). *Encuesta para estudiantes de escuelas normales y UPN de Puebla.* 4076 face to face surveys.

Ramírez Raymundo, R., Esquivel, G., Encinas Nájera, A., & Pérez Benítez, N. (2016). *Reforma en materia educativa: Un análisis de su diseño y aplicación, 2012-2016* (1st Edn.). Mexico City: Instituto Belisario Domínguez, Senado de la República.

Reimers, F. (2018). Reformar la escuela pública para el siglo XXI. Los desafíos para México. In O. G. Roldán, X. P. de la Mora, & E. O. B. Torres (Eds.), *Fortalecimiento de derechos, ampliación de libertades: Vol. I. Fondo de Cultura Economica.*

Reimers, F. (Ed.) (2020a). *Empowering Teachers to Build a Better World. How Six Nations Support Teachers for 21st Century Education.* Singapore: Springer Briefs in Education. https:// doi.org/10.1007/978-981-15-2137-9

Reimers, F. (Ed.). (2020b). *Audacious Education Purposes: How Governments Transform the Goals of Education Systems*. Switzerland: Springer International Publishing. https://doi.org/10.1007/978-3-030-41882-3

Reimers, F. M. (2020c). *Educating Students to Improve the World*. Singapore: SpringerBriefs in Education. https://doi.org/10.1007/978-981-15-3887-2

Reyes, A. (2018, November 20). *Skype interview*.

Schmelkes, S. (2018, November 28). *Skype interview*.

Secretaría de Educación Pública. (2002). *Decreto por el que se crea el instituto nacional para la evaluación de la educación*. Diario Oficial de la Federación, 2002. https://www.inee.edu.mx/index.php/normateca-descentralizada/documentos-del-inee/normateca/normas-internas-del-inee/normas-sustantivas-del-inee/presidencia-del-inee/decreto-de-creacion-del-instituto-nacional-de-evaluacion-para-la-educacion/detail

Secretaría de Educación Pública (SEP). (2015). *Seguimiento a los Consejos Técnicos Escolares. Informe general de la 1a a la 3a Sesión Ordinaria, Ciclo escolar 2014–2015*. Mexico: Secretaría de Educación Pública. http://www.setse.org.mx/ReformaEducativa/recursos_evaluacion/curso_evintern/materales/anexos/Bloque%203/Anexo%208.pdf

Secretaría de Educación Pública (SEP). (2016). *El modelo educativo 2016*. El planteamiento pedagógico de la reforma educativa. Mexico: Secretaría de Educación Pública. https://www.gob.mx/modeloeducativo2016/articulos/introduccion-46873

Secretaría de Educación Pública (SEP). (2017a). *Aprendizajes clave para la educación integral*. Mexico: Secretaría de Educación Pública. https://www.aprendizajesclave.sep.gob.mx/descargables/APRENDIZAJES_CLAE_PRA_LA_EDUCACION_INTEGRAL.pdf

Secretaría de Educación Pública (SEP). (2017b). *Lineamientos Generales para la prestación del Servicio de Asistencia Técnica a la Escuela en la Educación Básica*. Mexico: Secretaría de Educación Pública. https://basica.sep.gob.mx/escuela_al_centro/documentos/eventoQro2017/Lineamientos_Qro.pdf

Secretaría de Educación Pública (SEP). (2017c). *La Escuela al Centro: Gestión y acompañamiento, presentación a la reunión con supervisores*. Mexico: Secretaría de Educación Pública. https://basica.sep.gob.mx/escuela_al_centro/documentos/eventoQro2017/LEC_Qro.pdf

Secretaría de Educación Pública (SEP). (2017d). *Ruta para la implementación del modelo educativo*. Mexico: Secretaría de Educación Pública. https://www.gob.mx/cms/uploads/attachment/file/207248/10_Ruta_de_implementacio_n_del_modelo_educativo_DIGITAL_re_FINAL_2017.pdf

Secretaría de Educación Pública (SEP). (2017e). Carta. In *Los fines de la educación en el siglo XXI*. Mexico: Secretaría de Educación Pública. https://www.gob.mx/nuevomodeloeducativo/documentos/carta-los-fines-de-la-educacion-en-el-siglo-xxi-2

Secretaría de Educación Pública (SEP). (2017f). *Aprendizajes clave para la educación integral: Educación Inicial: Un buen comienzo*. Programa para la educación de las niñas y los niños de 0 a 3 años. México: Secretaría de Eduación Pública. https://www.planyprogramasdestudio.sep.gob.mx/descargables/biblioteca/inicial/1Educacion-%20Inicial_Digital.pdf. Accessed 25 Feb 2019.

Secretaría de Educación Pública (SEP). (2017g). *Modelo Educativo. Marco para el desarrollo de la formación docente continua*. Educación Básica.

Secretaría de Educación Pública (SEP). (2018). *Nuevo modelo educativo*. Mexico: Secretaría de Educación Pública. https://www.gob.mx/sep/documentos/nuevo-modelo-educativo-99339

Secretaría de Educación Pública (SEP). (2020). *Comisión Nacional para la Mejora Continua de la Educación*. https://www.gob.mx/mejoredu

Sindicato Nacional de Trabajadores de la Educación (SNTE). (2015). *La evaluación del desempeño docente*. Mexico: SNTE. https://www.snte.org.mx/pdf/Folleto_Evaluacionwebok.pdf

Tirado, F. (2018). *Member of the governing board of UNAM*.

Tuckman, J. (2013, February 27). Elba Esther Gordillo – Mexico's famed union boss – accused of embezzlement. *The Guardian*. https://www.theguardian.com/world/2013/feb/27/elba-esther-gordillo-mexico-union-embezzlement

Unidad del Sistema para la Carrera de las Maestras y los Maestros "USICAMM". (2020). *Convocatorias del proceso de Admisión ciclo 2020–2021*. Retrieved from: https://serviciprofesionaldocente.sep.gob.mx/

Woldenberg, J. (2012). *Historia mínima de la transición democrática en México*. El Colegio de Mexico AC.

World Bank. (2018). *Learning to realize education's promise*. World Bank Group.

Paul Moch Islas holds a B.A. in Political Science from the Instituto Tecnológico Autónomo de México (ITAM) and studied in Sankt Gallen University, Switzerland. He is a graduate of the International Education Policy program at the Harvard Graduate School of Education where he also worked as a research assistant for the Harvard Ministerial Leadership Program and as Teaching Fellow, where he published case studies of Colombia and Mexico's education reforms. He previously served as Deputy Director at Mexico's National Institute for Adult Education (INEA), as a consultant for the United Nations Population Fund and the United Nations Development Program, and as advisor to Mexico's Deputy-Minister of Communications.

Anne K. Calef was born and raised in Oakland, California. Anne worked as a public elementary school teacher for 6 years prior to pursuing a Master of City Planning at the Massachusetts Institute of Technology. She is a passionate educator whose firm belief that all students deserve the resources they need to succeed drove her to study housing, community and economic development at MIT. Anne graduated from Pomona College in 2012 with a BA in Asian American Studies, and earned her Master of Science in Educational Studies while teaching full-time in 2015. She has worked for Mexicanos Primero in Mexico City, and studied in Spain.

Cristina Aparicio is a 2020 Ed.M graduate in International Education Policy at the Harvard Graduate School of Education. She has worked as a Graduate Student Civic Engagement Fellow for the Institute of Politics at the Harvard Kennedy School. She received her B.A. in International Development Studies at the University of California, Los Angeles, and an M.A. in Latin American Studies at the California State University, Los Angeles. She has over 10 years of work experience in higher education at the University of California, San Diego office of Enrollment Management where she worked as an International Admissions Officer, recruited students mainly from Mexico and Panama. She recently completed an internship through David Rockefeller Center for Latin American Studies (DRCLAS) Harvard at AMEXCID a development agency within the Ministry of Foreign Affairs in Mexico.

Chapter 5
The Punjab Schools Reform Roadmap: A Medium-Term Evaluation

Rastee Chaudhry and Abdullah Waqar Tajwar

Acronyms

AEO	Assistant Education Officer
CEO	Chief Education Officer
DDEO	Deputy District Education Officer
DEA	District Education Authorities
DFID	Department for International Development (UK)
DMO	District Monitoring Officer
EVS	Education Voucher Scheme
FAS	Foundation Assisted Schools
LND	Literacy and Numeracy Drive
MEA	Monitoring and Evaluation Assistants
NLNS	National Literacy and Numeracy Strategy
NSF	National Science Foundation (U.S.)
NSP	New School Program
NTS	National Testing Service (Pakistan)
OECD	Organization for Economic Co-operation and Development
PCTB	Punjab Curriculum and Textbook Board
PEC	Punjab Examination Commission
PEF	Punjab Education Foundation
PISA	Programme for International Student Assessment (OECD)
PITB	Punjab Information and Technology Board
PMIU	Programme Monitoring and Implementation Unit
PSRR	Punjab Schools Reform Roadmap
QAED	Quaid-e-Azam Academy for Educational Development
SED	School Education Department
SMU	Special Monitoring Unit

R. Chaudhry (✉) · A. W. Tajwar
Harvard University Graduate School of Education, Cambridge, MA, USA

© The Author(s) 2021
F. M. Reimers (ed.), *Implementing Deeper Learning and 21st Century Education Reforms*, https://doi.org/10.1007/978-3-030-57039-2_5

SSI   Statewide Systems Initiatives
TALIS   Teaching and Learning International Survey (OECD)

5.1   Introduction

In 2010, the challenge of education reform in Pakistan was threefold: scale, capacity to deliver, and political will (Barber, 2010, p. 7). To make matters more urgent, an amendment to the Constitution of Pakistan had just been passed that gave all children between the ages of 5 and 16 the right to free education while simultaneously devolving education autonomy, formerly a federal matter, to the provinces (Government of Pakistan, 2010). During this dynamically changing political and administrative landscape, a reform to Pakistan's most populous province – the Punjab – was launched by then Chief Minister of the Punjab Mian Shahbaz Sharif (Barber, 2013; Pakistan Bureau of Statistics, 1998). This reform came to be known as the Punjab Schools Reform Roadmap (PSRR) and was a direct response to the challenges of education in the province.

The PSRR targeted the entirety of the Punjab and called for the systemic overhaul and transformation of the entire education delivery and monitoring apparatus of the province. The key themes under this reform included the capacity-building of management in the public education system, the capacity-building of teachers, the collection of reliable and timely data, and the expansion of access to education through public private partnerships (Barber, 2013).

This chapter studies the outcomes of the PSRR and analyzes the sustainability of these outcomes 5 years after the conclusion of PSRR (this time period is henceforth referred to as the medium-term) with an emphasis on management capacity, teacher capacity and monitoring & information systems dimensions of the reform. Specifically, we discuss the above with reference to increasing access to and quality of education in the province.

We start with reviewing the literature on whole-system reforms and institutional capacity building to drive change within education systems. Next, we discuss the design elements of the reform, followed by an analysis of the interventions, outcomes and sustainability of the reform in the medium term. Lastly, we conclude with recommendations and a discussion of the way forward.

5.2   What Are Whole System Reforms and Capacity Building?

5.2.1   Whole-System Reforms

A whole-system reform (also known as a large-scale reform) is a reform that focuses on the improvement of every school within a district, every district within a province, and every province within a country. This contrasts to a targeted reform that focuses on improving outcomes for a subset of schools, communities or districts (Fullan, 2009).

"The moral and political purpose of whole-system reform is ensuring that everyone will be affected for the better, starting on day one of implementing the strategy" (Fullan & Levin, 2009). Since before the turn of the twenty-first century, this large-scale reform theory has been applied in several countries and states within individual countries to drive change at scale in their respective educational landscapes. One of the first countries to use this reform theory posited by Michael Fullan was the United Kingdom in 1997. The United Kingdom formulated a National Literacy and Numeracy Strategy (NLNS) that aimed to improve learning levels of 11-year-old students in all primary schools across the country (20,000 schools in total).

One of the key architects of NLNS was Sir Michael Barber, who also played a foundational role in the design and implementation of the PSRR. Barber's implementation strategy for NLNS rested on six key fundamentals. Namely, (i) ambitious standards, (ii) good data and clear targets, (iii) devolved responsibility, (iv) access to best practice and quality professional development, (v) accountability, and (vi) an increased focus on low performing schools (Fullan, 2009). An evaluation of the NLNS concluded that this strategy led to a significant improvement in student achievements over a relatively short span of time. However, there was concern about its sustainability in the long term due to the strategy being largely centralized and target-driven from the center (Fullan, 2010).

Another major example of a whole-system reform is a series of reforms launched in the United States in the early 1990s by the National Science Foundation (NSF). These systemic reform programs were intended to influence most, if not all aspects of the school system in the U.S. (Supovitz & Taylor, 2005). The NSF first launched the Statewide Systemic Initiatives (SSI) program in 1991, which provided up to $10 million to 25 states and Puerto Rico to assist with beginning whole-systems reform efforts in science, mathematics and technology education at the K-12 grade levels. Two years later, the NSF initiated the Urban Systemic Initiatives program to catalyze changes in policy and resource utilization in 28 of the largest U.S. school systems. The NSF also launched subsequent programs such as the Rural Systemic Initiative and the Local Systemic Change Initiative (Supovitz & Taylor, 2005; Zucker et al., 1998).

The SSIs were born out of a desire to improve student performance in mathematics and the sciences to improve the nation's economic competitiveness (Earle & Wan, n.d.; Zucker et al., 1998). Over the course of the 3 years following the SSIs' launch in 1991, the NSF negotiated 5-year cooperative agreements with competitively selected states to undertake such initiatives (Supovitz & Taylor, 2005; Zucker et al., 1998). While results have been varied due to the spread of the reform, the SSI program generally brought overall improvements in the practices of school systems in participating states. Evaluations of the program speak about the legacy of new or improved curriculum frameworks, positive changes in various state policies, new institutions and partnering arrangements, and an increased number of competent state and local leaders of reform. Additionally, evidence from selected states shows that some SSIs had a modest, positive impact in improving student learning outcomes in mathematics and science (Zucker et al., 1998).

5.2.1.1 Implementation and Delivery Chains

How Are Whole-System Reforms Implemented?

The NLNS serves as a useful case study on the efficacy of whole-systems reform theory and its implementation strategy respectively. Fullan has since directly worked with the Canadian government in Ontario, designing an implementation strategy that draws on lessons learnt from the United Kingdom while adjusting to the context of Canada. However, the fundamentals of the implementation strategy do not drastically differ. The whole-system reform implementation in the eyes of Fullan still rests on the foundation of focusing on a limited number of core policies and strategies, and working on them in tandem while ensuring strong leadership at the top that does not lose sight of the intended focus (Fullan & Levin, 2009). As a result of such an implementation strategy, the impact of well-executed large-scale reforms has been similar (significant impact in a short time period) and with similar potential pitfalls (sustainability concerns due to a top down implementation strategy).

Whole-System Reform Delivery Chains

Another approach to effectively achieving whole-system reform is by giving prime importance to the implementation strategy (Fullan, 2009). This approach has been pioneered by Michael Barber and is called 'Deliverology' (Barber, Moffit, & Kihn, 2011). Deliverology outlines a delivery chain that effectively manages and monitors all steps of the implementation of a reform with the aim of producing the highest impact on desired outcomes.

This approach has three key components. The first step is the establishment of a Delivery Unit that is limited in size but is only comprised of highly skilled and talented individuals who can oversee, inform and improve all aspects of the implementation process. The second foundation is effective and robust data gathering and analysis to ensure evidence-based progression at all steps and stages of the implementation. Third, the establishment of routines in order to assess performance and subsequently ensure a timely delivery of the reform. Relationship building across all levels of the hierarchy of the delivery chain (from top leadership to district officials and teachers working on the ground) is another component that is imperative to achieving optimal implementation of the reform (Barber et al., 2011).

In the next section, we frame this idea of institutional capacity and how it has been built in education systems worldwide to achieve both whole-system reforms or marginal scaling-up reforms.

5.2.2   Strengthening Institutional Capacity

An institution (or system)'s capacity refers to the capability of the institution to "plan, implement, manage, or evaluate policies, strategies or programs" (Cohen, 1995a, 1995b, p. 409). Institutional capacity has two arms: human resource capacity and management capacity. Thus, strengthening these capacities require the strengthening of the following components (Dill, 2000, p. 214):

- Strengthening human resource capacity requires the strengthening of "training, recruitment, effective utilization and retention of skilled public sector personnel."
- Strengthening management capacity requires strengthening of the ability of a public organization or agency to anticipate and adapt to change through policy levers and implementation policies, effective management of resources, and evaluation of performance for continuous feedback.

To put it more explicitly, building institutional capacity entails targeted interventions that build human resource capacity and management capacity, the latter of which strengthens the organization and can lead to institutional reform. This section explores how countries have (successfully) attempted to build institutional capacity in their education systems, including best practices and the building of institutional capacity through the use of data.

5.2.2.1   International Best Practices

The Organization of Economic Cooperation and Development (OECD) identifies Canada, Finland, Japan, Shanghai-China and Singapore as having high-performing education systems, formulating lessons from these systems as guidelines for other countries (OECD, 2011, p. 228). Among the lessons from these high-performing education systems is the development of capacity at the point of delivery, which includes attracting and developing high-quality teachers and developing the capacity of school leaders. These systems also place large emphasis on the development of management capacity, giving autonomy to school leaders coupled with strong accountability mechanisms and incentive alignment. Further, the systems embed a culture of developing "ambitious, focused and coherent" standards for education and system coherence that incorporate the alignment of policies and practices, and reform based on continuous feedback (OECD, 2011, p. 233).

In terms of student learning outcomes, Hong Kong, South Korea, Shanghai and Singapore rank among the top five high-performing countries, based on the OECD's Programme for International Student Assessment (PISA) assessments in 2009 (Jensen, 2012). These countries owe their success to an unrelenting focus on implementation in tandem with policy, using effective education strategies and well-designed programs that target teaching as well as learning. Among their strategies is the provision of high-quality teacher education, mentoring for teachers, treating teachers as researchers in the field and giving them more responsibility and avenues for career growth. These are unsurprisingly similar to the practices identified by OECD (2011) above, emphasizing the importance of common themes of teacher capacity, management capacity and policy reform in high-performing education systems around the world.

5.2.2.2 Capacity Building through the Use of Data

High-performing systems place a strong emphasis on continuous feedback to see what is working and areas in which further investment is required (OECD, 2011). One method to measure teacher and school leader capacity is the OECD's Teaching and Learning International Survey (TALIS) (OECD, 2019). TALIS brings forth three dimensions of policy recommendations for nations, of which two relate to the professional growth of teachers and school leaders, and attracting quality teachers and school leaders (OECD, 2019, p. 27). These resonate strongly with the practices of high-performing systems that build institutional capacity, providing the data which informs and enables the adjustment of specific policy levers as a result.

Hong Kong is one of the world's highest performing education systems (Jensen, 2012). From 1999 to 2012, Hong Kong implemented holistic whole-system reforms to its education sector to improve student learning (Jensen, 2012, p. 26). Hong Kong guided its reforms around an in-depth analysis of its education system, which revealed major gaps in student learning and teaching practices (Jensen, 2012, p. 27). Following this, Hong Kong conducted comprehensive consultations with stakeholders and key actors to understand the gaps needing reform in its education system and ultimately improve student learning (Jensen, 2012, p. 27). Hong Kong has significantly reformed its education system, becoming one of the highest-performing education systems in the world, through systematic reforms which were guided significantly by in-depth analyses of the state of its system, feedback loops, and engagement and consultation of stakeholders.

While understanding international best practices is important, it is imperative to remain cognizant of the specific context of Pakistan (and of the Punjab province in particular) and how capacity building (stemming from gaps identified by robust data) relates to this context. India is a country that can illuminate such a situation due to its contextual similarities to Pakistan.

The Indian government established federal and provincial institutes to build the capacity of government officers driven by an analysis of gaps in the system, for example the professional development of government officers to allow them to undertake more challenging and complex tasks (Aijaz, 2010, p. 388). While the (management) capacity building interventions seemed beneficial for those attending the sessions, the study found that many personnel for whom the training was intended would nominate their subordinates to attend instead, not seeing the relevance of the training to themselves (Aijaz, 2010, p. 389). One of the key recommendations from this analysis, which is relevant to the Pakistani context, is that capacity building will fail to reach those it is intended for and thus will fail to achieve its objective of strengthening the capacity of the institution as a whole if the concerns and attitudes of the targeted personnel are not addressed, or perhaps if participation is not incentivized.

5.3 Design Elements of the Reform

The Punjab has an intricate system of interconnected bodies and actors that collectively provide and monitor public education in the province. This system and the interactions within are what led to the formation of the PSRR. Thus, to understand the PSRR we must first understand the system on which it is based.

In 2010, the Eighteenth Amendment to the Constitution of Pakistan was passed (Government of Pakistan, 2010). This amendment had two major implications for education in the country. First, the amendment added Article 25-A to the constitution, which stipulated that all children between 5 and 16 years of age had the right to free and compulsory education. Secondly, the amendment devolved education autonomy to the provinces, making "the curriculum, syllabus, planning, policy, centres of excellence and standards of education" fall within the provincial purview (Dawn, 2010). As a result, the Government of the Punjab was now responsible for providing free and compulsory education (previously a federal matter) to all children 5–16 years old, putting new pressures on the previously limited provincial system of education delivery.

PSRR was born during this period, looking to reform and strengthen the system of public education delivery in the Punjab at a time when such an undertaking was becoming necessary. PSRR was built on a thorough understanding of the system, having been led by then provincial Chief Minister Mian Shahbaz Sharif and the Pakistan Education Taskforce (Barber, 2013). The Pakistan Education Taskforce was developed by then Prime Minister of the United Kingdom Gordon Brown & President of Pakistan Asif Ali Zardari; it was co-chaired by Sir Michael Barber (referenced above) and Shahnaz Wazir Ali.

5.3.1 The System

The Punjab's public education system is comprised of numerous bodies and agents, each responsible for different components of education delivery. At the provincial level, the network of formal schools falls under the purview of the School Education Department (SED), while non-formal education falls under the Literacy & Non-Formal Basic Education Department and the Technical Education & Vocational Training Agency. Higher education falls under the Higher Education Commission's Punjab chapter, and standardized assessment at higher levels is the responsibility of the Board for Intermediate and Secondary Education. Since the PSRR was concerned with strengthening the system of public education primarily in relation to

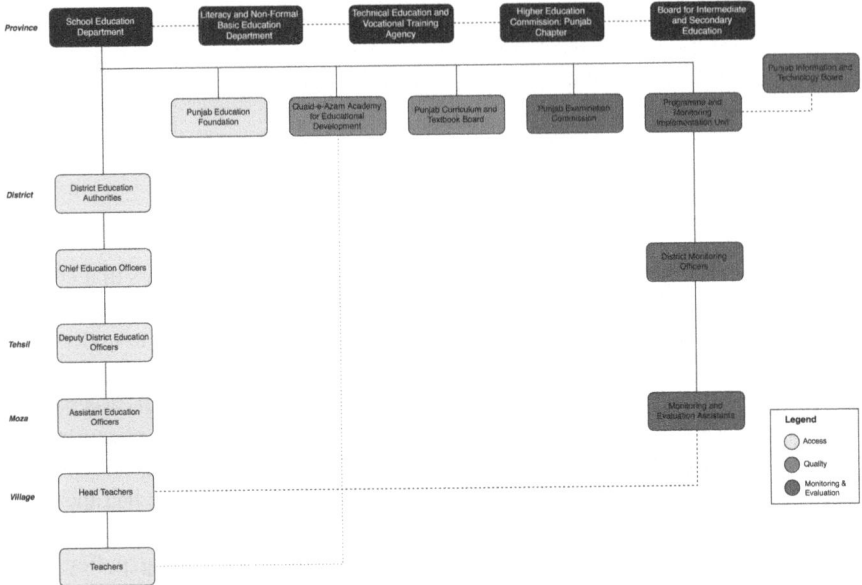

Fig. 5.1 System map of education in the Punjab

Article 25-A (formal education for children 5–16 years old), it focused on the SED and the bodies/actors within.

This system of public education delivery has been extensively mapped out through secondary research and interviews of relevant actors within the system to produce. Figure 5.1 details the other bodies that work concurrently with the SED, the numerous bodies within the SED and the specific channels of public education delivery that the reform targets. Mapping of the system has also been color-coded to display the channels within the system that cater to (a) access, (b) quality, and (c) monitoring & evaluation – the three dimensions of the PSRR.

5.3.2   Theory of Change

As stated above, PSRR separated the system of public education into three dimensions: access, quality and monitoring & evaluation. The overarching goal of the reform (the 'impact') was to provide quality education to the children in the Punjab through a strengthened and well- functioning provincial education system. It aimed to achieve this by producing three major outcomes:

1. Greater access to schools for school-aged children.
2. Improved quality of education being imparted in public schools.
3. Robust monitoring & evaluation mechanisms for evidence-informed service delivery and improved accountability, embedded in each layer of the system.

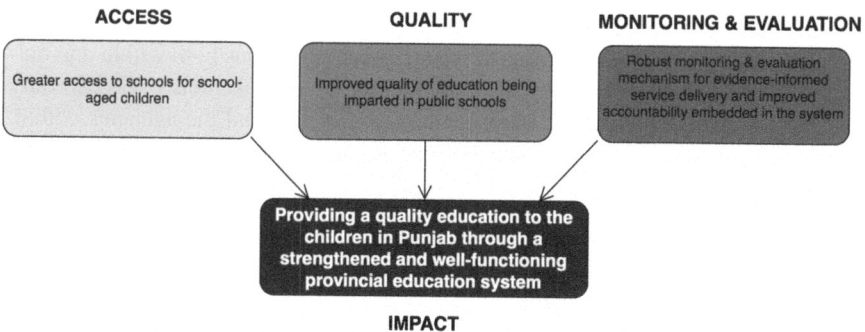

Fig. 5.2 From outcomes to impact - theory of change of the reform

A visual representation of this relationship is given in Fig. 5.2 above, following the same color-coded themes as defined in Fig. 5.1.

5.3.3 Interventions

To achieve its ambitious goals under the impact and outcomes statements described in the theory of change above, PSRR developed a portfolio of ambitious yet achievable activities, each targeting a series of outputs that would ultimately and collectively enable the achievement of the outcomes described above. This portfolio of interventions has been re-constructed for this study in consultation with stakeholders and through secondary research. The full portfolio can be found in Table 5.1 in the Annex, while relevant components are elaborated on in the evaluation section that follows.

5.4 A Medium-Term Evaluation: Where Do We Stand?

Given that it has been a decade since the PSRR was launched in 2010, this section studies the outcomes of the reform and whether these outcomes have been sustained over time. The outcomes being studied are those resulting from the institutional capacity building component of the reform. Specifically, we ask whether the reform had a lasting impact on access to, quality of, and monitoring & evaluation mechanisms in the public education system through the building of management capacity, teacher capacity and monitoring systems in the Punjab. Furthermore, we situate our analyses within the five-point framework on education reform and evaluate the sustainability of the outcomes of the PSRR in the medium term according to the five perspectives of educational reform (cultural, psychological, professional, institutional and political).

We addressed our research questions conducting a series of interviews with stakeholders from a wide spectrum of organizations/ positions both within and outside of the public education system in the Punjab.[1] Each stakeholder was carefully selected to represent a specific component of the system and the agencies within, and care was taken to consider potential biases each informant might bring to our research.

5.4.1 Management Capacity

Building the capacity of management in the system was essential to all three dimensions of the reform. Improved management capacity results in a greater ability of management to scale its services (addressing access to education), to improve the quality of services (quality of education) and to utilize feedback from the system to inform the first two components (monitoring & evaluation). This section discusses the activities implemented under the reform to build management capacity and their outcomes, and the sustainability of these moving forward.

5.4.1.1 Activities and Outcomes

The reform adopted a multi-pronged approach to building management capacity. Primarily and most noticeably, it did so via the adoption of frequent accountability meetings driven by data at all levels of management hierarchy in the public education system. Secondly, it directly addressed inefficiencies in the system, such as by placing an emphasis on ensuring all hiring was now done on merit, a process that has historically suffered from political interference and nepotism in Pakistan. Thirdly, it built management capacity by increasing the number of 'managers' in the system, realizing that a greater workforce was necessary to implement the new and more-demanding quality standards PSRR aspired towards.

The accountability component was arguably the largest element under the PSRR, based on the 'Deliverology' management approach developed by Barber. Deliverology is rooted in the use of reliable, relevant and timely data to inform feedback on performance and hold the system/actors accountable (Barber et al., 2011). Under PSRR, accountability was introduced in an almost identical format to Barber's Deliverology, employing widespread data dissemination, discussion and decisions based on data gathered under the salient 'monitoring & evaluation' dimension of the reform. In practice, the reform did this via the following interventions:

---

[1] 10 key stakeholders were interviewed spanning the core team that designed the reform, the bodies within the system that were targeted under the reform, civil society that was engaged with the reform, and other persons directly involved in the design or execution of reform interventions.

1. Generating and widely disseminating monthly data-packs assessing performance at all levels (from district to school) to all actors in the system (from the Chief Minister to head teachers).
2. Regular stock-take meetings at all levels of the system hierarchy to discuss progress and areas for growth, and to take action. These levels were:

   (a) Provincial: Meetings chaired by the Chief Minister and involving all key players in the system. These occurred every month for the first year, and every 2 months thereafter.
   (b) District Clusters: District Review Committee Meetings chaired by the District Coordination Officer and involving all Chief Education Officers of the District Education Authorities.
   (c) District: Pre-District Review Committee Meetings chaired by Chief Education Officers and involving all Deputy District Education Officers.
   (d) Tehsil: Meetings chaired by Deputy District Education Officers and involving all Assistant Education Officers.
   (e) Moza: Meetings chaired by Assistant Education Officers and involving all Head Teachers in the Moza.
   (f) School: Meetings chaired by Head Teachers and involving school teachers.

Next, under PSRR all new appointments and hiring were made on the basis of merit in order to ensure the most qualified personnel were being hired into the public education system. This was a result of the Chief Minister's political will and personal dedication to ensuring merit-based appointments were made, holding strong accountability measures in place for any violations of such a policy.

In addition to these changes, the capacity of the system to manage public education was enhanced by increasing the number of Assistant Education Officers (AEOs) in the system. This meant that there was a greater number of AEOs per Moza, reducing the number of schools each AEO was monitoring. This allowed each AEO to dedicate more energy towards the schools they were monitoring, now also acting as mentors and conducting classroom observations to provide feedback to teachers. Under the reform, AEOs were also hired from the private sector to get a more competitive pool of candidates, whereas they were formerly hired from the teaching cadre alone.

5.4.1.2 Sustainability

This systemic restructuring of education management in the Punjab has managed to take root in the province over the course of the last decade. The Punjab benefits from a period of prolonged political stability that helped in the continuation of policies put in place under the PSRR. Due to the dynamic nature of the reform, it is hard to provide an accurate quantitative causal measure of the impact of the reform on the system in the medium term. Therefore, our understanding and analysis of the impact relies more on qualitative stakeholder interviews.

The stable leadership and political will of the Chief Minister ensured that the accountability embedded within the reform was maintained and that regular stock-taking took place. Expectedly, the continuity of policies is often a prerequisite to sustainable outcomes. Looking at it from the five-point framework on educational reform discussed in the first chapter of this book, a stable positive change in the institutional capacity of the system can be viewed from both a political and institutional perspective. Expanding on the political perspective first, the strong political will of the Chief Minister towards PSRR meant that the interests and positions of the remaining stakeholders of the education system in the Punjab were also aligned with that of the center and this alignment was effectively maintained through a strict process of accountability.

The merits (and ethics) of such a top-heavy approach notwithstanding, the effectiveness of this political approach to the implementation of the reform can also be evaluated from the institutional perspective. Increasing the capacity of the education system while also restructuring district education departments of the entire province represented a fundamental shift in how education was managed in the Punjab. The digitization of data collection with reliability and its speedy dissemination, regular checks on district performance using said data, streamlining of teacher hiring processes with a focus on ensuring meritocracy and quality (measured, as of now, through academic qualifications of applications), restructuring the roles of AEOs and the literal expansion of teaching staff as well as student enrollment drives all serve to highlight the institutional restructuring of the education system in the Punjab. The institutionalization of this reform has been made possible due to sustained political will resulting in a successful cultural change within the entire system.

However, there are still shortcomings that hamper the functioning of the system in the medium term. With a change in government after the elections of 2018, the upward trajectory appears to have plateaued under the new regime. The stock-takes are no longer taking placing (a common theme echoed by our informants) and the original top-down accountability system appears to have lost momentum. The monitoring of the system is now being conducted sporadically, and that too by third parties rather than institutionally by the state.

In terms of accountability through technology, the PSRR has proven very effective in technologically upgrading the education monitoring apparatus of the Punjab with new, efficient and real-time digital data collection. This apparatus continues to enjoy widespread use among the public education delivery chain and the direct accountability benefits (tracking learning levels and school facilities, for example) remain. The systematic use of this evidence by the state is unfortunately less prevalent in the medium term.

5.4.2   Teacher Capacity

The capacity of teachers is essential to any well-functioning education system, especially considering teachers are the system's primary point of contact with students during their education. Building the capacity of teachers was thus particularly relevant to the quality dimension of the reform in addition to addressing access to education. This section explores the activities and outcomes of the PSRR's efforts to build teacher capacity (directly addressing teachers under a professional frame of the reform), as well as the sustainability of these activities and outcomes moving forward.

5.4.2.1 Activities and Outcomes

To build teacher capacity, the reform employed five major activities. The first activity was the hiring and training of a significant number of new teachers to increase the strength of the workforce in existing schools, relating to both quality and access. The remaining four activities directly dealt with improving the quality of instruction in order to bring about an improvement in the quality of education being imparted in classrooms. These included the development of teacher training modules, distributing these modules/guides, training teachers to use these guides, and hiring & training teacher coaches.

One of the most visible activities under the reform was the hiring of 80,000 new teachers into the system to ensure that each primary school had at least four teachers (Barber, 2013). This was imperative to improving and maintaining productive student-teacher ratios in public schools. Improving the student-teacher ratio means that teachers are better able to manage and deliver the material to their students and have more time to devote to lesson planning and lesson preparation, improving the quality of instruction. This also means that the school is able to cater to more students due to a greater number of teachers, increasing the access to education.

To further promote an increased quality of instruction, 75 new teacher training modules were developed to facilitate the professional development of teachers and the new emphasis placed on greater quality instruction. 60,000 copies of these modules (collectively known as 'teacher guides') were subsequently distributed across the province and 200,000 teachers were trained on using these guides.

As an additional source of support to teachers, 4000 teacher coaches were also hired and trained. This was a new resource for teachers to support improvements in instruction in classrooms and the design of classes, moving towards the greater quality standards set under the reform. These coaches acted as mentors to teachers and also conducted classroom observations to provide timely feedback to teachers, institutionalizing these greater quality standards by expanding the professional frame of teaching to include a new layer of quality assurance and support.

5.4.2.2 Sustainability

The efforts under PSRR have developed the teacher professional frame to one that has a greater emphasis on quality of instruction and one that is becoming more meritocratic. The meritocracy has been institutionalized by introducing a standardized and independent system for the hiring of teachers, where K-12 teachers are now hired through a standardized test conducted by an independent body called the National Testing Service (NTS). This step has made the hiring of teachers more meritocratic, reducing the former political nature of such appointments. Further, the pay scales of public-school teachers have now been increased to allow for the induction of young professionals into the profession of teaching, improving the pool of teachers in this professional frame.

The teacher training facility, Quaid-e-Azam Academy for Educational Development (QAED, formerly known as the Directorate for Staff Development), has also been significantly strengthened. QAED now provides an 8-week induction program for teachers that join the workforce and a 28-day leadership training for head teachers to enable them to lead their schools, signaling that the emphasis on quality under the PSRR is still an important area to the system (Javed & Naveed, 2019).

Despite these efforts, reports of unsatisfactory learning levels of students are still being seen[2] and rigorous evaluations on the impact of teacher trainings have not been conducted. This means that the actual efficacy and result of these teacher trainings and greater emphasis on quality is still in question.

Moving forward, the government needs to translate its emphasis on accountability under the PSRR into the teacher professional frame as well. Impact evaluations of teaching, for example, should be embedded into the system to diagnose why student learning levels are unsatisfactory and to design specific support mechanisms for teachers as a result. Further, the content-specific knowledge of existing teachers is an area that still needs more dedicated effort, especially via regular in-service trainings (Asian Development Bank, 2019). A final recommendation is to introduce a mechanism within QAED which allows for additional teacher trainings on a per-need basis, rather than a pre-determined arbitrary schedule. This would be a direct next step to the evaluations of teachers, providing additional support to any teacher that is not performing as expected.

5.4.3 Monitoring & Information Systems

Monitoring & information systems were a crucial component of the reform upon which the salient accountability model was built. These relate directly to the education monitoring and evaluation dimension of the reform and play a pivotal role in informing access and quality decisions. The accountability component of monitoring and evaluation has been covered under the management capacity segment

---

[2] 44% of Grade 5 students in rural areas could not read a second grade short story in their native language whereas 47% could not compute a double-digit division problem (ASER, 2019a). The students in urban centers fared marginally better however 36% of Grade 5 students were also unable to read a second grade short story in their native language and 35% could still not compute a double digit division problem (ASER, 2019b).

above, while the actual monitoring systems and data-collection processes are discussed here.

5.4.3.1 Activities and Outcomes

Strong monitoring and information systems require reliable data. PSRR achieved this through triangulating their data sources to check for accuracy and placing a large emphasis on the accountability of the data collection process itself. This was achieved by digitizing the data collection process used province-wide, conducting monthly assessments of learning, and contracting a reputable independent party to conduct biannual learning assessments with which to check the reliability of their own data.

Monitoring of the school education system in the Punjab is conducted by the Programme Monitoring & Implementation Unit (PMIU) under the SED, which monitors all public schools in the province. Before PSRR, this monitoring was a manual task whereby all data (of school facilities or student/teacher attendance) was collected by hand, manually entered onto a computer (creating a time lag and introducing human error) and then shared onward up the chain. Under PSRR, this mechanism was quickly shifted to one that was completely digitized (requiring all monitoring staff to use digital tablets for entry) and using state-of-the-art technology, such as verifying the location of data entered for a school by referencing the geographic coordinates at the point of entry of the data point against the location of the school.

In addition to routine data monitoring, learning levels of students was another salient component that had to be measured. To this end, monthly Literacy and Numeracy Drives (LNDs) were designed and conducted by AEOs in all schools to spot-check learning levels of random students across the system. With the lens of accountability, this data was then verified by contracting a reputable independent party to conduct their own biannual assessments of child learning to triangulate the state data with and verify reliability, which was crucial.

5.4.3.2 Sustainability

Efficient and real-time data collection and analysis was a major component of the PSRR. Since the data collected on district performance in education metrics also formed the basis of the stock-takes conducted by the Chief Minister, a robust and well-functioning data monitoring system equipped with the requisite technology was a requirement, if not an outright necessity. The province was successfully able to transition to a digitized model, with real time information on education statistics (including but not limited to student performance and teacher attendance) becoming freely available to the SED and the public in a record amount of time. This has persisted because of the sustained initial effort made by the government to structurally integrate this new monitoring mechanism into the operations of the system.

The monthly school performance numbers are still collected by the AEOs and made available on the PMIU website.[3] There is now a District Monitoring Officer (DMO) in every district office who is tasked with ensuring continuity of data collection. The Monitoring and Evaluation Assistants (MEAs) report to the DMO who in turn ensures that the data reaches PMIU in time: this is now a regular feature of the Punjab's education system as originally envisioned by PSRR.

This goal of the PSRR can also be analyzed through the institutional perspective of the five-point framework on educational reform. Framed as a core component of the PSRR, the upgrading of monitoring mechanisms to include robust and timely data collection and dissemination as well as its integration across all levels of the education system, the formulation of policy decisions (pertaining to student learning outcomes, teacher incentives, district management etc.) on the basis of evidence became more than a catchphrase. It has successfully become a fundamental cog in the running of the SED in the Punjab. Thus, this aspect of the reform has brought about an institutional change within the education system of the Punjab.

While data collection is still occurring in the medium term, the stock-takes have stopped taking place, primarily due to the change in government after the elections of 2018. However, the bureaucratic and accountability driven method of collecting data (via the AEOs and MEAs) may also need to be repackaged for teachers and head-teachers of public schools. One of our key informants stated that teachers continue to harbor resentments against the data collection regime, due to the fact that financial (or other) penalties can be imposed on teachers by MEAs if their school does not perform well or if a teacher is absent on the day the MEA visits the school. If the objective in the medium-term has shifted from expanding access to improving quality, then the next step has to involve reducing the trust deficit between the center and the teachers.

5.5 Way Forward

The PSRR was designed keeping in mind the specific challenges of education in the Punjab, looking to reform education by placing its emphasis on three frames that were most relevant to the context and the time. These were the institutional, professional and political. Institutionally, the reform embedded accountability into each layer of the system and built the capacity of those within the system to take action and hold the system accountable. Professionally, the reform placed a large emphasis

---

[3] This website can be accessed at https://open.punjab.gov.pk/schools/home/landing

on the teaching profession, building the capacity of teachers and incorporating support mechanisms for teachers as well as expanding the profession entirely. Politically, the reform was encouragingly cognizant of the political landscape within the province and the political powers that were distorting the system for personal gain. Together, these frames and the vision produced a reform that was highly context specific and had the potential to create real change.

Although an unfortunate learning crisis is still seen in the Punjab today, the education landscape in the province has drastically grown from where it was a decade ago. Large elements of success and structural transformation have taken place over this past decade, many of which appear to be both sustained and sustainable in the foreseeable future. At the core of the reform, we see a push in the system towards a deep accountability in all decisions that is informed by robust, accurate and timely data to provide quality education in the province. Further, we see increased capacity of management in the hierarchy to conduct diagnostics of the performance of their constituencies, which is a powerful tool. Lastly, teachers now being aware that their performance is constantly being monitored, through frequent school visits for example, is a tool that still holds significant power.

While the above is true, the work started under the PSRR now faces significant risks due to the reform being centralized in nature. The PSRR thrived due to strong accountability from the top, specifically due to the Chief Minister being personally invested in the reform. With the 2018 elections and the change in governance, the emphasis on accountability from the top seems to have faded; worryingly, this fading emphasis on accountability currently seems to be trickling down to the rest of the system. Monitoring is still taking place and robust data is still being collected, however the actions taken on this evidence are fewer, which is reducing the accountability within the system that took much effort to build.

This waning accountability from the top is not entirely surprising, given governance changes in a democratic system that are brought on when a new political party assumes power. This is why a reform should be robust to change in governance. In the short term and to keep the system from regressing to its prior state, one of the key pieces of advice we received from our informants was the need for a dedicated person ideally higher up in the hierarchy of the education delivery chain who would continue this unrelenting focus on evidence and accountability. At the same time and for a more long-term solution, a system of accountability must be developed and implemented that is robust to change in government and leadership. Each change in governance should not be a threat to the right to quality education for the Punjab's children. This means further research must be conducted into embedding accountability (ideally in a developing country context) from the ground-up, instead of limiting it to elements at the top of the management chain.

Annex

Table 5.1 Breakdown of the impact, outcomes, outputs and activities under the PSRR

Impact	Outcomes	Outputs	Activities
Providing a quality education to most of Punjab's children through a strengthened and well-functioning provincial education system.	Greater access to schools for school-aged children	Enrolling identified out-of-school children	Biannual enrolment drives
		Providing vouchers to attend non-public schools	Upscale and restructuring Punjab Education Foundation's Enrollment Voucher Scheme
		Improved infrastructure of schools across the province	Build 13,000 additional classrooms
			Upscale Punjab Education Foundation's Foundation Assisted Schools
			Introduce Punjab Education Foundation's New School Program
			Reduce missing facilities in schools
		Hiring more teaching staff	Hire 80,000 additional teachers to ensure each primary school has at least 4 teachers
		Hiring more administrative staff	Hire more AEOs to allow each AEO to monitor fewer number of schools for more effective monitoring
	Improved quality of education being imparted in public schools	Improved teacher training	Develop 75 teacher training modules
			Distribute 60,000 teacher guides
			Train 200,000 teachers to use teacher guides
		Improved support to teachers	Hire and train 4000 teacher coaches
		Improved assessments of learning	Punjab Examination Commission assessments of students in grade 5 and grade 8
			Independent biannual learning assessments conducted by an independent party (McKinsey)
			Monthly assessments of learning in grade 3 English, Mathematics and Urdu under the 'Literacy and Numeracy Drive' conducted by AEOs
	Robust monitoring & evaluation mechanism for evidence-informed service delivery and improved accountability embedded in the system	Less number of schools monitored by each AEO	Hire more AEOs (detailed above)
		Evidence-informed discussions on access and quality	Generate and distribute monthly data-packs at all levels of the system
			Regular stock-take meetings (every month / 2 months) led by the Chief Minister and involving all key players in the system
			Regular District Review Committee Meetings chaired by District Coordination Officer (DCO)
			Regular Pre-District Review Committee Meetings held every month chaired by the CEO of DEAs
			Regular accountability meetings held at each level (District level, Tehsil-level, Moza-level and school-level meetings) to discuss progress and areas for growth
		Digitization of PMIU	Digitize data-collection by PMIU through a collaboration with Punjab Information & Technology Board to collect real-time data with greater chains of accountability

References

Aijaz, R. (2010). Capacity building of municipal functionaries for good governance in Uttarakhand, India. *Habitat International, 34*, 386–391.

ASER Pakistan. (2019a). *Annual status of education report (ASER) Pakistan national (rural).* ASER Pakistan 2018: Islamabad.

ASER Pakistan. (2019b). *Annual status of education report (ASER) Pakistan national (urban).* ASER Pakistan 2018.

Asian Development Bank. (2019). School education in Pakistan: A Sector Assessment. *Country Sector and Thematic Assessments (Education).* Retrieved from https://doi.org/10.22617/TCS190039.

Barber, M. (2010). *Education reform in Pakistan: This time It's going to be different.* Brookings Institution.

Barber, M. (2013). *The good News from Pakistan: How a revolutionary new approach to education reform in Punjab shows the way forward for Pakistan and development aid everywhere.* London: Reform.

Barber, M., Moffit, A., & Kihn, P. (2011). *Deliverology 101: A field guide for educational leaders.* Thousand Oaks, CA: Corwin Press.

Cohen, D. K. (1995a). What is the system in systemic reform? *Educational Researcher, 24*(9), 11–31. Retrieved from https://doi.org/10.3102/0013189X024009011.

Cohen, J. M. (1995b). Capacity building in the public sector: A focused framework for analysis and action. *International Review of Administrative Sciences, 61*, 407–422.

Dawn News. (2010). 18th amendment and education. *Dawn Newspaper.* Retrieved from https://www.dawn.com/news/570524

Dill, D. D. (2000). Capacity building as an instrument of institutional reform: Improving the quality of higher education through academic audits in the UK, New Zealand, Sweden, and Hong Kong. *Journal of Comparative Policy Analysis, 2*(2), 211–234. Retrieved from http://search.proquest.com.ezp-prod1.hul.harvard.edu/docview/197269536?accountid=11311

Earle, J. & Wan, J.C. (n.d.). *The National Science Foundation and Systemic Reform.* Yale-New Haven Teachers Institute. Retrieved from https://teachersinstitute.yale.edu/pubs/A17/earle.html

Fullan, M. (2009). Large-scale reform comes of age. *Journal of Educational Change, 10*(2–3), 101–113. https://doi.org/10.1007/s10833-009-9108-z

Fullan, M. (2010). The big ideas behind whole system reform. *Canadian Education Association, 50*(3). Retrieved from http://michaelfullan.ca/wp-content/uploads/2016/06/13396082070.pdf

Fullan, M., & Levin, B. (2009). *The fundamentals of whole-system reform: A case study from Canada.* Retrieved from https://michaelfullan.ca/articles/fundamentals-of-whole-system-reform/

Government of Pakistan. (2010). *Constitution (eighteenth amendment) act.* The Constitution of the Islamic Republic of Pakistan. Retrieved from http://www.pakistani.org/pakistan/constitution/amendments/18amendment.html

Javed, U., & Naveed, S. (2019). *2013–2018: Five Years of Education Reforms PUNJAB Wins, Losses and Challenges for the Future 2018–2023.* Islamabad: Alif Ailaan.

Jensen, B. (2012). *Catching up: Learning from the best school systems in East Asia: Summary report* (pp. 1–115). Melbourne: Grattan Institute.

OECD. (2011). *Strong performers and successful performers in education: Lessons from PISA for the United States.* Paris: OECD Publishing.

OECD. (2019). *TALIS 2018 results (volume I): Teachers and school leaders as lifelong learners.* Paris: OECD Publishing.

Pakistan Bureau of Statistics. (1998). Population Census. *1998 Pakistan Census.*

Supovitz, J. A., & Taylor, B. S. (2005). Systemic education evaluation: Evaluating the impact of Systemwide reform in education. *American Journal of Evaluation, 26*(2), 204–230. Retrieved from https://doi.org/10.1177/1098214005276286.

Zucker, A. A., Shields, P. M., Adelman, N. E., Corcoran, T. B., Goertz, M. E., & Anderson, B. T. (1998). *A report on the evaluation of the National Science Foundation's Statewide Systemic Initiatives (SSI) Program*. National Science Foundation Directorate for Education and Human Resources.

Rastee Chaudhry holds a Master of Education from the Harvard Graduate School of Education (2020), specializing in international education policy. She has previously worked on education service delivery, research and policy in Pakistan – her country of origin. During this time, she worked on providing remedial education to out-of-school girls in rural Punjab, conducting systems-level research into the status of early childhood education across the province, and strengthening child rights in the legislature to protect children from physical and humiliating punishment. Currently, she is assisting with research on an early childhood development project in Sindh with the Harvard T.H. Chan School of Public Health.

Abdullah Waqar Tajwar is from Pakistan and has a Master's degree in International Education Policy from the Harvard University Graduate School of Education. He has previously worked in the education non-profit space in Pakistan, heading projects on education service delivery using technology for disadvantaged Pakistani youth. His most recent work has centered around female secondary education, in partnership with the Malala Fund with the objective of reintegrating girls who had dropped out after the primary level back into the formal education mainstream.

Chapter 6
Nurturing Every Learner's Potential: Education Reform in Kenya

Jeļena Fomiškina, Eve Woogen, Ama Peiris, Somaia Abdulrazzak, and Emma Cameron

6.1 Introduction

Kenya has made significant progress towards increasing access to basic education over the past few decades. Since 2017, attention has, therefore, turned to improving quality as well by starting a wide reform of the content and structure of the education system from primary through to tertiary. This is one of the most significant education reforms undertaken in Kenya since independence was declared in 1963, and major aspects of this reform include the adoption of a Competency-Based Curriculum approach and changes in educational structure, among others. While nominally focused on curriculum, in reality the reform encompasses multiple aspects of Kenya's educational system and ambitiously seeks to initiate major changes in school cycles, the structure of school systems, and several of the country's socio-economic spheres. While other countries have implemented either a curriculum or a structural reform at a given time, Kenya's reform is uniquely ambitious in its approach to dually tackle both spheres simultaneously and introduce major shifts in the general understanding of the education system. Additionally, analyzing the reform from Reimers' (2020) five perspectives on education change, we find that the curriculum reform is most appropriately framed from a cultural perspective with the long-term shifts in shared norms and practices that it calls for. At the same time, this structural reform presents more immediate infrastructural and logistical challenges. We, therefore, argue that this dual process presents distinctive challenges in balancing the disparate needs of each sphere. As reform implementation is still in an early stage as of 2020, this chapter examines the process to date. It begins with an overview of the country context in Kenya, followed by a more detailed

J. Fomiškina · E. Woogen · A. Peiris · S. Abdulrazzak · E. Cameron (✉)
International Education Policy, Harvard Graduate School of Education,
Cambridge, MA, USA
e-mail: jelena_fomiskina@gse.harvard.edu; ewoogen@gse.harvard.edu; amapeiris@gse.harvard.edu; Somaia_Abdulrazzak@gse.harvard.edu; ecameron@gse.harvard.edu

© The Author(s) 2021
F. M. Reimers (ed.), *Implementing Deeper Learning and 21st Century Education Reforms*, https://doi.org/10.1007/978-3-030-57039-2_6

description of the reform, its theory of change, implementation timeline, and stakeholder involvement. Finally, we analyze major challenges to the implementation process at the moment of writing and conclude by looking forward in anticipation of the remaining implementation process.

Unless otherwise cited, all information in this chapter was obtained from documents provided by the Ministry of Education (MoE), as well as through in-person interviews conducted in January 2020. Interviews were conducted with representatives from the MoE, the Kenya Institute of Curriculum Development (KICD), the Teachers Service Commission (TSC), the Kenya National Examinations Council (KNEC), the Kenya Secondary Schools Heads Association (KESSHA), the Kenya Primary Schools Heads Association (KEPSHA), and the Kenya Institute for Public Policy, Research and Analysis (KIPPRA). Additionally, we held individual and group interviews with headteachers, deputy headteachers, classroom teachers, and champion trainers at a number of primary and secondary schools in Kakamega, Kajiado, Kiambu, and Meru counties, where we also conducted classroom observations.

6.2 Country Context

After independence, Kenya along with Uganda and Tanzania (three of the six East African Community countries) adopted a structure of education that strongly resembled Britain's education system: 7 years of primary, 4 years of secondary, 2 years of high school and 3 years of tertiary education, or 7-4-2-3. Students completed region-wide exams after primary and then after secondary school – East African Certificate of Primary Education (EACPE), East African Certificate of Secondary Education (EACE), and East African Advanced Certificate of Secondary Education (EAACE). This system did not achieve the desired outcomes, however, and was felt to lack flexibility to adapt to labor market demands and was considered too academically-oriented (Wanjohi, 2011). These failings became the focus of an ongoing debate over unemployment throughout Kenya. After the collapse of the East African Community in 1977, Kenya changed the names of the two exams to just the Certificate of Primary Education and Secondary Education, CPE and KCE respectively. Not until 1985 however, under President Daniel arap Moi, did the government overhaul the education system to create a new structure: 8 years of primary, 4 years of secondary, and 4 years of tertiary, a system known as 8-4-4. Once again, the exams changed names to Kenya Certificate of Primary Education and Secondary Education, KCPE and KCSE, respectively. Since then, the curriculum has undergone review several times but with no major reforms up until now.

In terms of access to education, the introduction of the Free Primary Education program in Kenya in 2003, followed by the Free Day Secondary Education program in 2008, has had wide-ranging impacts on the country's education sector. With the reduction of school fees came an unsurprisingly significant increase in enrollment across the country with millions more students entering into the educational system since 2003. In 2000, prior to the reduction of school fees, net enrollment in primary schools was 59.6%, and 32.9% in secondary schools (UNESCO Institute of Statistics, 2000). In 2014, during the most recent national data collection, net enrollment in primary schools in Kenya had risen to 88.2%, and to 47.4% in secondary schools (Ministry of Education, Science and Technology, 2014a). While net enrollment in secondary schools is still significantly lower than primary net enrollment, the transition rate from primary to secondary was 98.8% in 2014 and by 2015 had further increased to 99.2% (UNESCO Institute of Statistics, 2016). Prior to 2014, the most recent data collection on transition rates dates back to 1980, at which point the transition rate stood at 85.6% (UNESCO Institute of Statistics, 2016).

The public education system in Kenya is administered along county lines, with schools in each of the country's 47 counties overseen by county Directors of Education responsible for implementing national education policies, programs, and initiatives across the country's 21,718 public primary and 7,686 public secondary schools (Ministry of Education, Science and Technology, 2014a). The National Education Sector Plan, released by the MoE in 2014, highlighted regional disparities as a key area for improvement in Kenya's education system. Female literacy rates, for example, ranged from 90% in urban areas such as Nairobi to below 10% in poorer northern areas such as Mandera, Turkana, and Wajir counties (Ministry of Education, Science and Technology, 2014b). Across Kenya, disparities in school funding and insufficient infrastructure were identified as impacting arid and semi-arid land regions, informal urban settlements, and other pockets of poverty in particular (Ministry of Education, Science and Technology, 2014b, p. 42). Increased primary school enrollment numbers had not been matched by an increase in staffing and infrastructure, and in some regions led to overcrowding far in excess of national averages. In 2014, the average student-teacher ratio for public primary schools in Kenya was 34.5:1. However, a number of counties had much higher ratios of 60 or 70 students per teacher. For public secondary schools, the ratio was only 20.2:1 with lower levels of disparity between counties but reached up to 50 students per teacher in some areas (Ministry of Education, Science and Technology, 2014a). While these averages are on the low end compared to many other African countries, there is evidence – discussed in further detail later in this paper – that overcrowding in schools is currently a more serious concern than would be apparent based on these most recently reported statistics from 2014. While the Education Sector Plan cites population forecasts showing that the Kenyan population, which is currently primarily young, will age over the next few decades, it states that providing universal basic education will continue to strain the sector. The report also predicts a shifting trend in which overcrowding pressures will lessen in primary schools and instead increase at the secondary level (Ministry of Education, Science and Technology, 2014b).

6.3 Theory of Change and Reform Goals

6.3.1 National Curriculum Reform

It is within this larger context of educational change that a major curriculum reform was launched in 2017 with the expectation of full implementation by 2028. Despite the progress made in Kenya with regard to increased access to basic education, this curriculum reform is the result of a growing sense that Kenya's existing curriculum and educational structure are insufficient to meet the country's goals as set forth in Kenya Vision 2030 (Ji & Kabita Njeng'ere, 2017). The primary goal of Kenya Vision 2030, as articulated by the MoE in their 2014 statistical report, is to transform Kenya into a globally competitive country by 2030. An understanding of the education system as a core domain in working towards this vision became necessary. In working to achieve this goal, the report emphasizes the importance of education: "Within the social pillar, education sector plays a critical role in facilitating the process of inculcating knowledge, attitudes, and skills necessary for catapulting Kenya to a globally competitive country and acquiring new knowledge in a systematic way with a view to improving products and processes" (Ministry of Education, Science and Technology, 2014a). This shift in the focus of the educational system is expected to empower the next generation to be effective leaders in various domains of life.

In order for the education sector to support the achievement of this goal, a Competency-Based Curriculum (CBC) is in the process of being adopted across the country with the objective of equipping students with twenty-first-century skills and competencies and better preparing them to participate in a modern global economy. Such objectives reflect those that have been widely adopted in education systems across the globe, including in other sub-Saharan African countries such as Zimbabwe, as described in Chap. 7.

With the adoption of the CBC, the role of curriculum in leading the educational process toward a pre-defined set of goals (competencies) was introduced. In 2017, a Basic Education Curriculum Framework (BECF) was developed by the Kenya Institute of Curriculum Development (KICD) in collaboration with education stakeholders to guide implementation of the CBC. This framework was designed based on seven identified core competencies: communication and collaboration, critical thinking and problem-solving, creativity and imagination, citizenship, digital literacy, learning to learn, and self-efficacy (Kenya Institute of Curriculum Development, 2017).

In terms of pedagogy, the curriculum changes call for an overarching shift from traditional didactic teaching methods to individualized student-centered instruction in which teachers act as guides and facilitators of the students' learning process. Accordingly, the new curriculum calls also for a shift from a focus on infrequent, high-stakes summative assessments to the inclusion of more ongoing formative assessment to make learning more individualized and student-centered. This shift broadly seeks to re-define the role of student assessments in informing and supporting the learning experience through reshaping daily norms and practices around assessment within classrooms. In doing so, there has also been a recognition across stakeholders that this increase in activities requiring teachers to provide more individualized student attention will be challenging to implement in large classrooms in particular, and may exacerbate existing challenges of high student-teacher ratios.

While such pedagogical changes are more evident within the new curriculum framework than changes to the content itself, some content changes have also been introduced. Chief among them is the inclusion of personal values into various content areas, and teachers are expected to explicitly teach and assess certain core values and interpersonal skills. Assessment will be conducted through checklists and other tools for teachers to observe student demonstration of values and skills in regular classroom behaviors. In addition, the new curriculum explicitly incorporates parental involvement into learning activities with the hope of building a shared cultural mindset that sees education as an ongoing learning process with teachers, parents, and students all as active participants.

6.3.2 National Structural Reform

The second component of the national reform is a planned shift of the country's educational cycle from 8 years of primary school and 4 years of secondary school (8-4 cycle) to 2 years of pre-primary, 6 years of primary school, 3 years of junior secondary school, and 3 years of senior secondary school, i.e. a 2-6-3-3 cycle. One intention for the shift is to provide greater opportunities for learner specialization early on in schooling, with a particular emphasis on strengthening pathways for Technical and Vocational Education Training (TVET) (Ministry of Education, Science and Technology, 2014a). Once students complete primary and junior secondary schooling, they will have the choice of being offered and selected into three different planned pathways in senior secondary school: Arts and Sports Science, Social Sciences, or STEM. One possibility being considered is that students may also have the option to bypass senior secondary and continue straight to TVET programs. The three overarching pathways – with between two to four tracks within each pathway – are intended to allow students to pursue their interests and talents in secondary school rather than focusing solely on academic exam performance. In addition, they are intended to grant students a stronger sense of responsibility and ownership over their own education. Having these options for the students at a relatively early stage is believed to have a major impact on their performance and success in the educational system as well as their careers (Kenya Institute of Curriculum Development, 2017). This concept of pathways has been constructed by the MoE in an attempt to provide a broad curriculum that allows for specializations with the intention of combatting rising unemployment in Kenya, which rose from 8.9% in 2008 to 9.3% in 2019

(Kenya Institute of Curriculum Development, 2017; UNESCO Institute of Statistics, 2019).

In alignment with the move from summative to formative assessments driven by the curriculum reform, another feature of the structural reform will be an automatic promotion of students from primary to junior secondary school. In 2017, then Cabinet Secretary Fred Matiang'i had instituted a campaign of achieving a 100% transition rate from primary to secondary school called "Tupeleke Watoto Shule" (Let's take our children to school). This initiative was launched as part of a global campaign to provide all children with 12 years of basic education. As the new educational reforms promote the mindset that all learners have the ability to become successful and should continue to their schooling, the current Cabinet Secretary George Magoha is continuing the "Tupeleke Watoto Shule" campaign, partly through putting pressure on secondary school administrators to accept all students rather than restricting enrollment.

In further pursuit of this policy of 100% transition, President Uhuru Kenyatta announced in August 2019 that the KCPE (performance on which currently determines a student's secondary school options) will be dissolved by the end of the CBC rollout (Kenya Institute of Curriculum Development, 2017). Under the original 8-4-4 system, Kenya's secondary schools were classified into four groups: national, extra-county, county, and sub-county, with the names broadly referring to school catchment areas. Generally, students achieving top results in the KCPE would gain admittance to a national school, the next-best performers would be admitted to extra-county schools and so forth. However, some school leaders indicated in interviews that excellence in other areas could also secure admittance into a national or extra-county school, including students who were exceptional athletes or performers, particularly in the arts. Enrollment into a national or extra-county school is a strong predictor of admission into tertiary education, whereas students who attend county or sub-county schools more rarely continue onto higher education.

In part, the discontinuation of the KCPE is hoped to transform a culture of competitive high-stakes examinations and student rankings, and instead promote the vision that every learner has the potential to succeed. However, as of early 2020, it had not been announced how secondary school placement would be determined in the absence of student rankings based on the standardized exam results. Further complicating the question of secondary school placement is the stated intention of also dismantling the current hierarchy between school categories that places national schools at the top (Nyaundi, 2019). Instead, one vision is that each school would offer at least two of the three pathway options previously mentioned, and placement would be done on a more individualized level to best match students to schools based on these offerings and student competencies and interests.

6.4 Reform Implementation

6.4.1 Initial Stages

Between May and September 2017, the MoE ran an initial pilot program in 470 schools across Kenya. The purpose of the pilot was to test the feasibility and validity of the planned curriculum, teacher preparation, and assessment in different contexts and levels. One of the distinguishing features of the pilot was continuous assessments instead of the traditional one-off examination at the end of the term. The program was implemented in both public and private schools and in rural and urban settings to ensure representation across different types of schools in Kenya. For this reason, ten schools in each of the 47 counties were selected: five primary and five pre-primary, with one of the selected schools in each county being a school for learners with special needs.

Following this pilot, the nation-wide roll-out had been planned for 2018 but was postponed as the pilot revealed concerns around capacity and logistics of implementation as well as resource gaps in supporting teachers. The KICD identified a lack of training for teachers and inadequate amounts of relevant teaching materials. A KICD (2018) survey discovered that one in five Kenyan teachers reported feeling 'unprepared' to implement the new curriculum. Teachers also opposed plans to merge the administration of primary and secondary schools, which would be a requirement of the reform. In light of these findings, 2018 was devoted to preparing for the nation-wide implementation and devising a plan for teacher professional development, as well as conducting CBC training sessions for teachers in pre-primary through grade three of primary school.

6.4.2 Teacher Training

The teacher training plan was developed and implemented by the MoE in coordination with multiple other bodies such as the Teachers Service Commission (TSC), the Kenya National Examinations Council (KNEC), the Kenya Institute of Curriculum Development (KICD), the Kenya Institute of Special Education (KISE) and the Kenya Education Management Institute (KEMI). The training courses were designed to be rolled out in an annual sequence beginning with teachers instructing in pre-primary and up to grade three receiving training, then continuing with teachers instructing in each subsequent grade level the following year. The sessions were intended both to introduce the content of the curriculum and to familiarize teachers with the pedagogical strategies it calls for. In advance of CBC implementation in each additional grade level, all teachers of that level complete training sessions conducted over school breaks in either April, August, or December. Trainings are organized along county lines by regional Training Centres and facilitated using a train-the-trainer model. All trainings are intended to be conducted following a standard CBC Teacher Preparation Manual.

The duration of training varies by county density: in less populated counties, teachers may be able to receive 2 or 3 weeks of training in the year before the CBC is implemented in their grade level, while counties with greater numbers of teachers may have the capacity to provide only 1 week of training for individual teachers. At the start of the 2020 school year, it was reported that 228,000 primary teachers had been trained (Nyamai, 2020). In recognition of the limited time span relative to the amount of material to be covered, an online training course[1] was also developed by the KICD and made available for teachers nationwide. However, completion of this course is non-mandatory and dependent on individual teacher initiatives as well as on access to appropriate technology. Given these limitations, the course does not appear to be in wide use as only 4,817 teachers are currently using the platform (Kenya Institute of Curriculum Development, 2019).

In 2019, the first cohorts of students from pre-primary to grade three were introduced to the CBC curriculum nationwide (Kenya Institute of Curriculum Development, 2018) while simultaneously CBC training was held for teachers of grade four. Grade four students across the country began studying CBC in January 2020. 2020 is also a target year for the completion of development of the curriculum designs for grades six through twelve, and training will be held for teachers of grade five beginning in April 2020. In 2023, the first cohort of grade seven students will move to secondary school rather than continuing in primary school up to grade eight. The full implementation process is scheduled to be completed in 2028 when incoming students of the final grade, grade twelve, are scheduled to transition to the new curriculum.

6.5   Stakeholders Involved

The curriculum and structural reforms are a national collaborative effort that demanded the engagement of multiple agencies. Coordinated by the MoE, the effort also includes the Kenya Institute of Curriculum Development (KICD), the Kenya National Examinations Council (KNEC), the Teachers Service Commission, the Kenya Secondary Schools Heads Association (KESSHA), and the Kenya Primary Schools Heads Association (KEPSHA), among others. Apart from coordination during curriculum development, training of teachers, and roll-out, members from these bodies also sit on a 17-member Task Force overseeing the roll-out of the CBC. Task Force members are charged with key decisions about both reforms as implementation takes place, such as the decision that the new junior secondary grades would be housed within secondary schools rather than in primary schools.

---

[1] https://elimika.kec.ac.ke/course/cbc-online-training/

As mentioned previously, the education system in Kenya is administered along county lines, and the cascaded train-the-trainer model for the CBC is structured around these county lines. This model involves the engagement of County Directors, Sub County Directors, Curriculum Support Officers (CSOs) at the zonal level, and champion trainers who are selected teachers from schools within each zone. Despite this involvement in the training process, however, broad scope decision-making related to the reforms remains concentrated at the top level of administration. As of the first few years of implementation, there was little communication between the national government and stakeholders at the country, sub-county, or school level during the implementation process (Barchok, 2019). As of 2020, for example, stakeholders at the lower levels of administration had not been involved in decision-making processes regarding the many upcoming changes for the secondary level in terms of training, placement of students at schools, and teacher reassignment.

With regard to engagement of parents and families, during the early stages of reform implementation such efforts were organized primarily at the school level with the Curriculum Support Officers occasionally organizing meetings at the zonal level. While active Parent Teacher Associations at some schools facilitated this engagement process, many teachers saw the lack of a centralized parent outreach and communication strategy as a weakness of the implementation process. There was believed to be a low level of parental understanding of the goals and theories of the CBC, as well as a low level of support in providing many of the materials that curriculum activities called for parents to provide (Oduor, 2020a, 2020b; Owiti & Kamau, 2019).

6.6 Implementation Challenges

6.6.1 Framing the Reform

Having now provided an overview of the dual process of curriculum and structural reform currently being undertaken in Kenya, we see that the MoE has a clear aim of building a new culture around education across the country. As discussed in earlier chapters, culture in this sense is understood as "a set of shared norms and practices that define how education is understood by a society, meanings about how instruction should be conducted" (Reimers, 2020, p. 26). This includes ideas about what instruction should look like, what a student-centered approach means, what the role of the teacher is, what types of competencies students should have upon graduating a school system, what the purpose of examinations is, and how examinations inform decision making at classroom, school, county, and national levels. This is not to say that there are not also psychological, institutional, professional, and political dimensions to the reform. From an institutional perspective, education is seen as a system "structured by elements such as curriculum regulations, instructional resources, school structure and buildings, governance, staff, assessments and funding"

(Reimers, 2020, p. 35). The CBC reform in Kenya certainly attempts to make multiple such systemic shifts including through re-tooling of teachers and head teachers, providing new learning resources, and infrastructural developments. Similarly, from a political perspective, the reform seeks to negotiate the interests of various groups and resolve conflicts during the design and implementation of a reform (Reimers, 2020, p. 23). As described, the design and implementation process of Kenya's reform brought together a multitude of politically and technically relevant stakeholders, incorporating their interests and perspectives into the reform. Despite the relevance of these other perspectives to the reform process however, we find that an examination of Kenya's reform process from the cultural perspective to be most illuminating given the long-term significant cultural shifts necessary to fulfil the reform's theory of change.

With this framing in mind, we turn now to an examination of implementation challenges that have arisen thus far. Given the ambitious scope and long-term outlook of Kenya's education reforms, it is perhaps unsurprising that implementation has encountered an equally wide scope of challenges to date. Broadly, these challenges can be organized into three areas: mindset challenges, capacity challenges, and challenges related to the timeline of implementation. While some of these challenges may be unavoidable for any large-scale educational reform of this nature, we believe that many of them stem more directly from the attempt to implement curriculum and structural reforms simultaneously. In doing so, Kenya faces the difficult task of initiating far reaching long-term shifts in the fundamental culture of education while simultaneously balancing more immediate infrastructural and logistical needs.

6.6.2   Mindset Challenges

Among the perhaps unavoidable challenges with a reform of this type was what many interview participants described as a general "resistance to change." A number of teachers, school leaders, and government officials all identified this resistance to change amongst both parents and teachers as the chief source of opposition to the CBC reforms. The previous 8-4-4 system had been in place since 1985, and was therefore the primary system experienced by many stakeholders.

In particular, the elimination of the high-stakes KCPE exam as the placement tool into secondary schools was the focus of significant opposition. Competitive, high-stakes exams were considered an indispensable part of Kenya's educational system. One ongoing challenge faced by the MoE, therefore, is to reduce the prominence placed on high-stakes exams in the country's cultural mindset. Due to their standardized nature, such exams are considered equalizers, offering all students a theoretically equal shot at being accepted into prestigious national secondary schools regardless of background. Many specifically feared that widespread corruption, tribalism, and a general lack of integrity would distort the secondary school placement process in the absence of the KCPE as an objective measure. On the other hand, despite their benefits, high-stakes exams were also acknowledged as a source of both significant anxiety for students and of frequent cheating. However, many teachers and school leaders were unable to envision viable alternate solutions for student placement. Such fears may have been exacerbated by the fact that as of January 2020, no decision had been made about what placement process would be followed starting in 2023. In the absence of an official direction, the process of mentally adapting to a new placement system could not begin, and concerns persisted amid this uncertainty. Apart from the question of exams, additional resistance to change centered on resistance to the general philosophy of "student-centered learning" and emphasis on formative assessment embodied by the new curriculum. While widespread, many believed that this resistance would be naturally overcome with time as both teachers and parents adapt and become more comfortable with these new elements.

6.6.3 Capacity Challenges

In addition to the need for changing cultural mindsets, a second widely identified challenge facing the reform was an anticipated insufficient capacity for the number of learners in the system in terms of both school infrastructure and human resources. Of course, the high student-teacher ratios in some parts of Kenya are not a result of the current reforms but have been a longstanding concern for the country as access to basic education was widely expanded, compounded by natural population growth and persistent understaffing of teachers.

However, there are several aspects of the reforms which are predicted to – or already have – put additional strain on the existing conditions. First is the commitment to the 100% primary to secondary transition policy, as previously discussed. The impacts of the policy had already been clearly felt by secondary schools as of the beginning of the 2020 school year as incoming classes of Form One (grade nine) students exceeded previous enrollment rates and placed significant strain on existing facilities. Second, the learner-centered pedagogical and continuous assessment strategies at the center of the new curriculum necessitate a more individualized approach to teaching. While many teachers recognized the educational benefits of such an approach, they also identified it as highly time-consuming and difficult to implement in large classes (Oduor, 2020a, 2020b). Designing, administering, and marking regular formative assessments was noted as particularly challenging with the existing student-teacher ratios. In recognition of these concerns, the MoE has identified potential decreases in quality of education – particularly with the goal of 100% transition – as one of its top priorities to address during the reform implementation process.

In addition to these ongoing capacity concerns, the structural component of the reform and the introduction of a junior secondary level creates entirely new challenges for secondary schools in particular. As announced by President Uhuru Kenyatta in August 2019, the government has directed that students in junior secondary grades will be housed in secondary school facilities (Nyaundi, 2019). As a result, those facilities will experience a double-intake of students starting in 2023 when the structural reform goes into effect. In that year, secondary schools will admit both the normal class of Form One students as well as incoming grade seven students (under the current plan, grade eight students in 2023 will remain at primary schools to finish out the 8-4-4 cycle). Eventually, once all grades have transitioned, there is a possibility that some facilities would house exclusively junior secondary students (grades seven through nine) and some senior secondary (grades ten through twelve). However, until facilities have been prepared for such restructuring, current secondary schools anticipate needing to accommodate two additional grades worth of students during the first few years of the transition. Accommodation will require serious infrastructure expansion of both classroom and living spaces, already a pressing need at many schools with the existing enrollment. Teachers will also need to be reallocated from primary to secondary schools to follow the shifting classes, an additional logistical hurdle as teacher certification requirements for the two levels differed as of the start of the reform. School leaders also expressed some concerns with integrating younger ages into secondary school bodies, particularly at boarding schools: staff anticipated the possibility of increased bullying and a potential need to hire additional caretaking staff for younger, less mature students.

In addition, the reform's introduction of three specialized pathways for senior secondary schools will carry its own capacity challenges for both infrastructure and human resources beyond those described above. Depending on which pathways are designated for individual schools to offer, many will need to add or expand specialized facilities in order to do so. While pathways will be matched to schools partially based on existing facilities, the reform's increased emphasis on "non-academic" learning areas such as TVET and the arts will necessitate an increased number of performing arts spaces, laboratories, and TVET facilities regardless. Staffing challenges are also anticipated with the introduction of the pathways, particularly for areas with few qualified teachers such as the arts and foreign languages.

As of January 2020, it had yet to be determined how many of the specifics of the structural reform would be carried out: how students would be placed into junior secondary schools (and therefore what the capacity needs at each individual school would be), which pathways would be offered at each senior secondary school and how they would be staffed, and which infrastructure projects would be planned and funded. All of these are complex and weighty decisions currently faced by the MoE, and, therefore, constitute a significant challenge at this point in the reform implementation process. In the meantime, secondary school leaders are left unable to begin preparations to meet the anticipated capacity demands, and many identified this lack of official directive as their top concern approaching 2023, particularly given the long timeframe that would be required for such intensive adjustments.

6.6.4   Timeline Challenges

Considering the long-term scope and the ambitious aims of the educational reforms in Kenya, a substantive roll-out period was necessary to phase in various stages of reforms. Even with a lengthy transition process, however, many teachers and other school staff across Kenya expressed concerns that the implementation was being rushed, particularly with its "re-tooling" of teachers. In part, concerns stemmed from the fact that each grade's curriculum designs were developed by KICD just one year in advance, and training materials and other resources could not be made available until each year's curriculum was complete. While waiting, teachers and schools were unable to begin to prepare themselves in advance despite believing that a lengthier preparation time would be necessary to implement the new curriculum with fidelity.

In addition, the simultaneous use of both the prior 8-4-4 system and new CBC system during this lengthy transition phase generated a number of difficulties. At the systems level, it was decided that teacher training institutions would continue to prepare teacher candidates to follow the 8-4-4 curriculum up until September 2020, although no new teacher trainees were admitted in 2019. The new class admitted in 2020 would then be the first to receive initial certification following the CBC. As younger grades had begun following the CBC starting in 2018, a consequence of this decision was several years of mismatch between teacher preparation and classroom needs, and a delay before schools would be able to fill positions with CBC-trained teachers. At the school level, a similar difficulty was encountered in 2020 when the CBC reached grade four. While younger grades are taught all subjects by a single teacher, starting in grade four teachers are generally subject-specific and teach older grades as well. Grade four teachers would therefore begin teaching some classes with the CBC and the new pedagogy while continuing to teach the remainder of their classes following the old curriculum until the CBC was fully rolled-out to upper primary grades as well. Several teachers described the challenges of switching back and forth throughout the school day and needing to divide their efforts and preparation time between the two systems. While these challenges will be resolved once transition has been completed in primary schools, in the meantime successful adoption of the new pedagogical strategies will continue to be hindered in the absence of full focus from teachers.

Finally, it had also been decided that while 2023 would be the first year of the structural reform from 8-4-4 to 2-6-3-3, students in grades eight and above that year would continue to follow the old system until it was fully phased out. In practice, this means that while the seventh grade cohort of 2023 will begin attending secondary rather than primary schools, the eighth grade cohort will likely remain at primary schools under the current plans. Similarly, the student populations of secondary schools may then become a combination of students placed there based on KCPE results under the old system, and students placed in the new, as of yet undetermined, method.

6.7   Conclusion

Kenya's curriculum reform is one that relies heavily on significant cultural shifts, calling for changes in mindsets towards education at multiple levels; parents, teachers, and even employers. This will by necessity be a long-term process. As Reimers emphasizes, "[the] cultural perspective underscores the need for relatively long cycles of reform" (p. 26, 2020). As Kenya's reforms are still in an early stage of this extended cycle, specific outcomes cannot be analyzed just yet. There are reasons for Kenya to be hopeful, however. Despite the significant challenges facing the implementation process as detailed above, many schools expressed optimism regarding the changes. With some exceptions, the general feeling as of early 2020 was a firm belief in the merits of the CBC. Most criticism was aimed towards an implementation process which was seen as rushed and insufficient, particularly towards the teacher training process (Nyamai, 2020), with the overall content and underlying theory of the reforms meeting wider approval.

On the other hand, while many schools and teachers have faithfully adapted their behaviors in alignment with the new curriculum and teaching methods, these behavioral changes have yet to be followed by the hoped-for changes in belief itself. Indeed, many of the current changes as a result of the reforms to date could be characterized as technical rather than adaptive change. One teacher, for example, when asked what had changed most in her classroom as a result of the reforms, saw terminological changes as most significant referring now to "assessments" rather than "exams", or "strands" rather than "topics." It remains to be seen at this point whether the corresponding changes in belief will eventually be realized at the national level.

Also remaining to be seen is whether the many logistical challenges facing the implementation process will be overcome. Given that the reform's most significant impacts for schools are still to come – the restructuring of secondary schools and redistribution of students and teachers – the concerns over a rushed implementation process must be taken seriously. It will be critical for those concerns to be addressed to allow for sufficient preparation time in order for later stages of implementation to succeed. Kenya currently faces the unique task of managing dual processes of long-term cultural shifts in beliefs called for by its curriculum reform as well as the short to medium term logistical challenges presented by the structural aspect of the CBC reform. If this difficult balancing act can be achieved, however, the impact on education across Kenya has the potential to be considerable and lasting.

References

Barchok, H. (2019, June 11). Four technical queries on CBC system. *Daily Nation.* https://www.nation.co.ke/oped/opinion/Four-technical-queries-on-competency-based-curriculum/440808-5151994-i1nd4bz/index.html

Ji, L., & Kabita Njeng'ere, D. (2017). *The why, what and how of competency-based curriculum reforms: The Kenyan experience.* UNESCO International Bureau of Education. Retrieved from https://unesdoc.unesco.org/ark:/48223/pf0000250431

Kenya Institute of Curriculum Development. (2017). *Basic education curriculum framework.* Retrieved from https://kicd.ac.ke/wp-content/uploads/2017/10/CURRICULUMFRAMEWORK.pdf

Kenya Institute of Curriculum Development. (2018, January). *Report on competence based curriculum activities.* Presented at The National Steering Committee. Retrieved from https://kicd.ac.ke/news/presentation-on-competency-based-curriculum-activities/

Kenya Institute of Curriculum Development. (2019). *Competency based curriculum course – Elimika LMS.* Retrieved February 20, 2020. https://elimika.kec.ac.ke/course/cbc-online-training/

Ministry of Education, Science and Technology. (2014a). *Basic education statistical booklet: Kenya Institute of Curriculum Development.* Retrieved from https://kicd.ac.ke/curriculum-reform/basic-education-statistical-booklet/

Ministry of Education, Science and Technology. (2014b, March). *Volume one: Basic education programme rationale and approach 2013/2014-2017/2018.* Retrieved October 2, 2019, from Kenya National Education Sector Plan website: https://www.globalpartnership.org/content/education-sector-plan-2013-2018-kenya

Nyamai, F. (2020, January 4). Teacher crisis: Are schools ready for Grade 4? *Daily Nation.* https://www.nation.co.ke/news/education/Are-schools-ready-for-Grade-4-/2643604-5406530-557dcg/index.html

Nyaundi, L. (2019, August 17). End of KCPE exams in new curriculum implementation roadmap. *The Star.* Retrieved from https://www.the-star.co.ke/

Oduor, A. (2020a, February 17). A year later, teachers yet to master new system. *The Standard.* https://www.standardmedia.co.ke/article/2001360714/a-year-later-teachers-yet-to-master-new-system

Oduor, A. (2020b, February 17). Why you're paying more under new curriculum. *The Standard.* Retrieved February 18, 2020, from https://www.standardmedia.co.ke/article/2001360715/why-you-re-paying-more-under-new-curriculum

Owiti, N., & Kamau, C. (2019, July 28). Education: Teachers want sensitisation of parents on CBC fast-tracked. *K24 TV.* https://www.k24tv.co.ke/news/education-teachers-want-sensitisation-of-parents-on-cbc-fast-tracked-4516/

Reimers, F. M. (2020). *Audacious education purposes: How governments transform the goals of education systems.* Cham: Springer.

UNESCO Institute of Statistics. (2000). *World Bank Indicators.* School enrollment (% net). Retrieved February 18, 2020, from https://data.worldbank.org/indicator/SE.SEC.NENR?display=graph%2D%2D%3E&locations=KE

UNESCO Institute of Statistics. (2016). *Progression to secondary school (%) – Sub-Saharan Africa (excluding high income) | Data.* Retrieved October 3, 2019, from World Bank Indicators website: https://data.worldbank.org/indicator/SE.SEC.PROG.ZS?locations=ZF

UNESCO Institute of Statistics. (2019). *Unemployment, total (% of total labor force) (modeled ILO estimate) – Kenya | Data.* Retrieved February 18, 2020, from https://data.worldbank.org/indicator/SL.UEM.TOTL.ZS?locations=KE

Wanjohi, A. M. (2011). *Development of Education System in Kenya since Independence.* KENPRO Online Papers Portal. Available online at www.kenpro.org/papers/education-system-kenya-independence.htm

Jeļena Fomiškina is an Ed.M graduate in International Education Policy at the Harvard Graduate School of Education with a focus on language policy and education in emergencies. Starting her career as a management consultant, she has advised corporate and government clients in the United States, United Kingdom, and the Falkland Islands. Since 2015, she has led an educational non-profit representing United World Colleges (UWC) in Latvia. In 2019, Jelena was appointed to serve on the UWC International Council.

Eve Woogen is a 2020 graduate from the International Education Policy program at the Harvard Graduate School of Education with a focus on language education policy and education in emergencies. She has a background in multilingual education, and since 2013 has worked at the district-level with Minneapolis Public Schools coordinating English Language Learner services.

Ama Peiris is an Ed.M graduate in International Education Policy at the Harvard Graduate School of Education. She previously worked as an Adviser and Research Officer at the Permanent Mission of Sri Lanka to the United Nations, where she focused on issues within the Economic and Financial Committee of the UN General Assembly. She is interested in education policy in conflict contexts and for post-conflict reconciliation.

Somaia Abdulrazzak is a Ed.M. graduate in the International Education Policy Program at the Harvard Graduate School of Education '20. She has a BS degree in Business Administration from the United Arab Emirates. Her work experience was primarily in education management corporations in the private sector with a focus on teachers' development and empowerment. Somaia is also interested in refugee education and education in conflict zones and emergencies in the Middle East.

Emma Cameron is an Ed.M graduate in International Education Policy at the Harvard Graduate School of Education. She has over 8 years of experience working in education both in the United States and abroad, the majority of which she has spent inside the classroom. Most recently, she served as an education specialist for the United States' Peace Corps in Rwanda, where she taught English at a rural secondary school, in addition to designing and implementing grassroots educational initiatives to address community challenges like gender equality, reproductive health, and disease prevention. Since graduating from Harvard, Emma has been working as a consultant for the World Bank and the Education Commission. Emma's current research interests are centered around the intersection of educational access, gender, and culture within different international contexts.

Chapter 7
From Content Knowledge to Competencies and Exams to Exit Profiles: Education Reform in Zimbabwe

Djénéba Gory, Jayanti Bhatia, and Venkatesh Reddy Mallapu Reddy

7.1 Introduction

The post-colonial era of the 1980s was marked with significant progress in Zimbabwe's education reform and policies. From making public schooling available for all to working on teacher training, the country seemed to be on the right track and was setting an example for other African nations. These remarkable efforts were praised by multilateral organizations such as UNESCO and UNICEF (UNICEF News Note, 2009). However, by the early 2000s amidst the political, economic, and financial crisis of hyperinflation, the tides turned in the opposite direction. The education system failed to keep pace and Zimbabwean students started struggling to meet the demands of the labor market. The political cadre in Zimbabwe saw the need for an ambitious education reform that could serve all children, and at the same time, held the potential to pull the country out of the turmoil and thereby pave Zimbabwe's way forward to economic development.

With this in mind, the government of Zimbabwe started working on enhancing the quality of education by shifting from content knowledge to competency oriented curriculum. The Ministry of Primary and Secondary Education (MoPSE) started developing the *Zimbabwe Curriculum Framework (ZCF)* in 2014. It was developed and finalized in 2015 and its phased implementation commenced in 2017. The framework provides a comprehensive plan (2015–22) for a rapid and sustainable transformation of Zimbabwe's education system. While Kenya's reform (Chap. 6) was ambitious in introducing both the curriculum and structural changes, Zimbabwe's reform focused mainly on curriculum. Everything else moved around

D. Gory
Harvard Kennedy School, Cambridge, MA, USA

J. Bhatia (✉) · V. R. M. Reddy
International Education Policy, Harvard Graduate School of Education,
Cambridge, MA, USA

© The Author(s) 2021
F. M. Reimers (ed.), *Implementing Deeper Learning and 21st Century Education Reforms*, https://doi.org/10.1007/978-3-030-57039-2_7

the curriculum and was an attempt of a systemic alignment to help implement the new curriculum. Additionally, analyzing the reform from Reimers' five frames theory on educational change (Reimers, 2020), we found that Zimbabwe's education reform was implemented addressing elements of each of the five perspectives. We argue, however, that when these perspectives are not adequately addressed, they present critical challenges in the success of the envisioned reform.

As of early 2020, the reform implementation is in its last leg and this chapter examines the progress to date. It begins with an overview of the country's education system and conditions that shaped the reform, followed by a more detailed description of the reform, its theory of change, and implementation timeline. It then analyzes the reform stages through the five perspectives of educational change (Reimers, 2020). The chapter concludes by presenting the results and challenges at the time of writing. All information unless otherwise cited has been obtained either from the Ministry of Primary and Secondary Education (MoPSE) or through several interviews and focus groups conducted during in-country research in January 2020. The references section provides more details under "In-Country Research" (2020).

a. Interviews were conducted with 52 officials from 6 departments of MoPSE – Curriculum Development and Technical Services Department; Human Resources and Discipline Department; Primary, Secondary and Non-Formal Education Department; Procurement Management and Business Development Unit; Centre of Education, Research, Innovation and Development; Finance Department.
b. Zimbabwe School Examinations Council (ZIMSEC); Zimbabwe Early Learning Assessments Team (ZELA); South East African Council for Monitoring Educational Quality (SEACMEQ).
c. Education Coordination Group partners such as World Bank, UNICEF, UNESCO, CSOs.
d. Textbook Publishers.
e. Provincial Education Directors, District School Inspectors, National Association of Primary School Heads and, National Association of Secondary School Heads.
f. Additionally, we held individual and focus group interviews in 7 schools in 3 out of 9 provinces in Zimbabwe where we interviewed 32 School Heads, 70 Teachers, 36 Parents and 38 Students.

7.2 Country Context

7.2.1 Zimbabwe's Education System

According to UNESCO (2017) figures, Zimbabwe has a young population, with 42% under the age of 14 (6.1 million of a total 14.4 million). Figure 7.1 shows the school-age population by level of education. Figure 7.2 further shows the widespread distribution of school types across primary (P) and secondary (S) grades. The vast majority of schools are rural and government-owned. In terms of literacy rate,

LEVEL	AGE GROUP (YEARS)	TOTAL POPULATION	ENROLLED POPULATION	PROPORTION ENROLLED
Preschool/pre-primary (ECD A-ECD B)	4-5	984,659	623,981	63%
Primary (P1-P7)	6-12	3,028,319	2,676,485	88%
Secondary (S1-S6)	13-18	2,146,723	1,075,325	50%
Total:	-	**6,159,701**	**4,375,791**	**71%**

Fig. 7.1 Zimbabwe's primary and secondary school enrolment (2017)
Source: UNESCO Institute of Statistics (http://uis.unesco.org/en/country/zw) Annual Statistical Digest (EMIS, 2017)

	PRIMARY (N)	PRIMARY (%)	SECONDARY (N)	SECONDARY (%)
Urban (P1/S1)	234	4%	205	7%
Semi-urban (P2/S2)	486	8%	336	12%
Rural (P3/S3)	5,403	88%	2,289	81%
Registered	5,107	83%	1,991	70%
Satellite	1,016	17%	839	30%
Government-owned	5,260	86%	2141	76%
Non-government-owned	863	14%	689	24%
Total schools	**6,123**	-	**2,830**	-

Fig. 7.2 Zimbabwe's school categories by demography, registry, and funding management
Source: Education Sector Analysis (2015)

which Zimbabwe defines as completion of at least Grade 3 for the population aged 15 and above, the country stands at 88.69% compared to 63.49% for Sub-Saharan Africa according to a World Bank report (World Bank, 2014). This is one of the highest adult literacy rates in Africa. According to the 2015 Zimbabwe Demographic and Health Survey data 73% of women and 77% of men aged 15–49 have also attended or completed secondary school or higher (Demographic and Health Survey, 2016).

However, despite the high literacy rate, Zimbabwe's education system was not adequately preparing students for life and labor market demands. Like many other former colonies, the system was designed based on the British system. Zimbabwe tried to add an additional year by addition of Grade 13 vis-à-vis Form 6, so as to increase the probability of all students closing their learning gaps because of an added school year. As depicted in Fig. 7.3, Zimbabwe's school system now comprises 4 years of infant education (including 2 years of early childhood education (ECE) and 2 years of formal primary), 5 years of junior education (ending in Grade 7 examinations), and 6 years of secondary school, with three sets of state exams at Grades 7, 11 (O Level) and 13 (A Level). Students progress automatically from one grade to the next until Grade 7. During the first half of Grade 3, a sample of students also take the Zimbabwe Early Learning Assessment (ZELA) that examines their Grade 2 competencies and generates evidence to help improve learning. All national examinations are set by the Zimbabwe School Examinations Council (ZIMSEC).

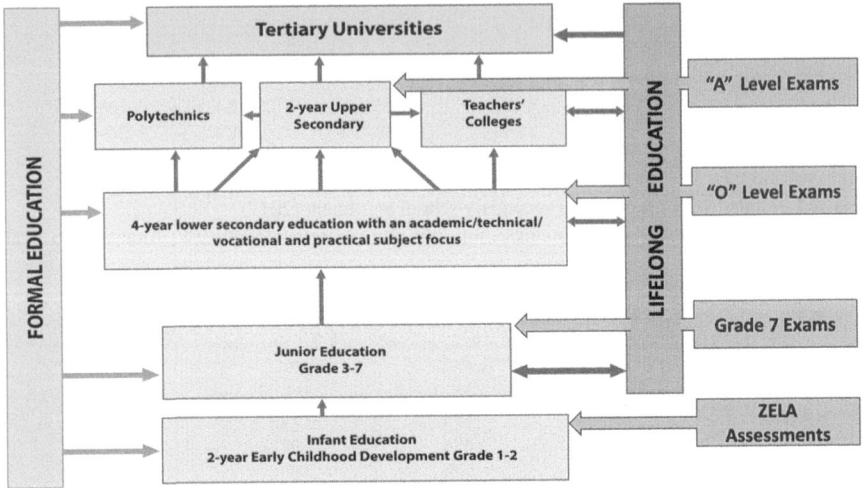

Fig. 7.3 Zimbabwe's education system
Source: Education Sector Strategic Plan (2016–20). Modified to highlight the exam and assessment levels

7.2.2 Conditions that Shaped the Reform

While the data above gives us a snapshot in time, it is also essential to know the numerous conditions that directly or indirectly shaped the reform. A country's education system does not sit in a vacuum but is rather situated within a complex web of economic, political, and financial spheres among others. Zimbabwe has been experiencing volatile conditions since over a decade. First, numerous ordeals, including cash shortages, fiscal deficits, unsustainable external debt arrears, unemployment, poverty and poor provision of social services, among other factors characterize the economic state of Zimbabwe (Universalia, 2019, p. 28). Second, in 2008, the country underwent a serious economic shock that was characterized by hyperinflation, collapse of living standards, and loss of international confidence (Universalia, 2019, p. 28). The hyperinflation has been continuing to date and the country suffered a currency crisis in 2018–19.[1] Third, on the political front, the 37-year president, Robert Mugabe, resigned amid threats of impeachment charges in 2017. All this halted and arguably even reversed the educational progress that the country had made in the post-colonial period between 1980s and 2000s.

These conditions additionally posed a barrier to some of the earlier attempts to address the educational challenges of Zimbabwe and thus further aggravated the gaps and challenges. One such significant attempt was made in 1999, by the then

[1]Inflation rates were at peak in mid-2000s, and while the World Bank does not have data for this peak period, Zimbabwe's central bank reported it at just under 80 billion % in mid-November 2008. Post this peak, the central bank stopped reporting monthly statistics.

president of the republic of Zimbabwe, Robert Mugabe. He assigned the *Commission of Inquiry into Education and Training (CIET)* to look into the structure and content of education for diagnosing the problems that were affecting the system because of phenomenal expansion. Following nation-wide consultations and international study trips, the team produced an invaluable report called the *Nziramasanga Report*. The country, however, could not act much on this for almost 15 years, because of fiscal constraints.

Like any other government or organization, faced with a similar challenge, the government of Zimbabwe had two options to overcome it during the 2010s. First was to act with urgency and opt for a full-fledged systemic overhaul in one go and second was to opt for a Singapore-like more gradual approach of ensuring implementation quality in one component of the reform before proceeding to the next. Zimbabwe chose the former i.e., a full-fledged reform from 2015 to 2022 that was phased out by grade-level to allow logistical and operational efficiency. However, planning is an oxymoron in such volatile conditions, especially amidst the financial crisis when it is hard to estimate what resources will be available. But does this mean that countries should put education in the backburner during such a crisis? Zimbabwe chose not to and worked hard to bring in a socio-economic transformation vision called *Zimbabwe Agenda for Sustainable Socio-Economic Transformation (ZimASSET)* which was a medium term 5-year plan for the country's economic reform and all-round growth (ZimASSET, 2015). Recognizing that the 15 years following the 1999 CIET Report had brought in various changes on the national landscape along with a global movement of the Information and Communication Technology (ICT), the blueprint underscored the need for a curriculum review albeit using CIET as a springboard. The goal was to reform the curriculum to develop students who would be prepared to navigate the evolving demands of the twenty-first-century.

A nationwide curriculum review process thus began in 2013 and was formally launched in October 2014. This process involved a nationwide consultation and culminated in the creation of the *Narrative Report* 2014–2015. This was followed by the approval of the new curriculum in 2015 and led to the creation of the *Zimbabwe Curriculum Framework (ZCF)* for Primary and Secondary Education (2015–22). During implementation, when finances went out of control, rather than abandoning the reform, the government chose to adjust the plan and continued moving forward, thereby ensuring continued progress even if it came at the cost of reduced quality and accountability in a few places.

Additionally, it is worth noting that the Global Partnership for Education (GPE) played a key role in supporting Zimbabwe's efforts of curriculum reform. GPE not only brought in the international aid to support all the reforms, but also helped shape the reform agenda through the Education Coordination Group (ECG)[2] which

---

[2] The national forum for multi-party stakeholder engagement in the Education Sector Strategic Plan (ESSP), consisting of the Ministry (MoPSE), Ministry of Finance and Economic Development (MoFED), Ministry of Higher and Tertiary Education, Science and Technology Development (MoHTESTD), World Bank (WB), UNICEF, UNESCO, Global Partnership for Education (GPE),

consists of International donor partners. While the reforms were planned and implemented primarily by the government and its associated ministry (MoPSE), the development of the reform itself was influenced by the ideas and technical expertise from GPE and other partners such as UNESCO, UNICEF, DFiD and ACER (ESSP, 2016). The focus on twenty-first-century skills, competencies, and Science, Technology, Engineering, Arts and Mathematics (STEAM) evolved from the global agenda[3] across the world for re-aligning education systems to twenty-first-century skill based curriculum and STEM education. This ultimately influenced the redesign of the curriculum and the development of learning areas and syllabus.

7.3   The Reform and its Theory of Change

As discussed thus far, the recommendations of the *Narrative Report* along with the ones from the earlier *Nziramasanga Report*, formed the basis for the *Zimbabwe Curriculum Framework (ZCF)* for Primary and Secondary Education (2015–2022). The Ministry of Primary and Secondary Education (MoPSE) recognized the need to shift the emphasis from content knowledge mastery to higher-order thinking skills and competencies. Several new learning areas were added to drive this shift. According to the ZCF document the goals of the reform were to (a) promote and cherish the Zimbabwean identity, (b) prepare learners for life and work in a largely agro-based economy and an increasingly globalized and competitive environment, (c) foster life-long learning in line with the opportunities and challenges of the knowledge society, (d) prepare learners for participatory citizenship, peace and sustainable development, and (e) prepare and orient learners for participation, leadership and voluntary service.

The theory of change, in particular, was that, if the curriculum is entirely overhauled from an outdated focus on knowledge transmission to focusing on the development of twenty-first-century skills and competencies, and if it is scaffolded by the provision of the updated syllabus and learning materials along with trained teachers to deliver the new curriculum, then the classroom experience and learning outcomes would advance for all students in the short-term. In the medium-term, students would achieve the desired exit profiles as defined in the new ZCF, and in the long-term, they would ultimately be able to meet the economy and labor market demands. Students would thus be better equipped to contribute to the country's socio-economic transformation.

The new curriculum supports students to build a strong scientific and technological mindset and to prepare them for the evolving needs of the twenty-first-century.

DFiD, and Civil Society Organizations (CSOs such as CAMFED and ECOZI) were named part of the Education Coordination Group (ECG).

[3] Finland, Singapore, Ghana had already implemented a twenty-first-century Competency-based Curriculum and began performing well on PISA scores which influenced the adoption of such curriculums across the world and Countries started redesigning so as to catch up to them.

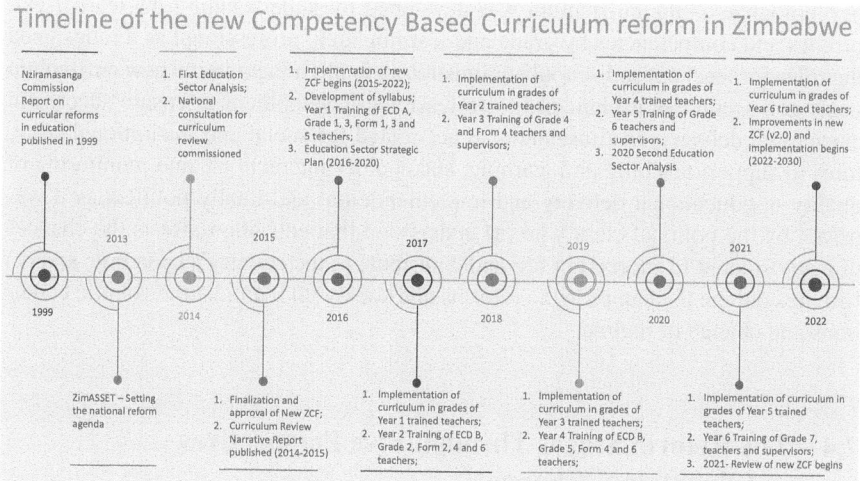

Fig. 7.4 Timeline of the new competency based curriculum reform in Zimbabwe
Source: Created by the authors (2020)

It has elements of adoption of a philosophical approach Ubuntu/Unhu/Vumunhu (i.e., self-respect and respect for others) along with an emphasis on STEAM and Information and Communication Technology (ICT). Additionally, humanities, agriculture, technical/vocational business, and commercial fields among other crosscutting themes such as civic, environment, finance, human rights, health, HIV/AIDS, climate change, and disaster risk reduction encompass a holistic education. The introduction of life-skills orientation programme (LOP), continuous assessments, and learner exit profiles are some of the other key features of the new framework.

As illustrated in Fig. 7.4 the implementation of the new curriculum started in 2017 with the plan to be phased in until 2022 as the first batch progresses from one grade to the next. To ensure a successful roll-out, MoPSE developed school packages in the form of CDs which contained the new curriculum framework document, the newly developed syllabi, and the continuous assessment tasks to be used by the teachers. Our field visits established that while few schools received these packages, others were still awaiting the materials.

Further on, as re-emphasized throughout the book, five main perspectives can be deployed to design and implement educational reforms: cultural, psychological, professional, institutional, and political (Reimers, 2020). We found that while certain perspectives outweighed others, all these collectively framed Zimbabwe's curriculum reform. The reform was cultural in terms of (a) government's attempt to incorporate voices of various stakeholders throughout the planning and implementation process, and (b) parents' understanding of the importance of education that drove their financial contribution even though they could hardly afford schooling;

psychological as the curriculum was developed by understanding the learner exit profiles and competencies by grade and learning area; professional as it redesigned the roles for teachers and school administrators to align them to the new curriculum goals and second as it planned for professional development to ensure successful curriculum delivery; institutional as it accounted for social and institutional structures to support teaching and learning, stakeholder interactions, and monitoring of quality of educational delivery and implementation; and finally political as it was driven by the political class who (a) understood that education affects the chances of every student to succeed in life and contribute to the country's economy, and (b) had the courage to champion the reforms and stick with it amidst the volatile conditions and change of regime.

7.4   The Reform Stages Through Five Perspectives of Educational Change

Zimbabwe's Education Sector Strategic Plan (ESSP), developed in 2016 with the technical and funding support of the Global Partnership for Education (GPE), aimed at providing appropriate coordination and phasing of all the required inputs for the best-in-class learning experience for all students. ESSP provides clear goals, describes the processes, and sets the agenda for regular monitoring of progress and timely adjustment if needed. ESSP laid out the following stages for educational development for the ministry to achieve its intended objectives – Development of the new competency-based curriculum (ZCF) and syllabus; professional capacity development on the interpretation and delivery of the new curriculum; preparation and availability of new learning materials such as student textbooks, teaching guides, science kits, and ICT and Science labs; and the introduction of continuous assessment. Followed by distribution of school packages to individual schools; continued professional upgrading and support for teachers; increased access to learning; right institutional architecture, great leadership, accountable management, efficient and effective resource utilization, and quality service delivery; EMIS/TMIS (Education/Teacher Management Information Systems) data reporting and collection systems along with bringing in research perspective to monitor and improve the delivery of services; improved learning environments; and finally increased equity (Universalia, 2018). These stages are explained below in detail and are analyzed using the five perspectives of educational change (Reimers, 2020).

7.4.1 Political Perspective

Reimers' political lens foregrounds how "education affects the interests of many different groups, and that those interests "may be in conflict" (Reimers, 2020). In the Zimbabwean context, the CIET commission and the blueprint for Socio-Economic Transformation of Zimbabwe (ZimASSET) were instituted by the government led by ZANU-PF and the country's former president Robert Mugabe. The government acknowledged that its economy was in a dire condition, and improving the economic conditions and bringing in growth and stability required multi-sectoral reforms. The same government was thus instrumental in starting the curricular reform in 2013, as they understood that education affects the chances of every student to succeed in life and thus positively impacts the country's economy. The government had the courage to champion the reform and stick with it amidst the volatile conditions and change of regime. The current president Emerson Mnangagwa was then the Vice-President and deputy to Robert Mugabe, and is continuing the implementation of the current reform.

On the one hand, as described in detail in Sect. 7.3.2, the ministry was able to involve the public to gather inputs on the kind of education and skills they desired for their children who would support their families and also the country's economy in the future, on the other hand, the ministry, however, did not continuously engage all stakeholders throughout the reform. Thus, not all teachers and parents were satisfied with the reform. The reform meant that teachers were not only expected to deliver the new curriculum and ensure that students had demonstrable competencies leading to exit profiles but also to assess students on these new competencies while the new assessment framework was delayed. All this was required of them using limited preparation through professional development training that focused more on the syllabus interpretation rather than delivery. Adding to the pressure were semi-annual performance assessments by the headmasters and district school inspectors (DSIs). These additional teacher duties arose during an economic crisis when inflation drastically eroded the value of teacher salaries from roughly 500 USD to 30 USD per month and they could no longer afford the education of their own children. The ensuing teacher strikes thus impeded the government efforts to change education. Additionally, a majority of the parents in semi-urban and rural areas could no longer afford their children's education as the annual school fees, purchase of new textbooks and associated workbooks to takes notes for the entire year for all learning areas exceeded their earnings, forcing them to take loans to sustain the education of their children. Parents who could not achieve this had to withdraw their children from school and were subsequently upset. The reform also translated into more effort and school time for teachers as well as students, where they now had to be in schools till around 4 PM rather than the initial 1 PM.

To navigate these differences, the government implemented a series of additional sub-reforms. First, in collaboration with ECG development partners, government schemes such as BEAM (Basic Education Assistance Module) and SIG (School Improvement Grants) were launched to support school enrollments and parental spending. BEAM prevents households from resorting to perverse coping mechanisms such as withdrawing children from school, in response to worsening household poverty, whereas SIG provides support to over 6000 P3 and satellite schools to provide textbooks, fee payment, and levies for vulnerable students.

Alongside this, the government initiated and finalized an amendment of the Education Act 2006, which guaranteed and protected every child's right to access and complete the basic education cycle. The same was adopted by the Constitution of Zimbabwe in 2013. This institutionalized the government's plan for having a national vision and goal for education within the Constitution, and was further used to bring in a host of associated educational policies to improve the quality of the education service across the country. Some of the many policies ranged from ICT for the education sector, school feeding, Inclusive Education, and Infant/Early Childhood policy to a policy for rationalizing School Development Committees and School Development Associations into a single entity and determining its aggregated responsibilities.

Lastly, though Zimbabwe was constricted in accessing international funding amidst sanctions from the United States ZIDERA 2001,[4] European Commission and the World Bank,[5] the government showed political will to implement this reform and managed to access funding from other international donors such as GPE, UNESCO, UNICEF, and DFiD through the GPE Fund and Education Development Fund (EDF). Additionally, the government managed to not only secure financial funding but also technical advisory expertise for planning and implementing the reform. It further managed to convince all the international donors and Civil Society Organizations (CSOs) to be a part of ECG, which participated in the reform design while MoPSE took the lead in planning and implementing the reform.

7.4.2 Cultural Perspective

The cultural perspective requires consideration of societal norms and values before undertaking the reform (Reimers, 2020). It considers what the society expects from schools or the education system in general and what the priorities are. This notion was considered throughout the planning and implementation phase in terms of incorporating voices of various stakeholders. To begin with, as part of the curriculum review process in 2013, the ministry had set up a nationwide consultation process involving technical working groups and held consultations across almost 20 platforms involving *"close to a million people (961,000) which included stakeholders like learners, parents, teachers, leaders in industry and commerce, farmers, church organizations, civil society, institutions of higher learning and government*

---

[4] Sanctions under the Zimbabwe Democracy and Economic Recovery Act of 2001 (ZIDERA) were renewed in 2018 for one more year till 2020 under the administration of President Donald Trump.

[5] Because of non-payment of dues amounting to 1.8 Billion USD (WB Zimbabwe Report).

ministries and departments. Furthermore, there was extensive media coverage which included advertorials, newscasts, features and interviews in all platforms" (Zimbabwe Curriculum Framework, 2015). The diverse perspectives allowed the MoPSE to ensure buy-in from relevant stakeholders and representatives of final beneficiaries, and more importantly, organizations and individuals who understood the needs of the labor market. As discussed earlier, this process culminated with the creation of the *Narrative Report* 2014–2015 (Narrative Report, 2014).

Additionally, the cultural perspective accounts to understand "a) how society values education and sees its relation to social purposes and values, b) how society views its teachers and learners, and c) how government involves its citizens in its reform agenda (Reimers, 2020)." In Zimbabwe, our meetings with the ministry officials and the focus group discussions with parents showed evidence that several parents saw education to be critical for their children's success in life, and for their socio-economic stability and upward mobility. This is evident when comparing government and parental spending on education. While the in-school expenditure of the ministry is close to about 950 Million Zimbabwean Dollars (ZWD), parental contribution on average is a little more at 1.2 Billion ZWD. In addition, some parents also annually donate anywhere between 150 and 500 ZWD to the school development committee (SDC) which helps sustain the improvement or management of the school infrastructure such as labs, various equipment, or other school facilities. This commitment signals a high-value and importance placed on education. It also signals that parents expect high returns for their children, expecting placement on the labor market. Overall, the total annual spending per child is anywhere between 2,400 and 6,000 dollars (ZWD) and covers school fees, uniforms, textbooks, stationery, and optional educational field trips.

Even though parents feel the economic hardships and their limited salaries do not meet the annual school expenses, many of them still sustain their children's education by taking loans as they view education as a key to their emancipation. In Zimbabwean society, parents highly value teachers and school principals. They listen to the teachers and school principals to cultivate a partnership of building their child's future through education. Some parents meet with teachers three times a year to understand their child's performance and learning gaps and to understand ways of collaboration with schools to improve learning outcomes. They build learning supports at home, based on the advice of their child's class teacher. When needed, some parents reported that they go the extra mile to provide for educational trips of their children which teachers say are critical for learning even if this means toiling hard by performing additional work to earn the required money.

7.4.3   Psychological Perspective

The psychological perspective requires us to consider the core questions of "what and when should students learn, how can students be supported in their learning, what and how should teachers teach, and how can teachers be supported to learn so that they can teach effectively (Reimers, 2020, p. 12)." To successfully implement the curriculum reform, the ministry re-imagined the learner profiles of students exiting the school system and aligned them with the demands of a twenty-first-century skills-driven workforce and economy by introducing new learning areas. The learner exit profiles are illustrated in Fig. 7.5 and draw upon from other high-performing education systems. The focus on Knowledge, Attitudes, and Skills is in line with the widely used CASEL framework of social and emotional competencies or the twenty-first-century skills (CASEL, 2017), whereas values and national identity account for the local context. These together encompass a wide range of learning areas ranging from Science, Technology, Engineering, Arts and Mathematics (STEAM), civic education, leadership, and innovation to vocational skills. Teaching of practical subjects such as Agriculture and Science along with vocational skills was envisioned to provide the necessary different pathways for students that would prepare them to become an engine of economic growth.

Based on the intended exit profiles (Fig. 7.5), the ministry then developed learning outcomes that students should have at the end of each school level[6] (Infant: ECD to Grade 2; Primary: Grade 3 to Grade 7; Secondary: Form 1 to Form 4; Senior Secondary: Form 5 and 6). To meet the objectives set in the reform, two teams within the Curriculum Development and Technical Services (CTDS) department of MoPSE were in-charge of this demanding task of curriculum and syllabus development. To undertake the development of the new syllabus and ensure its alignment to the adopted curriculum, the team started by developing 104 syllabi – 8 infant, 11 junior, 41 lower, and 44 upper-secondary level. The syllabus team worked alongside the curriculum team to ensure the alignment between syllabus and curriculum. However, while the curriculum team produced only broad statements for end of school level learning outcomes, the syllabus team produced more detailed learning objectives by learning area specific subtopics at grade level to assist in classroom teaching.

Thus, although the syllabus presents considerable level of detail, the curriculum mainly shows more general objectives that are not specific to grade levels but rather to junior or senior categories in general. Though this discrepancy in granularity between the two points to a potential misalignment, the ministry has assured that the two have been aligned by its CDTS team. Our visits also highlighted that teachers primarily rely on the syllabi, so this potential misalignment does not constitute a major threat to learning outcomes.

Further, in line with the science of learning, which advocates for multiple instructional methods to accomplish varied learner outcomes, the curriculum framework advocates for varied teaching methods ranging from discovery, project-based, and problem-based to design-based for supporting student learning of twenty-first-century skills (Education Encyclopedia, n.d.). These are typical characteristics of a learner-centric approach with the teacher acting as a facilitator.

---

[6] The learning outcomes are outlined in Sect. 3.6 of Zimbabwe's Curriculum Framework document.

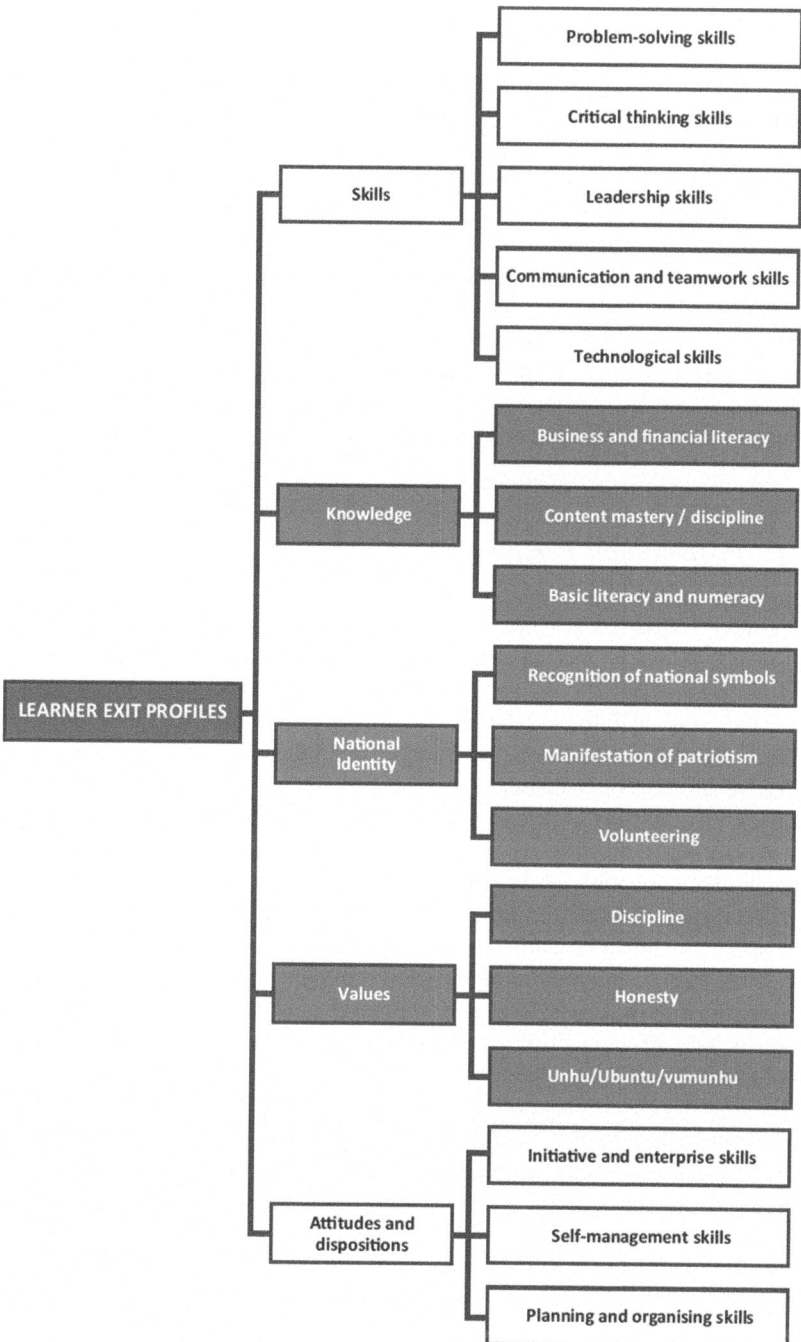

Fig. 7.5 Learner exit profiles
Source: Ministry of Primary and Secondary Education, Curriculum Framework Document (2015)

In terms of preparation and availability of learning materials to support student learning, the CDTS team was involved with the tendering, publishing, and distribution of textbooks while vetting their quality from multiple local publishers to ensure they are aligned with the syllabus and curricular requirements. MoPSE even considered the use of additional learning materials such as science kits. ECG partners supported MoPSE in the procurement and distribution of textbooks and science kits.

Alongside this, CDTS used the principles of science of teaching to design the teacher professional development experience for equipping teachers in their new role of a facilitator. It not only developed the content for the syllabus interpretation workshops but also undertook workshops for all trainers at all levels from provincial to district for delivering grade-level national teacher training workshops. It also produced teacher guides to support teachers in planning and delivering classroom instruction, especially for new learning areas. The professional perspective in the following section covers these aspects in detail.

7.4.4 *Professional Perspective*

The professional perspective requires us to consider the core questions of "rules about who can teach, what qualifications they need to have, how and when they could be employed, how could they be trained and developed professionally to deliver their responsibilities" (Reimers, 2020, p. 16). Professional development sets a foundation for in-classroom pedagogy and acts as a driver for change. As Zimbabwe shifted from a content knowledge to a competency-based curriculum, it was essential that the role of teachers also shifted from a content deliverer to facilitator of learning. This shift was crucial for the success of the curriculum reform and eventually for Zimbabwe's economy to bear the fruits of the hard work.

The ministry acknowledged this need and invested in teacher professional development to maintain and ensure the quality of teaching and instruction. Zimbabwe's Curriculum Framework thus defined a set of principles that must guide teaching and learning, and redesigned the roles of teaching staff to align them to the new curriculum goals. One of its positive aspects was the focus on not just teachers but also school heads.[7]

The ministry rolled out several measures to bring its teaching force up to speed with the curriculum reform and to be able to effectively use teaching methods such as discovery, project-based, problem-based, and design-based.

This shift in expectations, attitudes, and behaviours of the teaching workforce was considerable and challenging. The preparation of teachers thus began with the launch of the Teacher Capacity Development Programme in 2014, which aimed at (a) upgrading teachers' educational qualifications to effectively contribute to the

---

[7] A table describing the new roles of teachers and school heads under the CBC, as defined in the new curriculum framework is provided in Fig. 7.6.

The Teacher	The School Head
• Uses a wide range of methods adapted to the learner's situation and needs in the context of interactive pedagogies • Reinforces connections between learning areas and disciplines and promotes integrated learning • Is able to integrate cross-cutting issues, such liberation history as part of the struggle for human rights and education for participatory citizenship; peace education; education for sustainable development; gender equality • Possesses intercultural understanding; life skills; health education; economic and entrepreneurial education; media education; ICT and e-learning • Is interested and participates in the development of customized curricula and learning materials, as well as the establishment of flexible plans of study in compliance with the school autonomy principle • Possesses the capacity to identify learning problems and provide appropriate support • Is interested in progress and formative assessment with a view to providing guidance, counselling, motivation and support to learners • Communicates and integrates well with learners, parents and other stakeholders • Facilitates learning for learners and engages them in meaningful activities • Is interested and able to engage in teamwork and participates in communities of practice.	• Provides a learner-friendly, safe, pleasant and enabling learning environment • Involves stakeholders and education partners in school decisions • Provides for differentiated learning and choice in the context of a broad curriculum • Monitors continuous assessment and learner profiles • Provides for consistency across the school ("whole-school approach") in promoting learner-centred teaching in their establishment • Engages in school networking to promote exchanges on, and mutual learning from effective practices of learner-centred teaching and learning elsewhere • Supports school-based teacher in-service training and mentoring as a means to improve the teaching skills of staff by combining theoretical and practical aspects in real school life situations • Collaborates with stakeholders in crafting school vision and mission and strategies in sync with the Ministry direction. • Works in collaboration with stakeholders in designing a school development plan and accountability procedures during implementation • Pay special attention to implementing the principles and practices of inclusive education by taking into account and addressing diversity and the different learners' needs.

Fig. 7.6 New roles of teaching staff
Source: Ministry of Primary and Secondary Education, Zimbabwe Curriculum Framework (2015)

curriculum, and (b) addressing their technical and vocational training needs. Since then there have been continuous teacher capacity development efforts. At a high-level, the ministry focused on the dual approach of in-service training and teacher guides to equip its teachers in effective implementation of the new curriculum.

In Zimbabwe, in-service training comes under the purview of MoPSE. As per the ministry website (February, 2020) there are 127,091 teachers, Head of Departments, Deputy Heads, and Heads of school located in 8953 primary and secondary schools across Zimbabwe. The ministry planned for a phased training schedule, which was in-line with the phased curriculum roll-out. This meant that the teachers were trained a year before the curriculum was supposed to be rolled-out for their respective grades. This ensured all teachers were expected to be prepared before the curriculum roll-out (Fig. 7.4). Further details of the in-service training methodology have been covered under Sect. 7.4.2.

The second key component to equip teachers was the development and distribution of teacher guides to aid teachers in classroom instruction. It was believed that sharing of tangible resources such as reference documents would further benefit the teachers in the new curriculum implementation because they usually led independent classrooms without any external support or supervision. For effective classroom delivery, the ministry thus planned to publish teacher guides that would complement the pupil textbook. These are available for each learning area at grade level (infant, primary, and secondary), and cover topics ranging from syllabus interpretation, sample lesson plan, curriculum delivery, and assessment and evaluation to competency matrix. The guides are readily available on the ministry website and have hard copy versions to account for low internet penetration. While most of these materials have been distributed, there is evidence that some schools have been either missed out or have received insufficient quantities (Universalia, 2018).

Alongside in-service training and teacher guide publication, the ministry also focused on other essential teaching aspects such as (a) teacher recruitment to fill the vacancies, (b) reducing the pupil-teacher ratio (PTR) to increase classroom engagement, and (c) reassigning existing teachers who teach outside their areas of specialization, to teach in their areas of specialization. We do not have data on teacher recruitment and reassignment, but the PTR either stayed stagnant or increased between 2013 and 2017. At 12%, the highest increase was observed in ECD ratio whereas the secondary ratio remained static (Universalia, 2019, p. 97). While this is not a positive development, it is alleviated by the fact that pupil to trained teacher ratios (PTTRs) declined across all levels during the same period. Again at 43% decline, ECD observed the biggest improvement, whereas both primary and secondary observed a modest decline.

7.4.5 Institutional Perspective

The Institutional perspective requires us to consider the core questions of "how the social and institutional structures supported teaching and learning, how various stakeholders interact with each other, and how their quality of educational delivery and reform implementation was monitored at various levels (Reimers, 2020)." In addition to this, the perspective also considers how the federal and local governments are coordinating with other stakeholders in not only ensuring the reform implementation but also monitoring its quality. In the Zimbabwean context, we try to analyze this through three lenses (a) Coordination between Stakeholders (b) Alignment of monetary funding and spending, and (c) Assessment reforms and insights.

(a) ***Coordination between Stakeholders:*** The ZCF reform was not driven by the ministry alone, but rather involved several stakeholders. ECG is a crucial entity in this regard. It provides consultation and promotes dialogue between the government and its partners on the development of the education sector in Zimbabwe. The World Bank, UNICEF, UNESCO, and GPE contributed to the GPE Fund which supported the development of the new curriculum and the preparation of the Education Sector Strategic Plan (ESSP). Additionally, DFiD and KfW, a German state-owned development bank, contributed to the Education Development Fund (EDF) and additional educational programmes by funding CSO interventions. UNICEF is the grant agent for both these funds.

As seen earlier, the ministry also conducted nationwide consultations with nearly a million people during the development and finalization of the curriculum framework. Additionally, close to half a million people were consulted for gathering feedback and inputs about the ESSP development and implementation. The ECG met every 2 months after this, to discuss the progress of the ESSP development and formally approved the final ESSP in February 2016 to implement between 2016 and 2020 (Universalia, 2018). This was operationalized through the National (NOP), 9 Provincial (POPs), 72 District operational plans (DOPs), and through the individual school development plans (SDPs).

The curriculum reform was implemented at the provincial level under the mantle of the provincial education office and its director; at the district level by the District School Inspector (DSI) and the district level education officers; and at the school level by school heads. Any challenges in implementing the reform at the school level were flagged to be solved by the district level officers, and similarly for district level by the provincial education officers. Any major problems or delays in implementation were flagged at the national level and to the ECG members, and they were addressed by the ministry directly. The CSOs also were authorized to flag any field implementation issues at the provincial and district level at the bi-monthly ECG meetings.

(b) ***Alignment of monetary funding and spending:*** To receive the funding earmarked from the GPE fund, the ministry must first spend the amounts on completion of activities and milestones, and then raise a receipt for payment to GPE. It must submit regular updates on the achievements and progress made on completing the activities mentioned as part of the ESSP to ECG and GPE. Any major delay in completing activities or achieving milestones must be flagged to ECG and GPE for prompt payments from the GPE fund. GPE then audits the activities and the corresponding spend by matching them against the activities mentioned under the finalized ESSP, and only approves payments which strictly adhere to ESSP plans. Any activities which do not match the ESSP plans are rejected and must be financed from the ministry's annual budget. Once GPE approves the expenditure and reimbursement of the same, UNICEF which is the grant agent for the GPE fund, releases the payment to the ministry. This process ensures that the ministry sticks to the originally agreed upon activities under the

ESSP and ministry's continued commitment to the reform year on year under the multi-stage multi-year ESSP. This also ensures that the ministry has to finance any spending which is not aligned to the ESSP or is rejected by GPE. This has resulted in a strong internal audit compliance mechanism by the ministry's internal finance team, which has to report any departure from agreement to the Ministry of Finance, which then holds the MoPSE accountable for such deviations and makes sure MoPSE falls back on its own resources raised through various provincial, district, and school level levies.

(c) *Assessment reforms and insights:* Sound educational assessments are critical to measuring school performance, which, in turn, is a key to helping policy-makers plan interventions for school-improvement efforts. These could measure a variety of aspects ranging from students' performance in a subject to teacher's content knowledge or teaching. Without these, governments might end up spending limited resources of time and money on something that is not working. They are thus also imperative to decide where the education budget should be allocated based on what is working or its potential to do so versus what is not. It is then no surprise that as part of the curriculum reform, the government proposed a 360 degree/rounded/holistic approach to assessments. This includes assessing students through continuous assessments of knowledge, skills, abilities, values, and traits. The assessment is additionally planned to be both formative and summative, assessing the students' abilities and competencies from infant to secondary levels. For example, students' grade at junior level will be determined by a mix of continuous assessments and performance on the national examination. At the "O" level, the grade will be based on theoretical, practical, and continuous assessment percentage (Universalia, 2019).

An assessment framework policy at Infant level has been drafted and is currently under review and finalization by MoPSE, Zimbabwe (Universalia, 2019). A new assessment framework for primary and secondary grades is also being drafted by MoPSE. Zimbabwe School Examination Council (ZIMSEC), a parastatal of the MoPSE, Zimbabwe is mandated with developing all the examinations in the schooling system and is currently working on developing and implementing the new continuous assessment framework and methodology. Based on this assessment framework, the formative and summative learning assessments, including the end of level examinations such as ZELA[8], Grade 7, "O" Level, and "A" Level will be reformed to align with the new curriculum. There is also a possible move away from summative to continuous formative assessments coupled with practical year-end examinations (Universalia, 2018). The delays and implementation challenges of the assessment reforms have been covered in detail under 7.4.1.

---

[8] ZELA assessments are developed by the funding support of UNICEF, test development support of ZIMSEC and implementation by a sub-department "ZELA" team within the ministry; All other assessments are developed and administered by ZIMSEC.

7.5 Results and Challenges

The results and challenges of the Zimbabwean curricular reform have been closely monitored by both GPE and UNICEF through their annual evaluation reports. These can be grouped under three broad categories (a) Infrastructure and Implementation, (b) Teacher Capacity and, (c) Economic.

7.5.1 Infrastructure and Implementation

1. Curriculum Packets: 13,000 copies of Curricular CD packets containing soft copies of curriculum framework document, syllabi documents, teacher guides and assessment activities to be used by teacher were developed and delivered to all schools through district level distribution mechanisms
2. Syllabi development: 144 Syllabi were translated with support from GPE into 13 regional and 8 indigenous languages
3. Textbooks: Procurement and distribution of 4,090,763 textbooks to 5,441 primary schools completed
4. SIG grants: 6,057 schools received School Improvement Grants from UNICEF totaling around 12 Million USD
5. Science Kits: MoPSE and UNICEF procured 12,600 science kits for 4,377 primary schools – 2,100 supported by GPE, remainder supported by EDF; 100% of all secondary schools have been provided with science kits by UNICEF funds
6. ICT Labs: A total of 1,200 schools with computer labs were developed through the GPE grants from 2016 onwards
7. Assessment related results: ZELA assessment results in 2018 showed improvement in mean performance for mathematics (2.3%) but remained about the same for reading (ZELA, 2018). UNICEF and EDF grants have ensured that Zimbabwe has participated in ZELA assessments every year from 2015 onwards. Similarly, the country has participated in the 2013 SEACMEQ regional assessments, whose results are awaited, and as of January 2020, the country is also in the midst of planning implementation of SEACMEQ 2020.

In terms of challenges, some stakeholders reported that implementation of the new curriculum had been rushed, and this had led to inadequate levels of learning materials of certain learning areas and poor provision of textbooks. While the ministry has developed syllabi for all learning areas from ECD to Form 6 level, there are still few learning areas for which textbooks are yet to be published after 2 years of the reform. These are primarily new learning areas and thus the teachers are facing difficulties in delivering these because of a lack of learning area specific pre-service or in-service training. This could be because MoPSE could not get private publishers to keep up with the demands and did not anticipate enough the timeline required to get the support and validation from CDTS to get the new textbooks approved. Further, procurement remains a challenge as the purchasing of textbooks is slow because of the bureaucratic processes involved and inadequate funding, so the text-book–student ratio is still inadequate, which prevents students from having their own material to study and practice their lessons (Universalia, 2019). Our focus groups with the teachers and school heads highlighted that at times, the textbook–student ratio can be as low as 1:10 for core subjects and 1:50 for non-core subjects.

Second, while the CDTS has reviewed curriculum and syllabus for its alignment, quite a few teachers and parents also mentioned that the curriculum is not progressing at the right level. They felt that the content is heavy for early grades and there is not much to focus on for higher primary grades. As mentioned in Sect. 7.4.3, this could be because the curriculum had broad statements for each learning area, which had been synthesized at the end of school level, whereas the syllabus was more detailed and specifies the learning objectives by grades.

Third, it is important to note that the assessment framework has been delayed since the beginning of the ZCF implementation (2016) owing to capacity gaps within MoPSE and ZIMSEC. It should hopefully be implemented within the turn of this year (2020) or early next year considering the consultative process of engaging stakeholders for comments and revising the draft assessments framework before its finalization and approval. Until then, the continuous assessment methodology and tools for assessment are critically required reforms that are awaited on a priority basis across the Zimbabwean school system. This is critical because the teachers were only trained on interpretation of the new syllabi and not on how to assess students in a continuous manner. As a result, more than 95% of them are still resorting to assessing students using methods learnt while they were at teacher colleges training to be teachers – methods to assess students on their content knowledge and rote memorization rather than on demonstrable skills. Some of the assessment practices from the earlier systems of assessing students periodically – unit tests, monthly tests, end of year assessments – are still continuing but these again are reduced to knowledge based assessments based on the capacity and know-how of teachers.

Fourth, while ICT and practical training or labs are the engines of the ZCF, there are schools that do not have the relevant infrastructure – computer labs, science labs, or lab equipment. While some schools do have computer labs, there is no electricity to render computer benefits. Schools with electricity only receive it during the hours where the school is not in session. Even schools in urban areas complained of power outage and internet connectivity issues. Students, teachers, and parents thus are unable to access educational information for developing skills and competencies. Without these resources, the outcomes and results of the ZCF will be difficult to realize.

Lastly, promoting inclusivity has also been a challenge. Despite the fact that MoPSE involved a high number of stakeholders in this reform, the dialogue was mainly between structures at the national levels. At the sub-national level, there was a gap due to the dysfunctionality of district-level communities which lacked appropriate resources, direction, and capacity (Universalia, 2019).

7.5.2 Teacher Capacity

In terms of professional capacity development, in 2016 alone, over 70,000 teachers who started implementing the curriculum in 2017, were trained. Further, as of early 2020, the ministry has claimed that all teachers teaching the new curriculum have been trained either directly or indirectly through a cascaded training model. This implies all teachers except for Grade 7 (curriculum roll-out planned for 2021) have been trained.

However, the in-service training primarily focused on syllabus interpretation rather than the methodology of teaching. The parts that focused on methodology were not learning area specific. This is crucial to note because several new learning areas were introduced as part of the reform, so it was essential to receive training focused on these, especially for primary grade teachers, who are required to teach all subjects in Zimbabwe. Second, this was a one-time annual training rather than an ongoing training support. Additionally, given the cascading model of in-service training, teachers are not fully satisfied with the frequency and content of the training. Though this model ensures effective resource distribution, ultimately it leads to loss of information as it trickles down the levels. As a result, teachers do not feel prepared to deliver the content. They desire for learning area specific pedagogical examples and action-oriented practical methods for delivering ZCF. This is especially true of primary grade teachers who have to teach all learning areas but are not trained to do so.

Additionally, while the government has undertaken several essential measures for the teaching workforce, it is worth noting that amidst the economic turmoil, the best Zimbabwean teachers likely moved out of the education system. Thus challenges have been noted in relation with the recruitment of teachers to ensure that the ministry is able to react to turnover and that students are not left without teachers as they are essential to learning. During our visit, ministry officials reported that the country does have a long waitlist of about 15–20 thousand teachers waiting to be recruited. All eligible teacher students are required to register into the ministry's database to be eligible for selection into the teaching workforce. The ministry then recruits the teachers higher up in the waitlist based on their province preference. There is no inclusion of a quality or a competency criteria.

7.5.3 Economic

In Zimbabwean Dollar (ZWD) terms, the MoPSE budget increased more than 40 times from 200 Million Dollars to 8 Billion in 2019–2020 due to hyperinflation and programming changes under the curriculum reform. MoPSE budget currently accounts for nearly 15% of the total government expenditure and 6% of GDP. Alongside, donor funding continues to play a significant role, allowing MoPSE to initiate and implement numerous key reforms to implement interventions to expand access or enhance quality. Donor funding through the Education Development Fund (EDF), the Global Partnership for Education (GPE), and other sources has amounted to close to USD 230 million between 2014 and 2020 (Universalia, 2019). Substantial resources from the NGO partners also support education. The ministry is currently consolidating different grant funding programmes into a single harmonized approach as a part of the school financing policy, which has been drafted and is under review by the ECG partners.

However, limited financial resources at the MoPSE level prevented the implementation from sticking to the initial schedule. This resulted in an excessive reliance on donor and parental funding for non-salary expenditures which is not a sustainable strategy in the long-run. Education affordability and sharp decline in teacher salaries was another hindrance.

Second, as of early 2020, MoHTESTD continues to train the new workforce using the old curriculum. On average, MoPSE has been spending close to 3 Million USD on professional capacity development, especially due to duplication of efforts by re-training new teachers who were originally trained on the previous curriculum. This can be optimized to some extent if the curriculum of the teacher education colleges is aligned with ZCF. Alignment with higher education would ensure continuity and consistency between the two and redirect the saved budget on other critical reform aspects.

Lastly, while limited internet connectivity has been highlighted as a challenge under infrastructure, it is also worth noting that a major deterrent is the installation costs and annual internet access charges. This cost is generally borne by schools from their school development funds collected through pooled-in resources from parents. Since the successful ZCF delivery depends heavily on fully functioning ICT labs in all schools across the countries, MoPSE needs to align with the Ministry of Information and Communications Technology (MoICT) to make access to stable and affordable, if not free, internet a reality for schools to realize the ICT benefits.

7.6   Conclusion

Amidst the political, economic, and financial challenges, MoPSE did its best by taking the courageous step of undertaking a full-fledged systemic overhaul and adjusting the plan as required. The ministry was driven with the mission of making schooling relevant for all Zimbabwean children and has moved a step closer to it. The Zimbabwean Curricular Reform is also ambitious in that it addresses the five perspectives of educational change proposed by Reimers (2020). While the reform is in its last leg, with the ZCF rolled out for Grade 6 in 2020 and plans for Grade 7 roll-out in 2021, there is much to appreciate and learn from the progress thus far. Even though we heard mixed reviews from several stakeholders, all the criticism was primarily targeted towards implementation and contextual situations such as economic hardships in terms of hyperinflation, economic stability, and sanctions from other countries and development partners, which were not in the ministry's control. This criticism is similar to educational reforms in other developing countries such as Kenya.

The ZCF implementation is expected to be completed in 2022 and the preparations for curriculum review will start in 2021. Hopefully, the curriculum review process will benefit from the findings of the Education Sector Analysis and incorporate these in the next phase of curriculum improvement and implementation (CBC V2.0) from 2022 to 2027. It remains to be seen whether Zimbabwe would be able to learn from the challenges faced in reform V1.0 and address all gaps in its curricular reform V2.0. The extensive support from the ECG, belief from the political cadre in the general direction of the reform, and the strong will to continue improving and implementing the reform are on its side. Thus, with improvements in economic conditions, international sanctions, and other associated hardships, Zimbabwe has the potential to once again be at the forefront of the educational achievement and progress in the continent.

References

Collaborative for Academic, Social, and Emotional Learning (CASEL). (2017). *CASEL Wheel & Competencies*. https://casel.org/wp-content/uploads/2019/12/CASEL-Competencies.pdf.

Demographic and Health Survey. (2016). https://dhsprogram.com/pubs/pdf/FR322/FR322.pdf. Accessed February 5, 2020.

Education Encyclopedia. (n.d.). https://education.stateuniversity.com/pages/2099/Instructional-Strategies.html. Accessed June 3, 2020.

EMIS. (2017). *Annual Statistical Digest*. UNESCO Institute of Statistics. http://uis.unesco.org/en/country/zw

ESSP. (2016). *Education Sector Strategic Plan*. Ministry of Primary and Secondary Education, Zimbabwe.

In-Country Research. (2020). Conducted by Jayanti Bhatia and Venkatesh Reddy Mallapu Reddy.

Interviews were conducted with 52 officials from 6 departments of MoPSE – Curriculum Development and Technical Services Department; Human Resources and Discipline Department; Primary, Secondary and Non-Formal Education Department; Procurement Management and Business Development Unit; Centre of Education, Research, Innovation and Development; Finance Department.

Kageler, S. (2015). *Education Sector Analysis (ESA)*. Ministry of Primary and Secondary Education, Zimbabwe

Narrative Report. (2014). *Narrative Report (2014–2015). Curriculum Review Process*. Zimbabwe, Ministry of Primary and Secondary Education

Zimbabwe School Examinations Council (ZIMSEC); Zimbabwe Early Learning Assessments Team (ZELA); South East African Council for Monitoring Educational Quality (SEACMEQ).

Education Coordination Group partners such as World Bank, UNICEF, UNESCO, CSOs

Textbook Publishers.

Provincial Education Directors, District School Inspectors, National Association of Primary School Heads and, National Association of Secondary School Heads.

Additionally, we held individual and focus group interviews in 7 schools in 3 out of 9 provinces in Zimbabwe where we interviewed 32 School Heads, 70 Teachers, 36 Parents and 38 Students.

Reimers, F. (Ed.). (2020). *Educating students to improve the world*. Singapore: Springer.

UNESCO. (2017). *Zimbabwe demographics*. http://uis.unesco.org/country/ZW. Accessed June 6, 2020.

UNICEF. (2009). https://www.unicef.org/media/media_47915.html. Accessed June 3, 2020.

Universalia. (2018). Aslam, M., Rawal, S., & Outhred, R. (2018). *GPE 2020 Country-level prospective evaluations*. Zimbabwe first annual report.

Universalia. (2019). Aslam, M., Rawal, S., & Turner, F. (2019). *Prospective evaluation of GPE's country-level support to education*. Zimbabwe second annual report.

World Bank. (2014). *Literacy rate, adult total (% of people ages 15 and above)*. Zimbabwe: World Bank. https://data.worldbank.org/indicator/SE.ADT.LITR.ZS?locations=ZW. Accessed February 5, 2020.

ZELA. (2018). *An evaluation report of the 2018 Zimbabwe Early Learning Assessment (ZELA) cycle*. Report to the Ministry of Primary and Secondary Education from ZIMSEC and UNICEF.

ZimASSET, G. o. (2015). *Zimbabwe agenda for sustainable socio-economic transformation (ZIM ASSET): Towards an empowered society and a growing economy, October 2013–December 2018. (2015)*. Harare: Government of Zimbabwe.

Zimbabwe Curriculum Framework. (2015). *Curriculum framework for primary and secondary education report (2015–2022). Zimbabwe, Ministry of Primary and Secondary Education.*

Djénéba Gory is a French-Malian Master's in Public Administration graduate at the Kennedy School of Government at Harvard University. She started her career as a financial auditor based in Paris for 4 years. She moved to Cote d'Ivoire where she focused on humanitarian and development projects. She provided audit/advisory services to non-profits in more than 15 African countries (ie. Burkina Faso, Central African Republic, Djibouti, Nigeria, etc) for 3 years. More recently, she moved to Switzerland where she worked on humanitarian projects implemented worldwide. At Harvard, she focuses her studies on education policies, gender and women's empowerment. She is the co-founder of the Suadela which is a nonprofit organization whose mission is to increase West-African teenage girls' power by building their negotiation skills.

Jayanti Bhatia is a 2020 Ed.M. International Education Policy graduate from the Harvard Graduate School of Education. She believes that Social and Emotional Learning should be embedded within the mainstream curriculum to drive learning and life readiness for all children. After completing her Bachelor's in Physics Honors from Hindu College, Delhi University, Jayanti joined ZS, a consulting and professional services firm in 2012. Yet one cause that has always stayed close to her heart is quality education for all. Her self-fueled passion has driven her to lead many initiatives for children in slums, learning centers for migrants, and low-cost private schools across India (2011-Present). Consulting at the same time has empowered her to use her skills interchangeably, and simultaneously see the bigger picture and intricacies of ground projects. She is now looking forward to leveraging her professional skills in the domain of education to ensure the holistic development of all children.

Venkatesh Reddy Mallapu Reddy has more than 10 years of experience in the Indian education sector in both for-profit and not-for-profit organizations in Strategic Partnerships and Development, Project Management, Financials and Budgeting, Monitoring & Evaluation and Communications roles. Most recently, he was the Strategic Partnerships & Management Lead for 4 years with his last employer, handling all the strategic engagements with education ministries and senior government officials, international agencies and foundations like World Bank, UNICEF, UNESCO, USAID, MSDF, MacArthur, and partner CSO/NGOs. He has worked with education systems and stakeholders in India, Bhutan, Afghanistan, Maldives, Thailand, United States and Zimbabwe. He has managed multiple large-scale diagnostic student assessments (>30 K Students data collected) projects in India and helped collect more than 1.5 Million students learning outcomes data and interviewed more than 10,000 teachers and school heads. He is interested in using low-stakes diagnostic assessment data and student/teacher/school background data to improve service delivery by making education more personalized and targeted to individual stakeholders (for ex:

personalized learning and addressing of learning gaps\student misconceptions, targeted teacher training programmes which address individualized needs of teachers) and help implement better policies and decision making at all levels and levers in the system.

He is a graduate of the Master's Program in International Education Policy at the Harvard Graduate School of Education and has a passion for Comparative Policy Research and Analysis in International Education, Assessments based insights and reforms, Social-Emotional Learning and Early Childhood Education.

Chapter 8
Conclusions. Seven Lessons to Build an Education Renaissance After the Pandemic

Fernando M. Reimers

8.1 Introduction

When it is finally over, we will in all likelihood conclude that the COVID-19 Pandemic was, in many ways, a veritable global calamity. Millions of people were infected, hundreds of thousands died, millions of jobs were lost, economies slowed down, the institutional and financial capacity of governments was burdened crowding out the State's and private institutions ability to deliver on most fronts. In education, the Pandemic disrupted the normal functioning of education systems, creating challenges for students, families, teachers and systems. The inability to overcome some of these challenges created significant learning losses for many students, amplifying learning gaps within and among nations.

We can anticipate that the long term outcomes of those losses, for individuals and communities, will be dire. Some students will never return to school, others will finish school with less skills than they would have otherwise. These results of the inability to sustain educational opportunity during the Pandemic will influence the future employment prospects of many students, negatively impacting their communities and nations.

But the interruption in the regular functioning of schooling created also a new awareness about the importance of education, greater curiosity and interest about what it was that students were and should be learning in school, it generated more views and even contention about how best to educate students. Perhaps there will be, alongside the obvious education losses, also an educational dividend of the Pandemic, if this interest in making education more relevant and more effective carries on into the Post-Pandemic world.

If this renewed urgency about helping students develop the breath of skills they need to thrive in a world that is volatile and uncertain does indeed continue, we

F. M. Reimers (✉)
Harvard Graduate School of Education, Cambridge, MA, USA
e-mail: Fernando_Reimers@harvard.edu

© The Author(s) 2021
F. M. Reimers (ed.), *Implementing Deeper Learning and 21st Century Education Reforms*, https://doi.org/10.1007/978-3-030-57039-2_8

171

would do well to learn from other system level reforms that have attempted to do just that. The six reforms studied in this book offer seven valuable lessons about how to enhance the capacity of education institutions to pursue more ambitious education goals. These lessons focus on the mindsets about reform, the importance of the implementation process, the need for operational clarity, the journey of reform, sequencing and the role of first steps, staying the course and learning from experience. I expand on each of those seven themes below.

8.2   Lesson 1. The Importance of Mindsets About Education Reform

The six reforms examined in this book demonstrate that large scale system reform was already happening throughout the world preceding the Pandemic, as governments transformed education systems to pursue more ambitious goals. The approaches followed by these reforms can be usefully characterized using the five frames I have argued explain how reformers view the process of educational change: cultural, psychological, professional, institutional and political (Reimers, 2020). While each of these six reforms relies on more than a single frame, countries can be divided in two groups in terms of how they appear to have drawn on the worldviews that characterize these five frames.

Whereas in Ontario, Singapore and Zimbabwe there are clearly recognizable elements of all five frames, in Mexico, Pakistan and Kenya, only one or two frames are clearly dominant. While the three reforms that reflect a more comprehensive view of the process of change vary, with reforms in Ontario and Singapore having been in place much longer than Zimbabwe's, it is noticeable that Zimbabwe's reform appears to have attempted, and to some extent accomplished, ambitious change in an obviously tumultuous period characterized by considerable political and economic turmoil. In contrast, the reforms in Pakistan, Mexico and Kenya, reflecting a more limited set of worldviews in their implementation, appear to have faced more challenges, in particular regarding their ability to achieve the intended changes and in terms of sustainability.

Ontario's reform reflects a political and professional perspective, focusing on supporting the professional autonomy and development of teacher capacity, strengthened by political support from teachers and teacher unions. Significant reliance on creating structures and processes to shape the reform and to develop the capacity of teachers indicates strong use of an institutional perspective. In particular, the use of data and frequent feedback loops to guide instructional improvement and management decisions, and the attention to fostering coherence across the three levels of the system (the school, the middle and the system) reveal a distinct reliance on and institutional view of how to help various stakeholders develop a shared understanding of 'the system'. The reform leaders were clearly attuned to expectations of teachers and of the population to replace the conflicted nature of relations between government and school for more collegial relationships, and they relied heavily on consultative and participatory approaches early on, suggesting an awareness of elements of a cultural perspective. While the reform relied on ideas about improvement that had a base on academic knowledge generated by research, and several of the processes created had the purpose of strengthening the role of evidence based knowledge to guide the reform, a psychological perspective, relying on science based knowledge to guide the reform, was conspicuously absent as a strong professional perspective prioritized knowledge based on practice and generated by practitioners, over knowledge based on academic research.

Singapore's reform of teacher education reflects also a blend of psychological, professional and institutional worldviews. In aligning the preparation of teachers with an ambitious curricular vision this reform drew on learning sciences to design deep learning experiences for teachers, and created institutional changes to sustain those reforms over time. There is no apparent reliance on a cultural frame, other than in the fact that the reform continued and deepened a 'culture of education' which had already established the importance of twenty-first century skills as an aspirational goal to drive reform efforts. The deft use of political worldviews is evident in the absence of political contention regarding the reform, as the reform benefited from a solid understanding of how change is accomplished in Singapore's education system, with an incremental approach, building on and honoring previous efforts, and with quiet, but palpable, support from the higher levels of education leadership in the Ministry of Education and in the National Institute of Education, and perhaps also in the Cabinet.

Mexico's reform is first and foremost an institutional and political reform, incorporating only in subsequent stages components reflecting a psychological and a professional perspective. There is no evident use of a cultural frame in the design of an unapologetic top down reform, although arguably the reform built on a widespread perception that the education system was not adequately serving the needs of students. While consultative processes were deployed once the reform began to formulate the curriculum component, 3 years into the reform, and the design for the reform included structures and processes designed to cultivate local participation and support, very much along the lines of Ontario's, those components were only announced once a public narrative opposing the reform had crystalized. The opposing unions and other detractors of the reform created a narrative about the reform as a punitive, anti-labor effort, from which it never recovered. The contrast between Mexico's reform and Zimbabwe's is interesting, as both aimed at significant elevation of curricular goals. Even though Zimbabwe's reform was launched in a much more embattled political and economic context, it rapidly sought to advance a multiplicity of components at once, whereas Mexico, in a much more favorable political and economic situation, advanced the institutional reforms rapidly, but was more gradual, arguably slow, in bringing about the curricular and professional changes, in effect running out of time and of political capital to effectively achieve those. While counterintuitive, Zimbabwe's bold move to attempt the impossible, to do much without apparent political, financial or institutional capital to achieve it, may have worked better than the more conservative, gradual, approach followed by Mexico.

Punjab's reform is principally an institutional reform, benefiting from skillful and consistent political support over an extended period. Through institutional mechanisms, the reform also tried to professionalized teaching, for instance changing the rules for teacher appointments to be more meritocratic, increasing the number of teachers in schools so that teachers could spend more time preparing their lessons, increasing the number of school coaches so that they could devote more time working with teachers on improvement strategies. There is no evidence that a cultural perspective informed what was unquestionably a top down reform with strong political support from the Prime Minister, as had been the case with the British reform on which the Punjab's reform was inspired. The absence of insights from learning sciences that characterize a psychological perspective is conspicuous in Punjab's case.

Kenya's reform draws largely on worldviews reflecting cultural and institutional frames, comprising a curriculum reform that requires responding to and supporting changes in broadly held expectations about schooling and its ways, and changes to structures to support the new curriculum. There is no obvious reliance on a political perspective, other than in the initiation of the reform via a pilot, which allowed to test not only the components of the reform, but the readiness of key stakeholders to embrace it. A psychological perspective is absent, except in the definition of some of the competencies which are included in the new curriculum. For example, the reliance on a train the trainer model, with very limited extended support in school to teachers, to build the capacities of the ambitious goals and pedagogies that are the core of the reform, ignores much of the research-based knowledge on effective teacher education. A professional perspective is also lacking in the reform, in glaring contrast to the reforms in Ontario and Singapore in that respect.

Zimbabwe is an institutional reform focusing on transforming a content based into a competency based curriculum. But the reform, at least in the early stages in which it is in 2020, relies also on worldviews that reflect cultural, psychological, institutional and political perspectives, even if somewhat superficially. The ambition of the reform, and the rapid pace at which it is being implemented, is counterintuitive given the high political and economic volatility in which it is taking place. It is possible that the reform is benefiting from the dividend of what was for decades a relatively highly professionalized education system, until successive economic crises caused many of the teachers to abandon the system. Reflecting reliance on a cultural frame, the reform consulted extensively with parents throughout the design and implementation process. The psychological perspective is reflected in the competencies included in the curriculum and in the thoughtful design of the curricular sequences, as well as in the multiplicity of approaches and structures envisioned to support teacher professional development. It also recognized the need to develop the professional skills of teachers to teach the new curriculum, reflecting a professional perspective. An institutional perspective is visible in the deployment of social and institutional structures to support teacher and learning and monitor quality of delivery. Finally, the reform relied on top down political support for implementation, a mixed blessing in a context of high political volatility.

8.3   Lesson 2. Implementation Matters Considerably

Reforming education systems is as much about, if not more, implementing educational change than about designing policy reform. What is a reform that is not implemented, or that is implemented in a way that distorts the intended objectives?

There are at least two reasons the topic of implementation merits careful consideration when transforming education systems at scale in order to help students gain a broader range of competencies. The first is, to put it bluntly, that a reform is not more than what is implemented. Reforms that remain on policy documents have little use other than adorning government bookshelves or providing fodder for government rhetoric. In a world of almost instantaneous communication and increasing transparency, however, it is not easy to trick the public into believing in a reform which exists only in the imagination of its leaders, or on paper, at least not for too long. The process of implementation often 'translates' policy initiatives into rather different operational activities than those intended and that translation in effect 'recreates' reform. This was the powerful insight developed by Michael Lipsky in his seminal book 'Street-Level Bureaucracy' in which he explained how policy is sometimes implemented in unexpected and unintended ways as Street-level bureaucrats 'make policy' because they exercise discretion resulting from their professionalism and relative freedom from oversight and authority performing tasks which cannot be scripted (Lipsky, 1980). Anticipating what Frederic Laloux in his book 'Reinventing Organizations' describes as a 'Pluralistic' view of organizations, which will be explained later in this chapter, Lipsky explains that the transformation of policy may also result from Street-level bureaucrats disagreeing with the views of their managers.

As implementation defines the important details of policy, it is those details that shape the fate of reform. Fullan and Gallagher refer to the importance of developing a 'nuanced' understanding of those details of reforms:

> Two systems can each produce all of the right foundational documents (annual improvement plans, SMART goals, literacy strategies, even deep learning strategies). They can believe in and provide professional development for teachers and express trust in their school staff, but one gets results and sustainable change and the other, actually most, do not. In our view, it is in the details that the difference is made. It is found in details such as the ways in which trust is built, the degree to which the implementation is nimble and flexes as it needs to in response to what is happening in the situation. (Fullan & Gallagher, 2020, viii).

Sometimes the details that matter are not as nuanced as Fullan and Gallagher describe, but are reflected in clear and visible ways in how various terms that define the components of a reform are operationally defined. The reforms studied in this book show that the same terms are commonly used to refer to components that, in practice, are rather different. For example, all of these reforms included a component to 'build teacher capacity' in one way or another, but this component was translated into very different activities in each case. In Ontario, for example, the component to build teacher capacity included a saturation of structures and processes to increase the knowledge and skills, and more importantly the shared understanding, of a very large number of stakeholders, from teachers to staff in the provincial Ministry. Capacity building involved creating a specific unit in the Ministry (the Literacy and Numeracy Secretariat) where about forty specialists were tasked to design improvement strategies to build teacher and leadership capacity focused on improving student outcomes in literacy and numeracy. In addition, each school created a team tasked with developing and implementing a student success initiative. A specific network was established to mobilize knowledge and support of school-based improvement strategies, partnering the directors of the five highest achieving districts with those from the eighteen lowest achieving districts to support the development of literacy and numeracy improvement strategies.

In contrast to Ontario, which focused on developing teacher professionalism and building teacher capacity primarily in their schools focused on their literacy and numeracy instruction, the focus of professional development in Singapore was much broader than two subject domains. Focusing on teacher initial preparation, Singapore's reform of teacher initial preparation was aligned to a twenty-first century conception designed to help develop teachers holistically and included developing clear competency frameworks for teacher graduates, that included themes such as Values of learner-centeredness, teacher identity, and service to the profession and community, Skills required by an educator, and in-depth subject-matter Knowledge, and that focused on three domains: professional practice, leadership and management, and personal effectiveness. The aims of Singapore's reform included helping teachers develop their own teaching philosophies, developing the habit of reflection on their practice supported by an e-portfolio, providing teacher candidates opportunities to learn from experiential learning and other deep learning pedagogies.

Contrasting to Ontario and to Singapore, the Mexican reform also included components to build teacher capacity but the specific operational mechanisms were developed in much more general terms than in Ontario or Singapore, were announced much later in the implementation cycle, towards the end of the term of the administration, and received limited funding and support from the States, with the ensuing limitations to implementation. Whereas in Ontario and Singapore the reforms began with professional development, this component in Mexico was an afterthought to the institutional and political reforms.

The Punjab reform, which also aimed at strengthening teacher capacity, did this in ways that are, by comparison to Ontario and Singapore, significantly more superficial, lacking the intensity of efforts that was apparent in these two reforms. In Punjab, professional development involved developing teacher training self-instructional modules, providing training to use them, and hiring teacher coaches to work with teachers. This 'dosage' of opportunities to develop new skills, contrasts to the rich set of structures, processes and opportunities that Ontario established to strengthen teacher capacity or to the deep changes that Singapore introduced in teacher preparation to help teachers develop twenty-first century competencies, and is more similar to what was done in Kenya through a train the trainer approach and short courses, which the pilot of the reform showed was insufficient to develop the capacity to teach an ambitious curriculum.

Kenya's reform, which attempted more ambitious curriculum change than the Punjab's or Ontario's, also relied on building teacher capacity. A pilot of the curriculum reform shows how easy it is to underestimate the needs for professional development to implement a demanding reform. The full implementation of the reform was postponed once the pilot revealed that the professional development which had been planned, consisting of 1–3 week courses to familiarize teachers with the new curriculum and the associated pedagogies, with some reinforcement during breaks, delivered via a train the trainer model, was deemed insufficient by the teachers participating in the pilot to equip them with the skills to teach the new curriculum. The contrast of this train the trainer model implemented in short sessions with the approach followed in Ontario could not be greater, even though both reforms included teacher professional development as a crucial reform component.

Zimbabwe's reform, similar to Kenya's in its focus in replacing a content-based curriculum with a competency based curriculum, followed in turn a different approach to professional development, also relying on a train the trainer model, but extending into supporting teachers in schools, more similar to the approach followed in Punjab, and what was planned in Mexico, but more shallow than what was done in Ontario.

Just as the operational translation of the concept of building teacher capacity in these six reforms reveals consequential differences, similar important differences in the details of implementation of these reforms are found with respect of other components. Not least among them the operational definition of the student learning outcomes that these reforms attempted to influence. All of the reforms studied in this book were predicated in preparing students for the increasing demands of the twenty-first century, with two of them, Ontario and Punjab, translating this aspiration on a sharp focus on literacy and numeracy, and also access to school in the case of Punjab and high school graduation in the case of Ontario, and four of them focusing on a wider set of learning goals for students. Those aspirations, however, were translated into different operational descriptions of what particular competencies students should be developing. In Mexico, the new education model outlined a detailed, ambitious and comprehensive taxonomy of competencies which guided the curriculum, arguably the most comprehensive and clearly developed of the six reforms studied in this book, and the one most aligned with the breadth of competencies discussed in Chap. 1. In Singapore, similar ambitions were articulated not for students but for teachers, in order to help them lead twenty-first century instruction. None of the other reforms examined in this book had similarly clear and ambitious expectations for what teachers should learn in order to lead twenty-first century education.

In Ontario, in contrast, the learning goals were initially narrowly focused on literacy and numeracy, and even as those goals expanded partway through the reform, the expansion was still largely about broader ways to understand literacy and numeracy as foundations to a broader set of competencies. In Pakistan, education quality was also translated into an operational focus on literacy and numeracy.

In Kenya the ambition to prepare students for the twenty-first century translated into a competency-based curriculum, a goal to help all students begin secondary school, eliminating exams, and creating a variety of pathways at the secondary level with an emphasis on technical and vocational tracks. Kenya's curriculum focused on seven core competencies: communication and collaboration, critical thinking and problem-solving, creativity and imagination, citizenship, digital literacy, learning to learn, and self-efficacy, all of them broader than the learning goals in Ontario or Punjab, more in line with those in Singapore, considerably less detailed than those in Mexico.

In Zimbabwe, the shift from a content based to a competency based curriculum emphasized higher order thinking skills, the development of national identity, preparing learners for life and work, for life-long learning, for participatory citizenship, peace and sustainable development, and for participation, leadership and service. These goals too were broader than those pursued in Ontario or Pakistan, and very similar to those pursued in Kenya.

This variability in the operationalization of education policy goals suggests that we need a language of implementation. Much of the language we have is more adequate for policy reform, than it is to guide the implementation process. It is high level conceptual language, useful for logical analysis, but insufficient to guide the operational planning of reform. The robust literature on the 'drivers' of policy change, the 'policy levers' that may lead to higher student outcomes, yields a working consensus on what policies matter, even as that knowledge may be limited by the limited range of countries where the research from which those drivers were identified was conducted as discussed in the first chapter of this book. But that literature is thin when it comes to defining what those terms mean for implementation, as a result the most critical details to inform the design of implementation strategies are left to the discretion of administrators and other Street-level bureaucrats. It is one thing to say that reforms should have clear goals for students, or even that those goals should equip them with twenty first century skills in cognitive, interpersonal and intrapersonal domains, it is another thing altogether to translate those aspirations into specific standards and curriculum, with the level of operational details that would allow two different people to have shared clarity as to what those goals mean in practice.

We often refer to the combination of policy levers, to the mix of components that are included in a reform, and to the assumptions we make about how the actions that a reform will support will produce particular results, as a theory of action. A theory of action can be expressed with a methodology called the logical framework approach, which makes explicit the underlying hypotheses of a policy or a program about how particular inputs will support activities which will in turn lead to immediate results and eventually to long term outcomes. A theory of action is a statement that makes visible how a policy is supposed to achieve its intended results. It's implementation 'in theory'.

For example, the National Literacy and Numeracy Strategy advanced in the United Kingdom by Tony Blair, which served as the inspiration for the reforms in

Ontario and the Punjab, comprised six key foundations: define clear and ambitious standards, use data to monitor performance towards targets, devolve responsibility to teachers and schools, access best practice and high quality professional development, create accountability, and focus on low performing schools. These are all elements that can be integrated in formulations of the sort 'if I do A then B will happen'. For example, 'If standards are clear and ambitious and teachers are given the freedom to design how to improve, and they are provided the support from peers and access to networks of colleagues, they will discover more effective ways to teach, will enact changes to their pedagogies and as a result students literacy skills will increase'.

In Ontario, for instance, the basic theory of action of the reform was that increasing teacher professionalism and accountability would lead to improvements in literacy, numeracy and high school graduation rates. The key hypotheses of the reform could be phrased as: 'if educators are provided the autonomy, and the professional development and support, to design their own plans for improvement, their pedagogical efficacy in literacy and numeracy will increase, leading to gains in student learning outcomes in those domains and greater personalization in high schools will lead to greater student engagement and to increases in graduation rates.'

In Singapore, the basic theory of action was that in order for teachers to help their students develop twenty-first century skills, they themselves must display them, and in order for them to be able to lead deeper learning processes, they must have experienced such teaching and learning. Teacher education was aligned to an explicit and ambitious framework of teacher competencies, and a number of changes to the preparation programs were introduced to specifically develop those competencies.

In Mexico, the theory of action was that greater teacher professionalism and an ambitious curriculum would support students to develop twenty-first century skills. To achieve greater professionalism the reform changed the rules governing access to and promotion to the teaching career, designed a new educational model, which specified not only a curriculum, but more autonomy and local participation for schools. An implicit theory of action driving the reform was that the control of the teacher union over the careers of teachers had to be eliminated and replaced by public rules and processes that recognized professional effort, skills and efficacy in order to develop the education system towards greater professionalism.

In Pakistan, the basic underlying theory of the reform was similar to that of the British reform on which it was inspired, although the goals included access to school, which was not a goal in the United Kingdom. Both reforms aimed at improving quality in public schools and at strengthening the capacity for monitoring and evaluation to improve accountability at all levels of the system. The reform was based on strengthening management capacity, largely creating systematic reporting of information on the status of implementation of reform activities to various management levels in the system. While there was also a component to strengthen teacher quality, through new norms for teacher recruitment, increase in the number of teachers, in-service professional development through self-instructional modules and with support from teacher coaches, these activities were in the shadows of the much more salient emphasis on using information systems to strengthen management capacity.

   In Kenya and Zimbabwe the basic reform theory was that a competency based curriculum, supplemented by teacher professional development, would lead to changes in the core of instruction which would in turn help students gain the competencies necessary to meet the demands of the twenty-first century. The necessary support for teachers to be able to teach the new curriculum seems to have been underestimated in both cases. In Kenya, a pilot implementation concluded that the 1–3 week training on the new curriculum was insufficient. In Zimbabwe financial constrains limited the implementation strategy.

   Given the variability in the operational definitions of the core policy components of system level reform included in the theories of action of system level reforms, without an explicit guide to translate the theories of action of reform into operational strategies, the operationalization will be left to administrators and teachers who will make consequential decisions about what it is that will actually be implemented. The fate of the reform is entirely contingent on those choices of street level bureaucrats, taking place with much less scrutiny than the public debate that accompanies the identification of policy alternatives. One valuable role for using a Logical Framework is that it makes such translation transparent and open to public scrutiny. This is critical for project management and for evaluation. As we take stock of how reforms have been implemented we complement the existing knowledge about 'policy reform in theory' with essential knowledge about 'policy reform in practice'. To build that knowledge base we need greater focus on the implementation of reforms, examining the operational translations of policy ideas, not about policy ideas themselves, as the various chapters in this book do.

   A second reason more attention to implementation is necessary is because reforms depend on unexamined mental models that relate policy change to implementation as much as they depend on the particular components and mix of actions that form the policy.

   A theory of action is not just about the particular components of the policy and how they are expected to work in practice. While most typically implicit and invisible, there is a second order set of assumptions undergirding a theory of action. These are assumptions about of how education organizations work, and they form mental models, much like the mental models I represented in the five frames about reform discussed earlier. They are often based on a theory of mind about what explains the behavior of the people who make an education system work.

   A common mental model is: 'If a policy mandates a change, people will comply'. The model assumes that through instruments of incentives and coercion, the education authority can influence and predict the behavior of implementors. An example of that model in practice would be the assumption that 'If the education authority provides each classroom with classroom libraries, and directs teachers to provide students the freedom to pick books of their choosing and to read them, teachers will comply, students will pick the books, and read them'. This mental model, that people will do as told by those in positions of formal authority, is widespread and often unexamined. It assumes compliance and assumes that particular roles provide individuals in position of authority the power to restrict or encourage behavior in others. This is clearly a top-down mental model that sees an educational institution as a command and control hierarchy. Lipsky's book 'Street Level

Bureaucrats' challenged the validity of this model suggesting that implementors could subvert a policy rather than comply. A significant contribution of Lipsky's book is in helping those in organizations, policy makers as well as implementors, recognize that different people may hold different mental models about how organizations work. This understanding is crucial, it is a powerful idea to help develop a more complex theory of mind to the assumption that people are cogs in a machine, so that those in the organization can communicate and collaborate.

It is certainly the case that some education organizations work as command and control hierarchies, and that many see them as 'machines' where people are 'cogs', but it is also the case that not all of them do, and that they may not be the most adaptive form of functioning to address certain education challenges. Furthermore, people working in organizations that operate as command and control hierarchies may differ in how they view the value of operating in that way for the task at hand. In education organizations the 'cogs' have a mind about whether they and others are indeed 'cogs' in a machine or instead people with agency and choice.

There are clear advantages to command and control hierarchies. They provide predictability, allow the organization of human effort in service of large goals, whether those include organizing agricultural societies, building cathedrals or pyramids, engaging in battle, manufacturing cars, or rapidly expanding access to school to enroll most children, as was done in the decades following the inclusion of education as a human right in the Universal Declaration of Human Rights. From the vantage point of this mode of organization enhancing implementation is about enhancing the institutional capacity of the implementation machine to execute policy, as implementors learn to do as told. Activities such as building the technical skills of people at various levels of the system or using information more effectively can enhance capacity, namely 'the capacity to do as instructed'. The Punjab reforms reflect this organizational mental model.

But command and control hierarchies have their limitations too, especially when the challenge is not to achieve predictable results in a stable world, but to respond to major changes in context – as in a Pandemic, where teachers who are close to students and families may have more knowledge about the conditions the children are in, or their needs, than education authorities – or to invent new ideas or products – as in reforming education to make it more relevant to a world that is volatile and uncertain.

Frederic Laloux offers a valuable conceptualization of the evolution of organizations over the course of human history (Laloux, 2014). In Laloux's account of the historical development of organizations, they have evolved trough the following seven stages:

Reactive, the earliest developmental stage taking place between 100,000 to 50,000 BC. These organizations were bands of a few people who associated for survival.

Magic, these were tribes forming about 15,000 years ago of up to a few hundred people organized mostly for survival and to handle the demands of the present.

Impulsive, forming about 10,000 years ago and comprising chiefdoms and protoempires. The major breakthrough in these early organizations was division of labor and role differentiation.

Conformist, starting around 4000 BC in Mesopotamia these represent a shift from chiefdoms and survival horticultural societies, to the organization of agriculture, states and civilizations, institutions, bureaucracy and organized religion. These are the first organizational forms that can achieve long term goals, shaping the future.

Achievement, the product of the Renaissance and of the Enlightenment, these complex organizations enabled significant material progress and much liberation and advancement to individuals. This stage "moved us away from the idea that authority has the right answer (instead it relies on expert advice to give insight into the complex mechanics of the world) and brings a healthy dose of skepticism regarding revealed truth. It has allowed us to engage for the first time, in the pursuit of truth regardless of religious dogma and political authority, without having to risk our lives. We have become capable of questioning and stepping out of the conditions we were born in, we are able of breaking free from the thoughts and behaviors that our gender and our social class would have imposed upon us in earlier times." (Laloux, 2014, p. 25).

Pluralistic, a form of organization that acknowledges that all perspectives deserve equal respect, not only 'what works'. "It seeks fairness, equality, harmony, community, cooperation and consensus" (Ibid p. 30). "For people operating from this perspective, relationships are valued above outcomes. For instance, where Achievement-Orange seeks to make decisions top-down, based on objective facts, expert input, and simulations, Pluralistic-Green strives for bottom-up processes, gathering input from all and trying to bring opposing points of view to eventual consensus" (Idem p. 31).

Finally, Laloux argues there is an emerging form of organization, which he calls evolutionary-Teal characterized by self-management, wholeness and evolutionary purpose.

I find Laloux's conceptualization and idea of a developmental continuum – in the lives of organizations, in how individuals see organizations and in which organizational forms become dominant at various historical periods – valuable to understand the evolution of education systems and also valuable to understand the task of implementing educational change at scale.

Since the public education system is a product of the Enlightenment, along with Democracy and with the modern research university, one would hope that the most apt organizational form to describe it would be the achievement organization, with its respect for expertise, reliance on evidence, and healthy skepticism to arbitrary authority and dogma. If this is the minimum standard, leadership or management approaches reflecting magic, impulsive or conformist organizational forms would be pulling the institutions of education backwards, not helping them progress. To a great extent, the language of 'delivery systems' is an apt language for the Achievement organizational model, in particular in its reliance on evidence to support decision making and in making policies 'visible' in their operational strategy and carefully monitoring implementation while creating accountability for delivery and results. In this view, the education system is in fact an 'implementation machine', a good clockwork model created in a Newtonian world in which the laws of science help us understand events, predict them and control them. Relative to a conformist organization, characterized by the arbitrary use of power, where dogmas are unquestioned, this Achievement organization represents considerable progress, and since many education systems function as Conformist organizations, helping them transition to an Achievement stage seems like a worthy goal.

But the Achievement model can reflect a rather static when it comes to accepting social norms and institutions, more apt to reinforce the power and privileges of dominant groups than to challenge them, more fit perhaps to conserve social norms and institutions than to change them. The Punjab reform, as well as the reforms in Mexico, Kenya and Zimbabwe were top down reforms, they depended largely on strong support not just from education authorities, but from the President and the Prime Minister. Arguably the legitimacy of those leaders rests of the legitimacy of the process through which they reached their position and if the leaders are legitimate they should have the authority to 'command' an education delivery system to achieve the goals set for them, which to some extent reflect the goals of the electorate, the 'mandate' they have given their elected authorities. Other stakeholders however, parents, or teachers, or students themselves, may have various views on the legitimacy of political authorities to determine education goals or means. Even if they accept the legitimacy of the President or of the Prime Minister as political authorities, they may not confer them with the authority to represent the educational needs or interests of the students. There is an obvious conservative undertone to an Achievement organization, great to 'get things done', but perhaps not great to produce social change.

A view that sees all perspectives as deserving equal respect, as reflected in a Pluralistic view of organizations, can be at odds with the view of Achievement organization's that those at the top should direct the organization. But isn't this pluralistic view the perspective from which various liberation movements emerged, movements that advanced the rights of women, or people of color, of the poor, or those with different learning needs? If democracy is a living organism, it is because the notion of who 'belongs', of who has rights, is dynamic, contested, always in flux. A pluralistic perspective, or an evolutionary purpose view of organizations, creates the space that allows for that continuous evolution to take place.

How do these ideas about the nature of organizations relate to the reforms studied in this book? Each of these six reforms is based on an implicit view of the education system as an organization, the Achievement view is dominant. As such, each of these reforms serves as a self-fulfilling prophecy to further consolidate that education system into that organizational form. Can education reforms help systems 'move forward' towards more complex organizational forms? When I wrote 'Educating Students to Improve the World' the implicit view of educational institutions covered a narrow spectrum between Achievement or Pluralistic organizations, two view of organizations I had recognized in my earlier book 'Informed Dialogue', in which I had contrasted top down approaches to change with 'learning organization' approaches that honor the diversity of views of various stakeholders affected by education (Reimers & McGinn, 1997).

At present, I find Laloux's theory about organizations considerably richer and more capacious as a way to enhance the Institutional perspective on educational change I included in 'Educating Students to Improve the World'. I now think that the language of educational change as strengthening a 'delivery system' conjures up a particular mental model about the implementation process that is top down, command and control, perhaps a good fit to an Achievement organization in a rather stable and predictable world, but not nearly as adequate in a world in flux, where good ideas can come from anywhere, or for a Pluralistic or Evolutionary Purpose organization, where we must actively cultivate and honor dissent.

I can appreciate how an education reform that reinforces an Achievement model of organization represents progress in systems that need to be liberated from more primitive organizational forms, where capture of the public education system by private interests subordinates them to tribal forms of governance characteristic of Magic and Impulsive organization, or to the pre-Enlightenment conservative forces of Conformist organizations. Clearly the reforms in Mexico and Pakistan, in changing teacher appointments to make them more merit based, where inducing exactly that kind of transition from Conformist to Achievement organizational functioning. The reforms in Ontario, Pakistan and Mexico, in using data on student achievement to drive accountability and improvement where trying to replace arbitrary decision making, characteristic of conformist organizations with public evidence decision making characteristic of Achievement organizations. But it is unclear to me whether a reform that consists of building capacity by strengthening the capacity to do as told, helps in any way to evolve that system towards more pluralistic or evolutionary forms of organization, where multiple perspectives are valued, and where individuals can self-manage, be whole and achieve evolutionary purpose. The slow progress of the Ontario's reform towards educating students for a breath of skills, in spite of the significant investments in building capacity an professionalism, are a cautionary tale on the power that reforms based on one implicit model of how organizations function to reinforce that particular model, and prevent evolution towards more complex forms of functioning.

To sum up, because implementation details in effect are what becomes of policy intent, and because implementation depends on our mental models about how change happens and about how education systems evolve, implementation matters greatly to thinking about the process of educational change. As those mental models become open and subject to scrutiny, they can inform more sophisticated theories of mind that can allow more effective communication, collaboration and collective learning, and perhaps support the development of education organization towards more complex pluralistic and evolutionary forms.

8.4   Lesson 3. The Need for Operational Clarity

People cannot support, or carry out, that which they do not understand. The appeal of approaches to reform that focus on the core literacies rests not only on the fact that building and sustaining trust is easier if reformers commit to a few narrow goals and pursue them with laser-like focus, but also on the fact that because educators have focused on those goals for a relatively long time, there is widespread agreement about that these goals mean, about their importance, and about how to measure and even support them. Such focus on a few goals was the cornerstone of the British education reforms carried out during the administration of British Prime Minister Tony Blair, on which the reforms that McGuinty pursued in Ontario were inspired, and which inspired also the reforms of the Punjab. The similarities between the three reform are not accidental. Sir Michael Barber was one of the architects of the British 'National Literacy and Numeracy Strategy'. He was also a key figure in the design and implementation of the Punjab reforms. In turn, one of the advisors to Ontario's reforms, Michael Fullan, had studied the National Literacy and Numeracy Strategy, and was inspired by it in designing Ontario's reforms, adding some important modifications in the form of more support for professional development.

To be sure, even as these three reforms prioritized the 'basic' goals of literacy and numeracy, there are some disagreements on what is meant by literacy – they form the basis of the well known 'reading wars' – or on the most appropriate approaches to advance them or measure them, but given that the scientific study of literacy spans many decades, those disagreements are minor compared to the state of consensus in domains such as self-efficacy, or perspective taking, or grit, or with respect to the vast set of constructs that are covered in the area of competencies for the twenty first century as discussed in the first chapter of this book. I recall once a conversation with the founder of the Partnership for Twenty First Century Skills, Ken Kay, in which he explained that as a result of working with various states in the United States advocating for broadening the goals of the education standards, he had realized that it was very difficult for most people to focus on a large number of goals, so he made the decision to narrow the focus of the Partnership's advocacy, from a dozen or so outcomes to 'Four Cs' (Critical Thinking, Creativity, Collaboration and Communication). Perhaps this is also the reason UNESCO's Commission on Education for the Twenty First Century, distilled 3 years of global consultations on the goals of education, and thousands of pages in background documents, to Four Pillars' (learning to know, learning to do, learning to live together and learning to be). Michael Fullan also, whose recent writings reflect an expansion of his earlier focus on the basic literacies into a broader set of outcomes, focuses on six Cs: Character, Citizenship, Collaboration, Communication, Creativity and Critical Thinking (Fullan & Scott, 2014).

But it isn't just the sheer number of competencies that a focus on 'breadth of skills' could require that makes some reformers leery of them, it is also the fact that there is less consensus on what those outcomes should mean, or on how to measure them. Clearly a focus on literacy and numeracy is a safer way to go if one is looking for a few clear goals, which don't cause much controversy, and on which there is widespread agreement on how progress is to be measured.

The downside of excessive operational clarity on a few narrow goals is that it may unduly constrain the focus of improvement. At its worst, if a reform defines as its goals to improve student test scores, this could lead to a narrow instructional focus where teachers teach to the test or to other shortcuts to improvement, such as focusing on teaching to the children who are just below the cutoff test scores, such that the improvements which are measured are spurious. That is a frequent criticism of standards based reform as discussed in the first chapter. The challenge for reform is to be understood with sufficient depth that means are not conflated with end goals, so that no one reaches the absurd conclusion that learning is 'that which the tests measure'. Especially if we view an education system from a pluralistic or evolutionary perspective, it is essential that all stakeholders can think with clarity about what are the goals that matter, and that they know the limits of any particular operational definition. This is hard to achieve, even in the context of reforms that invest heavily in teacher capacity and professionalism, as was the case in Ontario's reform. Midway through this reform, which was initially narrowly focused on literacy and numeracy, the definition of those constructs was broadened to encompass broader skills. Even as more policy documents began to include references to a broader range of competences and deep learning, that expansion did not easily translate into implementation. As I will explain later in this chapter, the initial steps in a reform have a long lasting legacy that shapes much of the future reform trajectory.

8.5   Lesson 4. Large Scale Reform Is a Journey: Coherence, Completeness and the Five Frames

If education reform is more about implementation than it is about design, it is obvious that changes to the day to day practices that constitute teaching and learning, for all students, at scale, is a demanding task that will require time. There are at least two reasons such time is necessary. The first, organizing and executing the activities that support such changes in educational practice takes time. The second, individuals, and organizations, need time to assimilate what they are learning in a way that translates into practice and eventually replaces 'old ways'. This is the sense in which changing 'the culture of education', to use Jerome Brunner's apt term, is a process of cultural change: possible, but slow. The dynamics of such process of educational change are aptly captured in the metaphor of 'geological layers' used by Tyack and Cuban in their study of education reform in the United States, in which they argue that federal mandates reach schools in the form of 'geological layers' that pile on top of layers created by previous mandates (Tyack & Cuban, 1997, 76).

If education reform is a journey it is necessary to (a) sequence activities, because not everything can be done at the same time, (b) for the journey to stay the course over time, and (c) to be able to course correct based on learning from experience. Sequencing, continuity and course correction require a reform that is complete and coherent. I now turn to explain how the five dimensional theory of educational change can support completeness and coherence in design, to then address the subjects of sequencing, staying the course and learning from experience.

Any reform is based on a set of assumptions about how the education system functions and how to change it. I have explained how those assumptions could be usefully categorized as five frames: cultural, psychological, professional, institutional and political (Reimers, 2020). A recognition of those frames could be useful in various ways to the design and the analysis of education reforms. First, it could help assess the internal coherence and completeness of the proposed reform in terms of the frame within which it was operating. Second, it could help develop a more robust reform by identifying blind spots in the proposed reforms as highlighted by the frames which had not been considered. Finally, it could help produce coherence in how various stakeholders understood the reform, and their particular role in it, as it provides a shared language and set of mental models that facilitated communication about the reform across the many people whose collaboration is essential in a large scale education reform. Coherence results when different stakeholders share an understanding of what a reform is attempting to do, how and what their own role in it is supposed to be. Laloux's theory of the developmental stages in the history of organizations has profound implications for how we interpret coherence. For organizations which are in an Achievement developmental stage, or in a previous stage such as Conformist, lack of a shared understanding of what a reform is trying to do can be interpreted as lack of capacity of those tasked to implement it, or lack of power of those leading the implementation of the reform to persuade or coerce implementors to 'do as they are told'. From this frame of mind, it makes sense that 'training' or using information to strengthen 'delivery chains' is a useful way to increase coherence. In other words, the root cause of lack of coherence is ignorance or lack of will to comply, and the response is capacity building or incentive and accountability structures to compel individuals into compliance.

However, from the more complex worldviews of organizations represented by pluralistic or evolutionary purpose organizations, following Laloux's taxonomy, lack of coherence could be more than the mere expression of ignorance or unwillingness to comply, as rightly articulated by Lipsky in his study of street level bureaucrats. Those organizational forms require valuing different perspectives of those in the organization, and continuous learning together, which in turn require a theory of mind, the capacity to understand the beliefs, intentions, knowledge and worldviews of others. Because different individuals may operate from various of the five frames (cultural, psychological, professional, institutional and political) integrated into my theory of educational change, such theory provides the means to develop a more complex theory of mind for each member of the organization, in understanding and appreciating the perspective of others, and consequently a capacious tool to facilitate communication, collaboration, and join learning. Such complex theory of mind is essential for teams to be able to recognize the shortcomings of any theory of action underlying a reform, and to identify ways to evolve together towards more a more capacious theory of action.

8.6   Lesson 5. Sequencing, Pacing and the Importance of First Steps

Deciding which particular components of a reform to address, and at what speed, requires reconciling the ambition of the reform goals and activities, with the existing capacity and resources. It may also require attention to the developmental stage of the organization. Some activities logically need to precede others, for instance, it is necessary to have clear standards before student knowledge and skills can be meaningfully assessed. From that perspective, it was contradictory that Mexico's reform developed a model of teacher assessment before the curriculum model that guided the reform was available, just the opposite of the more logical sequence Singapore followed in creating a framework for twenty-first century teacher education. Similarly, some organizational or individual capacity needs to be developed before certain functions can be carried out, for example, some coordinating mechanism of the functions of teacher selection, initial teacher education and in-service education, needs to be established in order to intentionally strengthen the continuum of teacher professional development. Without such institutional forms, Singapore could not attempt to develop a twenty-first century model of teacher, for example.

Is it necessary for education systems to stage reforms so that they first focus on creating the capacity to deliver simpler goals, before they can take on more ambitious goals? The reform in Punjab, for instance, focused on fairly narrow access, literacy and numeracy goals, as did the Ontario reforms which focused on literacy, numeracy and graduation rates. In neither case did the reform evolve towards addressing broader goals than those that were initially established. In contrast, the reforms in Singapore, Mexico, Kenya and Zimbabwe are all focused on broader education goals, even though it is unclear that any of them, except Singapore, are making progress towards changing the culture of education towards a broader set of outcomes, although in fairness Kenya and Zimbabwe's reforms are in too early stages of implementation to be able to expect impact on teacher practices or student learning outcomes.

From an organizational developmental perspective, are Mexico, Kenya and Zimbabwe's reforms attempting to pull above their weight in pursuing reforms to develop twenty-first century competencies? Would they be best served pursuing narrower goals, and using increased capacity gained from achieving those goals as a way to develop implementation capacity, to only subsequently pursue more ambitious goals? That seems to be the underlying assumption of the Punjab reforms. While the idea of taking small steps first, focusing on narrower goals, has intuitive appeal, Ontario's reform seems to disconfirm the notion that systems naturally transition to more complex and ambitious goals as they succeed in improving narrower goals. Even though the reform was quite successful in achieving large scale improvement in literacy, numeracy and graduation rates, and was sustained for a fairly long period of time, it has not yet transitioned to adopting a broader set of goals or implementing the necessary changes so that the culture of schools pursues them, even though one of the architects of the reforms (Fullan), who remains an influential thought leader in the field of system level change for educators of all political persuasions in the province and in the world, has increasingly written about the importance of pursuing such more ambitious goals.

Kenya's experience with the pilot of the new curriculum revealed that the needs for professional development had been underestimated and that the initially planned pace of the reform was too ambitious for the capacity of the system. The aim to change the curriculum, requiring more personalized instruction, while also changing the structure of the cycles of education, with automatic transition from primary to secondary schools, in a short timeframe, seems to have exceeded the capacity of the system with the logistical requirements of implementing such changes. For instance, the combined effect of new pedagogies, relying on ongoing formative assessment of student progress with much larger secondary classes created by the elimination of the exams created demands that are difficult to meet by the current teacher force.

In sequencing the implementation of a reform three critical considerations should include the ambitions of their goals, the existing level of implementation capacity, and the stage of development of the education system. Laloux characterizes the development of organizations as an evolutionary, staged, process, where certain stages in organizational development preceed higher levels. It may not be realistic to expect education systems functioning as proto-Achievement organizations, for example functioning within the rigid hierarchical stratification of conformist organizations, to carry out activities that require a pluralistic organizational mindset, without first helping them evolve into an achievement organization. In Laloux's description of a conformist organization I recognize the practices I have observed in many ministries of education, in fact Laloux's description is close to the way my colleague Noel McGinn and I characterized the internal structure of education systems in the book Informed Dialogue (Reimers & McGinn, 1997). What a huge leap forward it now seems,with hindsight, to expect the institutions operating out of that conformist worldview to transition into a professional culture of self-management, or even into the modes of democratic participatory decision making I advocated in the same book, or that are implicit in the ideas of schools as learning organizations or in the concept of collaborative professionalism advanced by Andy Hargreaves and his colleagues (Hargreaves, Shirley, Wangia, Bacon, & D'Angelo, 2018).

In a conformist organization: "Planning and execution are strictly separated: the thinking happens at the top, the doing at the bottom. Decisions made at the top get handed down through successive layers of management .... A whole catalog of rules is set up. Some among the staff are put in charge of ensuring compliance and handing out disciplinary measures and punishments for those found wanting ... The underlying worldview is that workers are mostly lazy, dishonest, and in need of direction. They must be supervised and told what is expected of them. Participatory management seems foolish from a Comformist-Amber perspective; management must rely on command and control to achieve results. Jobs at the frontlines are narrow and routine-based. Innovation, critical thinking, and self-expression are not asked for (and often discouraged). Information is shared on an as-needed basis.

People are effectively interchangeable resources; individual talent is neither discerned nor developed" (Laloux, 2014, 21–22).

While I endorse holding the aspiration that all education systems should become, in time, pluralistic or evolutionary purpose organizations, I recognize it may take some intentional sequencing to help some systems get there. Education reforms are the conduits to support that transition. I do not know, at this point, whether it is possible to plan for systems to 'leapfrog' stages in Laloux's sequence, but I do think there has to be alignment between the tasks and expected functioning in any particular stage of education reform and the organizational arrangements and practices that characterize how the education system functions. Those can change, just as 'the culture of education' can change, but slowly, with adequate support and skillful design.

From this perspective, a key difference between the reforms in Mexico, Punjab, Ontario and Singapore, are not just that Punjab and Ontario pursued rather narrow curricular goals, whereas Mexico and Singapore pursued more ambitious goals. But another fundamental distinction is that Mexico and Punjab's education systems were both in a proto-Achievement stage, whereas Ontario and Singapore where in an Achievement stage proper. Punjab's reform made as much sense as an instrument to help that organization transition to an Achievement stage as it did as an avenue to pursue improvements in access and literacy. Mexico's reform was also instrumental to help the system evolve into an Achievement stage, while pursuing a much more ambitious set of educational goals. The sequence followed by the Mexican reform made more sense as a path to help that organizational transition, than as a sequence to achieve a twenty-first century curriculum reform.

In contrast, Ontario and Singapore, both Achievement organizations, pursued goals of different level of ambition, narrower in Ontario than in Singapore. It is not evident that either of these reforms attempted to help those systems transition into a Pluralistic or Evolutionary Purpose stage, instead the reforms helped to consolidate those systems into an Achievement stage. With hindsight, Ontario might have more readily transitioned to teaching twenty first century skills following the intentional staged process followed by Singapore, rather than expecting that the successful implementation of a strategy focused on narrow goals would eventually lead the system there. Conversely, Mexico might have benefited from attempting a transition to an Achievement organization focusing on a narrower set of goals, as did Ontario, rather than attempting similar goals to Singapore's with an organization at a very different level of functioning.

On the other hand, Ontario, Punjab and Singapore benefited from sustained periods of educational continuity which eluded Mexico, and perhaps also Kenya and Zimbabwe, for reasons that are somewhat extrinsical to the particulars of the education reform, and contingent on national politics and economic developments. To some extent the role played by those external political circumstances, a change in government, government continuity, are not within the control of education reformers. We might think of them as just pure luck, good or bad. But perhaps there are steps that could increase the probability that a reform will be long lived, other than counting on good luck.

If there is something education reformers can do to secure the necessary continuity of a reform it is attending to the 'narrative' of reform, as it will inform how stakeholders at various levels of the system make meaning of it. In building a reform's narrative first steps are critical. They set the initial conditions of the reform in a way that will signal for many what the reform is about, and that can open possibilities for subsequent steps, when they build capacities or create essential units, as much as they can close them. The Mexican education reform provides a great example of the necessity of sequencing and of the importance of first steps. The reformers realized that before expecting teachers to be able to implement an ambitious curriculum reform, which required among other conditions high levels of professionalism and more autonomy at the school level, the norms that governed who could become a teacher should be aligned with a professional view. To this end, they eliminated the control of the teacher union over the process of teacher appointments, in favor of giving the state the authority to assess knowledge and skill of candidates to enter and remain in the profession. In terms of the evolutionary sequence described by Laloux this effort attempted to replace organizational practices appropriate to impulsive organizations, characterized by sheer and continuous exercise of power in interpersonal relationships to sustain the position of the chief, with practices aligned with conformist organizations, or even of proto-achievement organizations. The direction of the proposed change was sensible, at least using Laloux's theory, even though there were incongruencies with what further elements of the reform expected. For instance, the curriculum reform which was eventually approved, expected a level of teacher professionalism, and school autonomy, that would have required mindsets and practices typical of Achievement and Pluralist organizations.

But the challenge with beginning the reform replacing the process to appoint and promote teachers with one based on merit is that it allowed the opposition of the reform to see it as a 'punitive' reform, as a reform that was about an attempt on the part of the State to grab power over the teaching profession. That narrative allowed those opposing the reform to build sufficient support to slow the reform down, and eventually to cause the leading opposition presidential candidate to commit to undoing the reform. Even though this reform could have just as easily been framed as a reform to promote teacher professionalism, to increase school autonomy, to recognize a plurality of legitimate views about the goals of education, which were indeed goals reflected in elements of the reform, that narrative never crystalized because the elements that most clearly reflected them came later, with hindsight too late. Once the 'New Educational Model' was announced, the element of the reform most explicitly focused on curricular goals, several consultations were conducted. While there are clear parallels with the Ontario reform in how Mexico created opportunities for teacher participation and support, the key difference between both reforms is the moment at which those opportunities for participation were deployed. In Ontario, they happened very early, marking a start contrast with the conflicted relationship between teachers and government which had characterized the administration preceding the reform and therefore shaping the narrative of the reform from the outset. As a result the reform was perceived as 'educational' and as 'inclusive' even though it was as political as any of the other reforms examined in this book. In contrast, in Mexico, they happened late, 3 years into the reform, once a narrative about the reform had developed and opposition had formed and organized against it. While both of these reforms could claim that they sought teacher participation, the devil, to quote Fullan and Gallagher, is in the details of how *and when* this was done (Fullan & Gallagher, 2020).

8.7   Lesson 6. Staying the Course

Reform takes time, the most elusive of all resources. Time is needed to carry out all the activities that have been carefully sequenced to allow a reform to reach its goals. Time is needed for the policy mandates of a reform to eventually crystalize into a new pedagogical 'core' that effectively shapes the new 'culture of education'. But time is by definition elusive in a world that is volatile and uncertain. The COVID-19 Pandemic likely derailed the best laid plans of many educational institutions, forcing them instead to deal with a world with new demands and different means to deliver education.

Political discontinuities are the main threat to the stability that reforms need to consolidate. When a president changes, the minister of education is likely to change. When the minister changes, senior leadership teams can change. With those changes, the balance of power that supported the reform may change. There are clear benefits from long policy cycles, and big costs to rapid interruptions of reforms, before those have had a change to bear fruit. What accounts for continuity in education policy cycles? Is such continuity something that can only be recognized after the fact, a product of good luck perhaps, or is it something that can be planned a priory, that can be cultivated and sustained over time?

One key element influencing implementation continuity are national politics and their relationship to education. Political support from high levels of government is not only helpful, but frequently essential. The magnitude of the changes required to put in place and sustain an education reform to augment the ambitions of the curriculum are such that they require substantial financial resources and political capital. Singapore's long cycles of reform have benefited from considerable support from the Prime Minister. In Ontario the fact that Premier McGuinty made education a priority of his administration since his arrival in office in 2003, and political continuity and stability for a decade, were very valuable to sustain the priority of the reform, the continuity of key teams and a steady influx of resources. The strong political support for reform in Singapore or Ontario never became a liability, even when governments or education administrations changed. In contrast, the Mexican reform is a clear example of how the same political support that benefited the initiation of a reform, heavily identifying it with a particular administration, became a liability when a presidential transition to a candidate from an opposition party took place. The Mexican reform began as one of the key structural reforms that an incoming administration launched to restructure the State. It was perceived as central to the strategy of the administration, and benefited from considerable support from the administration for that reason. At the same time, such high level of support identified the reform with the administration, and made it an obvious potential target for groups opposing the President. When an opposition candidate launched his campaign against the incumbent party, the education reform was an easy political target, and opposing it allowed that candidate to obtain the support of groups opposed to the education reform. Dismantling the education reform became a campaign promise, even though the interests motivating the opposition were more about dismantling any legacy of the previous administration than specific interests around the education goals or strategies of the education reform per se. A reform less visibly identified with a Presidential administration would have made a less likely target in an electoral campaign. When the opposition candidate was elected President he had to fulfill his electoral promise.

Political discontinuity also ultimately interrupted Ontario's reform, but did so after a long period of implementation, which allowed enough of the culture of education to have changed for some of that change to continue under the leadership of schools and local organizations. In addition to the good fortune from that reform resulting from the continuity of a party in power, Ontario's reformers explicitly framed the reform as an educational reform from day one. They also intentionally sought to gain trust and support from parents and teachers early on. Mexico's reform was more top down, and insufficiently focused at the outset on curriculum and pedagogy, which was paradoxical for a twenty-first century education reform. The almost exclusive focus on institutional changes, important as those were both as foundations to the pedagogical reforms and as avenues to help the education system develop into more advanced organizational forms, allowed a narrative to develop about the reform from which it would never recover. That fact, and the limited implementation of the reform by the time a new government came into office made the reform very vulnerable to severe interruption.

The reform in Punjab, also benefited from a relatively long period of political stability in the province, and from consistent high level support from the Prime Minister. That kind of support and continuity were essential to the significant changes this reform enacted, changing rules to appointing teachers, for example, towards greater meritocracy, or increasing the number of local school supervisors who would work as coaches and pedagogical advisors in schools.

As an example of the benefit of long policy cycles to the implementation of a reform Singapore stands in a class of its own. It is clear that to some extent such continuity has resulted from the very long period in power of the ruling party, and from the very high political priority that education has received from the nation's leaders. Here too initial steps are very consequential. Lee Kwang Yew, Singapore's first Prime Minister, built two very powerful narratives in the early history of the nation that to this day provide impetus to education. One was that Singapore's future depended on the cultivation of the talent of the population, and that education was a cornerstone of strategic importance to shaping that future. The second was a certain modesty and awareness of the limited resources available in the early years of the nation's history, which cultivated an approach to reform consisting on building on what had been done previously, rather than replacing previous reforms. The narrative that the country's education system has evolved through four distinct phases, intentionally pursued, and that this has produced great results, sustains a view of reform as incremental continuous improvement, rather than one fell swoop change. In addition, the relatively small size of the nation state and of the education community, and the close ties between many who work in various roles in education, sustains a close knit profession where there are strong incentives to be respectful of the institutions, policies, programs and people that are in place and cautious in attempts to make too many changes at once. As a result, Singapore has, arguably, the strongest institutional education culture of all six countries examined here and this, in itself, is a driver of continuity and long policy cycles.

While support from high level political leaders, such as the support the reforms in Ontario and the Punjab received from their respective Prime Ministers, or the support the reforms in Kenya, Mexico and Zimbabwe received from their respective Presidents, are undoubtedly helpful, ultimately earning the support of students, parents and teachers may be more important to the long term continuity of the reform. The Ontario reform explicitly sought to earn the trust of society and of teachers, this may account for the significant continuity of the reform over a decade. It is difficult for elected leaders to undermine reforms which are widely valued by the voters. The Mexican reform, in contrast, does not appear to have invested as much in earning such support, while its detractors actively worked to undermine such trust, building a narrative that portrayed the reform as 'top down' and 'punitive'. The Punjab reform has lost support as a result of a change of political administration in the province, and because it never sought to gain support from teachers and parents, as Ontario's reform did, it is more fragile. Zimbabwe appears to have more intentionally sought support from the population by opening up consultations about the new curriculum than Kenya, but it is unclear how the larger political instability will influence such support and the durability of the reform.

8.8   Lesson 7. Learning from Experience to Build System Level Capacity

As explained earlier in this chapter, the theory of action of any reform is series of hypotheses about how it is that certain activities will produce certain immediate results and in turn contribute to larger educational goals. Good implementation of educational change is continuous course correction, adjustments based on what is learned as a result of attempting what the reform proposes. If programs of professional development are offered, will teachers participate? Will they learn from them? Will the programs contribute to changing their practice? If they change their pedagogy, will students develop new competencies as a result?

The reason methodologies such as the logical framework approach are useful is because making those hypotheses visible and public helps develop a shared understanding of what it is that a policy is trying to do and how. But the logical framework is also a management tool, helping to focus attention on the key activities that translate a policy or program into an implemented reality. Just as important, the logical framework is a tool to support evaluation, and continuous program improvement.

The pilot of the reform which Kenya implemented in 470 schools was a deliberate effort to test the new curriculum, teacher preparation, new assessment, in a diversity of contexts and levels. The use of continuous assessment in the pilot served to provide regular feedback to help develop shared understanding of what the curriculum reform would look like in practice and to make necessary adjustments as a result of what was learned.

Learning from the process of implementing the reform is essential not just to adjust the reform so it better achieves its goals but also to achieve coherence among the many stakeholders that must collaborate to make change happen. How we think about who precisely it is that must learn what depends on our mental models of organizations. In a Conformist organization, using Laloux's language, which supposes a clear differentiation between those who make policies and those who do as they are told in implementing them, those who make policy need to learn whether the hypotheses on which the reform is based are correct, and whether they are been implemented as intended, while those who implement it need to learn what is expected of them, and need to develop the skills necessary to do as they are told. In contrast, in an Achievement, Pluralistic or Evolutionary Purpose organization, people need to learn together whether the theory of action holds up. In those organizations good ideas can come from anywhere, and the insights of teachers, or of students, can be as valuable as those of a Minister. In addition, in Pluralistic organizations, people need to learn together whether the goals the policy is pursuing make sense, or whether they are sufficient or should be expanded. In an Evolutionary Purpose organization, they may also need to learn together whether the reform is helping advance the education system to higher levels of evolutionary purpose, or holding it back.

An example of a 'learning organization' perspective, reflecting a pluralistic or an evolutionary purpose view of organizations is provided by Michael Fullan and Mary Jean Gallagher in their recent book 'The Devil is in the Details'. These authors explain that coherence requires that people 'understand the system' in order to collaborate towards good system change. In their view good system change is the result of coherent work of people working at three interrelated levels of the system (the macro, the middle and the local). As people become aware of the worldviews of those in their same level, as well as of the worldviews of those in the other two levels, they can understand the system in which they work and come to understand the system dynamics of educational change (Fullan & Gallagher, 2020, 32–33).

The Ontario and Punjab reforms, which included accountability and data as instruments of school improvement, explicitly built into the theory of action of the reform feedback loops for improvement. In Ontario, for example, the assessment results were used by teachers to identify the extent to which each of the students was meeting curriculum expectations, and those data were used by principals to develop school improvement plans. Schools received data on the performance of their students, compared with the performance of students in other schools with similar demographics. The results were also used by school improvement boards and by the ministry to launch support initiatives. In this way, the same information, shared and used for different purposes across the three levels of the education system, helped shape a shared understanding of what the challenges were with respect to achieving the reform objectives.

In Punjab, the most significant activity to strengthen management capacity consisted of creating a monitoring and reporting system of all key actions involved in the implementation of the reform. Those reports were frequently discussed by teams at all levels of the implementation 'delivery chain' to facilitate course correction but also learning. The parallel with the approach followed in Ontario is not accidental, as that reform too, just like the reform in the Punjab, borrowed this emphasis on data utilization to strengthen delivery from the National Literacy and Numeracy Strategy in the United Kingdom.

In contrast, implementation of the Mexican education reform was hindered because states, which have substantial authority in education governance, had an uneven commitment to the reform. The top down nature of the reform, with most of the impetus coming from the Federal government, and with limited opportunities for input from the local and state level, prevented the development of shared learning of stakeholders across these various levels, resulting from access to similar information or from collaboration in efforts of improvement as was done in Ontario or in Punjab. The result, predictable, was limited coherence and limited buy-in and support from local and state levels.

8.9   Coda

The year 2020 was a pivotal moment in the history of humanity. Not only did the COVID-19 Pandemic extract a heavy toll on many lives and on societies, it disrupted many of the existing processes and social institutions that defined life as we knew it. The effects of that disruption are likely to be felt for a long time to come, even after the Pandemic is over. To a great extent, the educational costs of the Pandemic caused significant losses for individuals and nations. Some may never fully recover from those losses. These losses are all the more reason to reassert the importance of education for the future of humanity. This new awareness about the importance of education and about the need for reinvention present a challenging conundrum. The urgency to reinvent education will happen in a world heavily burdened by the results of the Pandemic, not least among those burdens will be the financial austerity that is likely to follow. We do not yet know how the Pandemic will accelerate pre-existing challenges and create new ones, but the study of past Pandemics teaches us that the challenges they create can have profound consequences for society.

A global pandemic is one of the most humbling experiences we could experience. In some ways a great equalizer, for a highly contagious virus knows no borders and no differences among classes of people, even though different forms of privilege influence the likelihood of contracting the virus and the fatality of losing one's life to the infection. Even so, that so many people around the world saw their freedoms constrained by this Pandemic provided a humbling reminder to all of our shared humanity, and an opportunity for deep empathy with others, of what it is to live without whatever privileges we may have grown accustomed to. It may have also provided time for some for deep thinking and reflection, for more attention to questions of purpose, of deep meaning, including questions about the purpose of education, in which societies invest so many resources and effort and in which we place so many hopes. Perhaps this global calamity will help us grasp the deep meaning in the powerful idea Terence put forth twenty centuries ago: *'to be human is to live so nothing human is foreign to us'*. Perhaps this crisis will remind us of the importance of solidarity, of the power of collaboration, of the power of reason, of the importance of science, or the power of good leadership, and above all of the need to make ethical choices.

In 1347 a ship brought the bubonic plague to Italy. In a year 25 million people had died. Over the ensuing decades, some of the social and economic disruptions caused by the Pandemic stimulated many questions about the pre-existing social order, along with an unprecedented social and economic mobility and many questions about the absolute authority of rulers, represented in the rise of the influence of the Medici family in Florence, where they would become patrons of a massive experiment in intellectual cross-fertilization that would in time bring about the Italian Renaissance.

In contrast, the 1918 Pandemic in Germany depressed municipal spending in ways which created challenges for the emerging Weimar Republic, and which radicalized many of those who felt excluded as their lives were negatively impacted by the economic impact of the Pandemic. Many of them would in time develop extremely intolerant views which contributed to the rise of intolerance, the development of the Nazi party and the breakdown of democracy (Blickle, 2020).

Whether our way out of this crisis goes one way or another, a Renaissance or a breakdown of democracy and social institutions, depends on how people make sense of the painful and confusing disruptions the Pandemic has brought about. Education can play a critical role helping people make sense of this time, and shaping the ethical choices that will define how we live after this crisis. Education will be critical so that at the end of this crisis there is a Renaissance, and not a return to the dark ages.

References

Blickle, K. (2020, May). Pandemic change cities: Municipal spending and voter extremism in Germany, 1918–1933. New York: Federal Reserve Bank of New York. Staff Reports No 921. https://www.newyorkfed.org/research/staff_reports/sr921. Accessed 28 June 2020.

Fullan, M., & Gallagher, M. J. (2020). *The devil is in the details*. Thousand Oaks, CA: Corwin.

Fullan, M., & Scott, G. (2014). *New pedagogies for deep learning*. Seattle, Washington: Collaborative Impact.

Hargreaves, A., Shirley, D., Wangia, S., Bacon, C., & D'Angelo, M. (2018). *Leading from the middle: Spreading learning, well-being, and identity across Ontario*. Toronto, ON: Council for Directors of Education.

Laloux, F. (2014). *Reinventing organizations*. Middleton, DE: Nelson Parker.

Lipsky, M. (1980). *Street-level bureaucracy: Dilemmas of the individual in public services*. New York: Russell Sage Foundation.

Reimers, F. (2020). *Educating students to improve the world*. Cham, Switzerland: Springer.

Reimers, F., & McGinn, N. (1997). *Informed dialogue*. Westport, CT: Praeger.

Tyack, D., & Cuban, L. (1997). *Tinkering towards utopia. A century of public school reform*. Cambridge, MA: Harvard University Press.

Fernando M. Reimers is the Ford Foundation Professor of the Practice of International Education and Director of the Global Education Innovation Initiative and of the International Education Policy Masters Program at Harvard University. An expert in the field of Global Education, Reform and System Level Change, his research and teaching focus on understanding how to educate children and youth so they can thrive in the twenty-first century. He is a member of UNESCO's high level commission on the Futures of Education.

He has written or edited thirty-three books, of which the most recent include: *Educating Students to Improve the World, Audacious Education Purposes. How governments transform the goals of education systems, Empowering teachers to build a better world. How six nations support teachers for 21st century education, Letters to a New Minister of Education, Teaching and Learning for the 21st Century, Preparing Teachers to Educate Whole Students: An International Comparative Study, Learning to Improve the World,Empowering Global Citizens,Empowering Students to Improve the World in Sixty Lessons. Version 1.0, Learning to Collaborate for the Global Common Good, Fifteen Letters on Education in Singapore, Empowering All Students at Scale*, and *One Student at a Time. Leading the Global Education Movement*.

Correction to: Implementing Deeper Learning and 21st Century Education Reforms

Fernando M. Reimers

Correction to:
F. M. Reimers (ed.), *Implementing Deeper Learning and 21st Century Education Reforms,*
https://doi.org/10.1007/978-3-030-57039-2

This book was inadvertently published with incorrect book title. The correct title of the book is as follows:

Implementing Deeper Learning and 21st Century Education Reforms

The book title has been corrected in the Cover and throughout the book.

The updated version of the book can be found at
https://doi.org/10.1007/978-3-030-57039-2

The manufacturer's authorised representative in the EU is Springer
Nature Customer Service Centre GmbH, Europaplatz 3, 69115 Heidelberg,
Germany. If you have any concerns regarding our products, please
contact ProductSafety@springernature.com

Printed and bound by CPI Group (UK) Ltd, Croydon, CR0 4YY
29/04/2026
02099458-0005